Surā

The Liquor and the Vedic Sacrifice

Reconstructing Indian History & Culture

(ISSN 0971-3824)

1. Society in Ancient India by Sures Chandra Banerji (ISBN 81-246-0000-7)
2. Political Thought in Ancient India by G.P. Singh (ISBN 81-246-0001-5)
3. Early Indian Historical Tradition and Archaeology by G.P. Singh (ISBN 81-246-0005-8)
4. Vasantotsava: The Spring Festivals of India by Leona M Anderson (ISBN 81-246-0011-2)
5. Ecological Readings in the Veda by M. Vannucci (ISBN 81-246-0009-0)
6. Vṛndāvana in Vaiṣṇava Literature by Maura Corcoran (ISBN 81-246-0024-4)
7. Social History of the Tamils (1707-1947) by P. Subramanian (ISBN 81-246-0045-7)
8. Ancient Indian Coinage by Rekha Jain (ISBN 81-246-0051-1)
9. Buddhism and Socio-Economic Life of Eastern India by Bimal Chandra Mohapatra (ISBN 81-246-0055-4)
10. Chandragupta Maurya by P.L. Bhargava (ISBN 81-246-0056-2)
11. Mṛtyu: Concept of Death in Indian Traditions by Gian Giuseppe Fillippi (ISBN 81-246-0072-4)
12. Yama: The Glorious Lord of the Other World by Kusum P. Merh (ISBN 81-246-0066-X)
13. Sacred Complex of Ujjain by D.K. Samanta (ISBN 81-246-0078-3)
14. Vedic View of the Earth by S.R.N. Murthy (ISBN 81-246-0091-0)
15. Society in the Atharvaveda by B.S. Kharade (ISBN 81-246-0093-7)
16. Orissan History, Culture and Archaeology by S. Pradhan (ISBN 81-246-0117-8)
17. Education in Ancient India by Mitali Chatterjee (ISBN 81-246-0113-5)
18. Surā: the Liquor and the Vedic Sacrifice by M.B. Kolhatkar (ISBN 81-246-0114-3)
19. Human Ecology in the Vedas by Marta Vannucci (ISBN 81-246-0115-1)

Reconstructing Indian History and Culture, no. 18

Surā

The Liquor and the Vedic Sacrifice

Madhavi Bhaskar Kolhatkar

with a Foreword by

C.G. Kashikar

D.K. Printworld (P) Ltd.

NEW DELHI-110015

Cataloging in Publication Data — DK

Kolhatkar, Madhavi Bhaskar, 1950 –
Surā: the liquor and the Vedic sacrifice.
(Reconstructing Indian history & culture ; no. 18).
Includes bibliographical references (p.).
Includes index.

1. Sacrifice — Hinduism. 2. Hinduism — Rituals.
3. Liquors — Religious aspects — Hinduism. I. Title.
II. Series: Reconstructing Indian history & culture ; no. 18.

ISBN 81-246-0114-3

First Published in India in 1999

Published by:
D.K. Printworld (P) Ltd.
Regd. office: '*Sri Kunj*', F-52, Bali Nagar
New Delhi - 110 015
Phones: (011) 545-3975, 546-6019; *Fax*: (011) 546-5926
E-mail: dkprint@4mis.com

Printed by: DP's Impressive Impressions, New Delhi - 110 059

To my husband

Who has always offered me
complete freedom
to pursue my own interests

Foreword

It gives me great pleasure to introduce the work *Surā, The Liquor and the Vedic Sacrifice.*

During the last few years, many scholars have written books on various Vedic rituals such as *rājasūya*, *cāturmāsyas*, *pravargya*, etc. In this line of the research-work, the present book on the *sautrāmaṇī* sacrifice is a welcome addition.

The offerings of *surā* (liquor) in the Śrauta sacrificial fire is the distinguishing feature of the *sautrāmaṇī* sacrifice. It is claimed in this work that the *punarabhiṣeka* (the reanointment) might have been the origin of the *sautrāmaṇī* sacrifice. This *punarabhiṣeka* has its roots in the struggle for supremacy between the brāhmaṇas and the kṣatriyas. It is of a redressing nature, as it were. It is performed for a kṣatriya sacrificer — the King himself — who has undergone the *abhiṣeka* (anointment) rite in the *rājasūya* sacrifice. Since he has temporarily become a brāhmaṇa during the sacrificial performance, he performs this *punarabhiṣeka* ceremony and attains his kṣatriya-hood again.

The present work highlights the sociological state of affairs in the Vedic period with special reference to the mutual relation of the brāhmaṇa and the kṣatriya in the context of the *rājasūya*, the *punarabhiṣeka* and the *sautrāmaṇī* sacrifice. In ancient India, there was a constant rivalry between brāhmaṇa and kṣatriya for the superior position. As a result of it, the kṣatriya sacrificer was denied the right of partaking of the sacrificial *soma*-drink in the *rājasūya* sacrifice and was given *surā* instead of it. Similarly, in the *punarabhiṣeka* ceremony also, he was given *surā* as his own drink. Thus, the *sautrāmaṇī* sacrifice plays an important role in the medicinal, sociological and ritualistic way of thinking of the Vedic people.

I would like to specially draw the attention of the readers to the anthropological importance of the myths. The myths in the *Brāhmaṇa*-texts are very closely connected with the sacrificial ritual. In the present work, due emphasis has been given to the myths and an effort is made to explain the mythological background of the *sautrāmaṇī* sacrifice.

I am of the opinion that the author has been quite successful in dealing with the complicated ritual procedure, as well as the conceptual background of this sacrifice in the Vedic texts.

Dr. C.G. Kashikar

Acknowledgements

I would fain offer my heartiest thanks to all who inspired and helped me first in preparing and then in publishing this study.

Dr. G.U. Thite, my *guru* encouraged me to formulate the problem and draw the inferences on my own. He always insisted on my making efforts to achieve clarity in expression and perfection in method.

Prof. M.A. Mehendale had suggested to me this interesting topic for research.

Prof. C.G. Kashikar made himself available to me whenever I wanted to get some points clarified and kindly agreed also to write a Foreword, even while he was not in the best of his health.

Prof. K.P. Jog went through the draft of my research and made a number of valuable suggestions.

Prof. M.K. Dhavlikar took interest in my work and drew my attention to various related references.

Prof. J. Gonda was kind enough to spare his valuable time to go through my paper related to the present work, and suggested to me some important modifications.

It was always a matter of delight to have the inspiring support of my friend Prof. Shrikant Bahulkar right from the beginning of the work.

The Poona University permitted me to publish this research in book form.

Prof. S.D. Laddhu introduced me to the publisher Shri Susheel K. Mittal of D. K. Printworld, who accepted to publish this work. He has been very prompt and efficient in every matter.

The members of my family have, as usual, offered their loving cooperation.

It is my pleasant duty to express my deep sense of gratitude to each one of these who made it all possible.

Pune **Madhavi Bhaskar Kolhatkar**
August, 1998

Contents

List of Abbreviations

AitBrā	*Aitareya-Brāhmaṇa*
ĀpaHauPari	*Āpastamba-Hautra-Pariśiṣṭa*
ĀpaŚS	*Āpastamba-Śrauta-Sūtra*
ĀśvaGS	*Āśvalāyana-Gṛhya-Sūtra*
ĀśvaŚS	*Āśvalāyana-Śrauta-Sūtra*
AV(Ś)	*Atharvaveda-Saṁhitā (Śaunaka Recension)*
BaudhŚS	*Baudhāyana-Śrauta-Śūtra*
BhārŚS	*Bhāradvāja-Śrauta-Sūtra*
DrāhyāŚS	*Drāhyāyaṇa-Śrauta-Sūtra*
GautDS	*Gautama-Dharma-Sūtra*
GopBrā	*Gopatha-Brāhmaṇa*
HirŚS	*Hiraṇyakeśi-Śrauta-Sūtra*
KāṭhS	*Kāṭhaka-Saṁhitā*
KātyŚS	*Kātyāyana-Śrauta-Sūtra*
KauśiSū	*Kauśika-Sūtra*
LāṭyāŚS	*Lāṭyāyana-Śrauta-Sūtra*
MaiS	*Maitrāyaṇī-Saṁhitā*
MānŚS	*Mānava-Śrauta-Sūtra*

MāṭhVṛ	*Māṭhara-Vṛtti*
Mbh	*Mahābhārata*
MīmāSū	*Pūrva-Mīmāṁsā-Sūtra*
PañcBrā	*Pañcaviṁśa-Brāhmaṇa*
ṚV	*Ṛgveda-Saṁhitā*
ŚāṅkhāBrā	*Śāṅkhāyana-Brāhmaṇa*
ŚāṅkhāGS	*Śāṅkhāyana-Gṛhya-Sūtra*
ŚāṅkhāŚS	*Śāṅkhāyana-Śrauta-Sūtra*
ŚatBrā	*Śatapatha-Brāhmaṇa*
TaiBrā	*Taittirīya-Brāhmaṇa*
TaiS	*Taittirīya-Saṁhitā*
VaikhāGS	*Vaikhānasa-Gṛhya-Sūtra*
VaikhāŚS	*Vaikhānasa-Śrauta-Sūtra*
VaitāSū	*Vaitāna-Sūtra*
VājaS	*Vājasaneyi-Saṁhitā*
VārāŚS	*Vārāha-Śrauta-Sūtra*
YV	*Yajurveda*

Introduction

THE Śrauta ritual comprises two sacrificial institutions: (1) The *soma*-sacrifices and (2) The *havis*-sacrifices. This division is based mainly on the oblation-material used in a sacrifice. It is obvious that in a *soma*-sacrifice, the main oblation is the juice extracted from the *soma*-stalks. In the *havis*-sacrifices, the oblations are given of milk, curds, ghee, clarified butter and various grains. Paddy, barley, wheat, *śyāmāka*, etc. are the sacrificial grains. Generally, rice pap or a cake made of the flour of the sacrificial grains is offered in *havis*-sacrifices. Sometimes, the grains are parched and the pop-corns are offered. An animal also is an oblation offered in *havis*-sacrifices. The animal-sacrifice is called the *nirūḍhapaśubandha*.

Besides the difference in the oblation-material, there are some other differences also between *havis*-sacrifices and *soma*-sacrifices. More priests are needed in a *soma*-sacrifice than in a *havis*-sacrifice. Further, the singing of the *sāman*[1] and the *avabhṛtha iṣṭi*[2] are peculiar to a *soma*-sacrifice; these are generally absent in the ritual procedure of a *havis*-sacrifice.

Among the *havis*-sacrifices is included the *sautrāmaṇī*-sacrifice.[3] It has two forms: (1) The *caraka* and (2) The *kaukilī*. The *caraka* is performed after the *rājasūya* and also after the *agnicayana* (the rite

---

1. *See* A. B. Keith, *Religion and Philosophy of the Veda and the Upaniṣads*, Part II, p. 314.
2. P.V. Kane, *History of Dharmaśāstra*, Vol. II, Part II, pp. 982 and 1228.
3. *sapta havissaṁsthāḥ sapta somasaṁsthāḥ* |
   tāsāṁ haviryajñasaṁsthānāṁ agnyādheyam agnihotraṁ darśapūrṇamāsau pākayajña iti |
   — *LāṭyāŚS*, V.4.22, 23; *see* also, *GautDS*, I.8.20; *VaikhāGS*, I.9.

of building the fire-altar). Occasionally, it is performed also for one who has vomited *soma* (*somavāmin*) or for one who is excessively purged by *soma* (*somātipūta*). The *kaukilī* is an obligatory (*nitya*) rite. Incidentally, it is performed for a *somavāmin* or a *somātipūta*. It is prescribed also for the fulfilment of certain desires. The oblations offered in it are those of rice, milk, clarified butter, etc. Animal-offerings also are to be made in the course of its performance. Three animals are offered to the Aśvins, Sarasvatī and Indra Sutrāman, and it is called both an *iṣṭi* and a *paśubandha* (animal-sacrifice, *ŚatBrā*, XII.7.2,12,21.) Besides these offerings, *surā* is also offered in this sacrifice. *Surā* is a kind of beer prepared from grains. Three cups are filled with it and are offered to the above-mentioned deities.

Surā, as we find it, is condemned in Vedic literature. It is grouped together with wrath, dice, etc. and is held to be the reason of various offenses and guilts, (*ṚV*, VII.86.6).[4] In *ŚatBrā*, V.1.2.10 in the discussion regarding the *vājapeya* sacrifice, *surā* is compared with the *soma* and it is said that *soma* is truth, prosperity and light, whereas *surā* is untruth, misery and darkness. Similarly, in *KāthS*, XII.11 and *MaiS*, II.4.2 also *surā* is said to be untruth.

Further, in *KāṭhS*, XII.12 and *MaiS*, II.4.2, *surā* is said to be unwiseness, thoughtlessness or foolishness of Prajāpati. It is also said: 'due to such nature of *surā*, the elder one and the younger one, the daughter-in-law and the father-in-law chatter foolishly after drinking it. Therefore, a brāhmaṇa should not drink *surā*. If he does so, he brings himself in contact with the evil.[5]

---

4. *na sa svo dakṣo varuṇa dhṛtiḥ sā surā manyur vibhīdako acittiḥ* |
— *ṚV*, VII.86.6.

5. The relevant passage reads thus:
ardhaṁ vai prajāpater ātmano dhairyam āsīd ardham mālvyam |
yad dhairyaṁ tat purastād akuruta |
yan mālvyaṁ tat paścāt paryauhata |
yad dhairyaṁ somo vai saḥ |
tato brāhmaṇam asṛjata |
tasmād brāhmaṇaḥ sarvam eva brahmābhi dhīro yan mālvyaṁ surā vai sā |
→

However, despite such severe condemnation, *surā* has found a place in the Vedic ritual. It is used in some *gṛhya* rites: *ĀśvaŚS*, II.5.4 prescribes that together with other oblations, *surā* also should be offered to the wives of the fathers. Also, the women present at a wedding or at an *ānvaṣṭakya śrāddha* are to be regaled with *surā* (*ĀśvaGS*, II.5.5 and also *ŚāṅkhāGS*, I.11.5).

Sūra is found used in the Śrauta ritual also. In the *vājapeya* sacrifice, seventeen cups of *surā* are drawn, they are shaken on the *mārjālīya dhiṣṇya* and then are partaken by some priests (*ĀpaŚS*, XVIII.7.2, 4, 8) or the Neṣṭṛ buys the cup of *madhu* in exchange of these *surā* cups (*KātyŚS*, XIV.4.16). According to the *AitBrā*, the sacrificer is given the *surā* drink in the ritual of the *rājasūya* and also in the rite *punarabhiṣeka*, which is perfomed at the end of the *rājasūya*. Remarkable is the glorification of it in the *rājasūya*, where it is said that *surā* gives, just like *soma* or any other food, pleasure and peace especially to a kṣatriya sacrificer (*AitBrā*, XXXIX.6).[6]

However, it is only the *sautrāmaṇī* sacrifice, in which *surā* is offered and even consumed by the sacrificer and also by the priests.

Interesting it is yet that, the same texts, which have condemned *surā*, have glorified it in this context. Thus, it is stated in *MaiS*, II.4.2 and *KāṭhS*, XII.12 that the kṣatriya is born from *surā*. He

---

← *tato rājanyam asṛjata* ।
tasmāj jyāyāṁśca kanīyāṁś ca snuṣā ca śvaśuraś ca surāṁ pītvā vilālapata āsata ।
mālvyaṁ hi tat ।
pāpmā vai mālvyam ।
tasmād brāhmaṇaḥ surāṁ na pibet ।
pāpmanā ātmānaṁ net saṁsṛjā iti ।
— *MaiS*, II.4.2; *KāṭhS*, XII.12.

6. *tad yathai'vā'daḥ priyaḥ putraḥ pitaraṁ priyā vā jāyā patiṁ sukhaṁ śivaṁ upaspṛśaty āvisrasaḥ evaṁ hai 'vai e'tenaindreṇa mahābhiṣekeṇā'bhiṣiktasya kṣatriyasya surā vā somo vā anyad vā annādyaṁ sukhaṁ śivaṁ upaspṛśaty āvisrasaḥ* ।
— *AitBrā*, 39.6

should be told this *brāhmaṇa* (portion) that one, who knowing this drinks *surā* does not get harmed by it. *Surā* is the vigorous form of Prajāpati; Prajāpati himself is vigour. He thus places vigour in himself.[7] Also, *surā* is said to be food, sacrificial food in *MaiS*, II.3.9 and *KāṭhS*, XII.11.[8]

Besides the use of *surā*, there are certain other peculiarities also in the ritual of this sacrifice. The *avabhṛtha*, which is performed generally after the *soma*-sacrifice is performed in this rite. It is found introduced in both the forms, the *caraka* and the *kaukilī*. Similarly, the singing of the *sāman*, which is a speciality of the *soma*-sacrifices is also prescribed, by some texts, in the ritual of the *kaukilī sautrāmaṇī*.[9]

The same tendency of establishing the similarity with *soma* is found in connection with *surā* also, which was, it should be noted, put in contrast with *soma* in connection with the *vājapeya*-sacrifice. In the *ŚatBrā*, the ingredients of *surā* are metaphorically said to be the stalks of *soma*. The various acts in the procedure of the preparation of *surā* are compared with the various acts in the procedure of preparing the *soma*-juice. Further, the ritual of the *sautrāmanī* itself is compared to that of the *soma*-sacrifice and the *sautrāmanī* is elevated to the dignity of *soma*-sacrifice. It is said to be not less than a form of the *soma*-sacrifice itself (*ŚatBrā*, XII.8.2.21).[10]

---

7. *tad u etad rāṣṭrīyāya brāhmaṇam brūyāt tad ya evaṁ vidvān surām pibati na vāi' naṁ drūṇāti* |
eṣā vai prajāpater vīryavatī tanūr vīryam prajāpatiḥ |
vīryam asmin dadhāti |
— *KāṭhS*, XII.12 and *MaiS*, II.4.2.

8. *annaṁ vai surā* |
medhyaṁ vā annam |
tena medhyā |
— *KāṭhS*, XII.11 and *MaiS*, II.3.9.

9. The singing of the *sāman* is prescribed in the *kaukilī* by *ŚatBrā*, XII.8.3.23; *KātyŚS*, XIX.5.1; *VaitāSū*, XXX.16 and *LāṭyāŚS*, V.4.16 and 21.

10. *sa vā pratyakṣāt somayajña eva yat sautrāmaṇi* |
— *ŚatBrā*. XII.8.2.21.

It is no wonder then that these peculiarities of the *sautrāmaṇī*-sacrifice have caught attention of the scholars. It is found described by Keith, Hillebrandt and others.[11] Weber[12] also has discussed it in connection with the *rājasūya*. G. Dumézil in his book *Tarpeia* has made a detailed study of *sautrāmaṇī*. He has suggested that the ritual of *sautrāmaṇī* has a close similarity with the Roman rite *Suovertaurilia*.[13] Gonda[14] has written a very valuable monograph on the *mantras* used in this sacrifice. Many scholars have studied, particularly the myth cited in connection with the origin of the rite and some of them have expressed their opinion about the origin of the rite based on the interpretation of these myths.[15]

Nevertheless, there have still remained some problems regarding the nature and origin of the *sautrāmaṇī*-sacrifice, the answers of which are not found in the works done herebefore. The problems are:

(1) How is it that the *surā* which is severely condemned in Vedic literature is accepted in the Śrauta ritual?

(2) Why is the *sautrāmaṇī* to be performed after the *rājasūya*? Further, is there any connection between the *punarabhiṣeka* and the *sautrāmaṇī*, since both of them contain the *surā*-ritual?

(3) What is the exact relation between the *agnicayana* and the *sautrāmaṇī*?

---

11. A.B. Keith, *op.cit.*, pp. 352ff.; A. Hillebrandt, *Ritualliteratur, vedische Opfer und Zauber*, pp. 159ff; P.V. Kane, *op.cit.*, pp. 1224ff.; G.U. Thite, *Sacrifice in the Brāhmaṇa texts*, pp. 83ff.; J. Gonda, *Die Religionen Indiens*, I, p. 173.

12. *See* G. Dumezil, *Tarpeia*, 1947, pp. 117, 158.

13. A. Weber, *Über die Königsweihe, den Rājasūya*.

14. J. Gonda, *The Mantras of the Agnyupasthāna and the Sautrāmaṇī*, pp. 63ff.

15. H. Oldenberg, "Indra and Namuci", in *Kleine Schriften*, pp. 635ff; M. Bloomflield, in *JAOS*, Vol. 15, pp. 143ff.; K. Rönnow, in *Le Monde Oriental*, Vol. 23, pp. 113ff.; A. Coomarasvamī, in *JAOS*, Vol. 55 (1935), pp. 373-7.

(4) Why is the *sautrāmaṇī* performed as a medicinal rite for a *somavāmin* or a *somātipūta*?

Similarly, among the myths cited in connection with the origin of the rite, only one particular myth is often taken into consideration by scholars and therefore, the correlation of that myth and the ritual has become lop-sided. The interpretation of other myths is really essential for understanding the full significance of the often discussed myth and the *sautrāmaṇī* ritual. This situation raises one important question viz. what is the purport of the myths which tell about the primeval performance of the *sautrāmaṇī*?

Consequently, I have tried here to offer answers to the questions which are related mainly to the origin and the nature of the *sautrāmaṇī*-sacrifice. These answers form the first part of my work.

In the next (i.e., the second) part, I have tried to give an account of the ritual procedure of the *sautrāmaṇī*, of both the *caraka* and the *kaukilī*. Weber[16] has taken into consideration the ritual of the *caraka* which is described in the *KātyŚS*, the *ĀśvaŚS* and the *ŚāṅkhāŚS*; he has discussed it in connection with the *rājasūya*. The detailed description of both the forms is arranged in the *Śrautakośa*[17] also. This work gives a detailed account of the ritual in the *sūtra*s one after another. However, it has not dealt with the ritual description and the explanations occurring in the Saṁhitās and the *Brāhmaṇa*s. Further, one finds it difficult to get a clear idea of the differences or similarities which are found in the *sūtra*s in respect of the different rites in the ritual procedure of the *sautrāmaṇī*. Therefore, it was felt necessary to discuss the ritual which we find in the Saṁhitās and the *Brāhmaṇa*s and also to rearrange the ritual described in the *sūtra*s. With this purpose in view, I have taken into consideration one rite after another and have tried to note the various procedures found in different texts and traditions. The ritual of the preparation of *surā*, I have dealt with separately and have compared it with the procedure of its preparation found

---

16. A. Weber, *op.cit.*, pp. 92ff.
17. *Śrautakośa* English Section, II, pp. 899ff.

in other civilizations. It must be stated, nevertheless, that my task would have been much difficult without the help of the *Śrautakośa*.

Then I have noted the differences between the two forms of the *sautrāmaṇī* and have mentioned, in the concluding chapter, the social and ritual significance of the *sautrāmaṇī* and its place in the Vedic ritual as well. I have tried to trace out the development and the changes in its ritual also.

Part I

1

The Place of the Sautrāmaṇī in Vedic Ritual

THE *sautrāmaṇī* has two distinct forms: (1) The *caraka* and (2) The *kaukilī*. That which is included among the *havis*-sacrifices is called the *kaukilī*.[1] It is obligatory (*nitya*), incidental (*naimittika*) and optional (*kāmya*). The *sautrāmaṇī* which is to be performed after the *rājasūya* or the *agnicayana* is called the *caraka*.

The description of both these forms is found in the Saṁhitās, the *Brāhmaṇa* texts and in the *Śrauta Sūtras*. The *mantras* and also the *Brāhmaṇa* portion regarding the *caraka* are collected in *MaiS*, II.3.8-9; II.4.1-2 and IV.12.5, and only the *mantras*, regarding the *kaukilī* are cited in *MaiS*, III.11.1-12 and IV.14.18. In the *KāṭhS*, the *mantras* and the *Brāhmaṇa* are cited at XII.9-12; XVI.1 and XVIII.21. The *mantras* of the *kaukilī* are collected in *KāṭhS*, XXXVII.18 and 38. Only four *mantras* and a very brief *Brāhmaṇa* of the *caraka* is collected in *TaiS*, I.8.21. It does not contain the description of the *kaukilī*. In the *VājaS* the *mantras* of the *caraka* are cited at X.31-34 and those of *kaukilī* are collected in XIXth, XXth and XXIst *adhyāyas*.

Among the *Brāhmaṇa* texts, *ŚatBrā*, V.5.4.1 to 35 describes the ritual of the *caraka* and XII.7.1.1 to XII.9.3.16 that of the *kaukilī*. In the *TaiBrā* the *mantras* of the *caraka* are cited at I.4.2 and the *Brāhmaṇa* portion of it, at I.8.5-6. As regards the *kaukilī*, the

1. Cf. *GautDS*, I.8.20; *HirŚS*, XXIII.1.1; *LāṭyāŚS*, V.4.33. *BaudhŚS*, XXIV.4 includes it optionally in the *havis*-sacrifices.

Brāhmaṇa gives only the *mantras* at II.6.1-20. In the *GopBrā* the ritual of the *kaukilī* only is described at II.5-6.

Among the *Śrauta Sūtras*, the *BhārŚS* does not contain any description of the *sautrāmaṇī*. In *BaudhŚS*, XVII.31-38; XXIII.16; XXVI.22; XIV.23, 30 and in *VaikhāŚS*, XI.1-6 the ritual of only the *caraka* is described, whereas the *VaitāSū* describes the ritual only of the *kaukilī* in the XXXth chapter. The ritual of both the forms is described in the *ĀpaŚS*; the *HirŚS*; the *MānŚS*; the *VārāŚS* and the *KātyŚS*. The duties of the Hotṛ in connection with the *sautrāmaṇī* are described in *ĀśvaŚS*, III.9 and *SāṅkhāŚS*, XV.15; *LāṭyāŚS*, V.4.11-15 and *DrāhyāŚS*, XIII.4.5-8 also describe the ritual of the *sautrāmaṇī*, mainly in connection with the singing of the *sāman*.

Even though, both the forms of the *sautrāmaṇī* are described in the Saṁhitās and the *Brāhmaṇas*, the names of the forms do not occur there. They are found in the *sūtras*. Thus, the name *kaukilī* is found in *ĀpaŚS*, XIX.5.1 — *athātaḥ kaukilīṁ vyākhyāsyāmaḥ*, 'Now we will describe the *kaukilī*', in *MānŚS*, V.2.11.1 — *kaukilyāḥ sautrāmaṇyāḥ sa kalpo ya aiṣṭikyāḥ*, 'The procedure of the *kaukilī sautrāmaṇī*' is like that of the *aiṣṭikī* (i.e., the *caraka*) *sautrāmaṇī*'; and in *VārāŚS*, III.2.8.1 — *kaukilyās te kāmā pūrvasyām anye ca*, 'The purposes of the *kaukilī* are those (stated) in the preceding one (the *caraka*) and some others.'

It is only in the *LāṭyāŚS* where both the names are mentioned. Thus in *LāṭyāŚS*, V.4.20 it is stated — *dve sautrāmaṇyau kaukilī carakasautrāmaṇī ca*, 'There are two types of the *sautrāmaṇī*; the *caraka* and the *kaukilī*.'

It is curious, however, that no explanation of the names is found anywhere in Vedic texts. Hillebrandt[2] has tried to establish some relation between the *caraka sautrāmaṇī* and the Caraka school of medicine which very much honours the *surā* drink. According to Keith[3] the *caraka sautrāmaṇī* seems to be a reference to the school

2. A. Hillebrandt, *Ritualiteratur*, p. 160.
3. A.B. Keith, *The Religion and the Philosophy of the Veda and the Upaniṣads*, p. 353.

of the *Black YV*, which is often so mentioned. Weber also holds a similar opinion.[4] He has convincingly argued that when we come across the references to the views of the *carakādhvaryus* in the *ŚatBrā*, these might have specific connection with the views expressed in the *Taittirīya Saṁhitā*. He has tried to establish some relation between the views of the *carakādhvaryus* and those expressed in the *Kāṭhaka Saṁhitā* also. However, he has stated at the end, 'for the time being, I am not sure about it'.[5]

He has further conjectured that the Kaṭha is a branch of the Caraka tradition, as the colophon of every *adhyāya* in the *Kāṭhaka Saṁhitā* reads as *śrīmadyajurveda-kāṭhake carakaśākhāyāṁ*, 'Thus in the *Kāṭhaka Yajurveda* in the Caraka branch'.[6]

Regarding the name *kaukilī*, however, Weber is certain that the information about this sacrifice is given by one prince called 'Kokila Rājaputra'.[7] The reason given is: this prince is the seer of *KāṭhS*, XXXVIII.3 (this contains the *mantras* of the *kaukilī sautrāmaṇī*) as is mentioned in the *Ārṣādhyāya* of the *KāṭhS*.

Although the names *caraka* and *kaukilī* are not explained in Vedic texts, the name *sautrāmaṇī* is explained in some of them. The word *sautrāmaṇī* is derived from the word *sutrāman*, an epithet of Indra. The rite which is performed for Sutrāman Indra is called the Sautrāmaṇī. A myth is cited in *ŚatBrā*, V.5.4.2. to 12 for explaining the words *sutrāman* and the *sautrāmaṇī*. The myth is (in brief) as follows:

> Indra killed the son of Tvaṣṭṛ, who thereupon became angry with him and brought *soma* to perform a Sacrifice. He did not invite Indra to that sacrifice. So Indra, using his force, went there and drank the *soma*-juice. However, since the *soma*-juice was drunk in an improper way, it came out

---

4. A. Weber, *Über die Königweihe den Rājasūya*, pp. 92, 93.
5. A. Weber, *Indische Studien*, Vol.3, p. 454.
6. A. Weber, *Über die Königsweihe den Rājasūya*, pp. 92, 93; *see* also L. Renou, *Les E'coles Vediques*, pp. 150, 151.
7. *Ibid*. p. 94, fn. 3.

> from all his organs. At that time, the Aśvins cured him with the help of this *sautrāmaṇī* and restored to him his sensual strength and power.

At the end of the myth occurs the explanation of the name *sautrāmaṇī*. Thus, it is said in *ŚatBrā*, V.5.4.11,

> *te devā abruvan sutrātum batai 'nam atrāsatām iti tasmāt sautrāmaṇī nāma* ।
>
> Aha! these two have saved him, the well-saved hence the name Sautrāmaṇī.
>
> (tr. by Eggeling, part III, p. 131)

A similar explanation of the name occurs also at the end of the myth which is cited in connection with the *kaukilī*. Thus it is said in *ŚatBrā*, XII.7.1.14,

> *tāv aśvinau ca sarasvatī ca indriyaṁ vīryaṁ namucer āhṛtya tad asmin punar adadhus tasmāt pāpmano atrāyanta sutrātam batai 'nam pāpmano'trāsmahīti tad vāva sautrāmany abhavat tat sautrāmanyai sautrāmaṇītvam* ।
>
> The two Aśvins and Sarasvatī, having taken the energy, or vital power, from Namuci, restored them to him (Indra) and saved him from evil. 'Truly, we have saved him from evil so as to be well-saved (sutrāta)' they thought, and this became the Sautrāmaṇī: and this is the (saving) nature of the Sautrāmaṇī. . . .
>
> (tr by Eggeling, pt.V, p. 217)

Even though, the myth is cited in almost all Vedic texts, it is only the *ŚatBrā* that has offered an explanation of the name Sautrāmaṇī on the basis of it. In other texts, the myth has occurred only to tell about the origin of the rite.

Further the word is found explained in the commentaries on the *VājaS*. The commentators Uvaṭa and Mahīdhara have first explained the word *sutrāman* and then presented its meaning in the ritual context. Thus, Uvaṭa while explaining *indrāya sutrāmṇe pacyasva* (*VājaS*, 10.31) has stated,

> *sutrāmṇe śobhanatrānāya sutrātavyāya vā bhaiṣajyaṁ hīndrasya kartavyam sautrāmaṇyā* ।
>
> The word *sutrāmṇe* means for one who has fine protection, (to offer to somebody else) or for one, who is to be well-protected, since by the performance of the *sautrāmaṇī* a medical treatment is to be given to Indra.

Mahīdhara also has explained the word *sutrāman*. He has stated,

> *suṣṭhu trāyate iti sutrāmā tasmai sutrāmṇe śobhanatrāṇakartre sutrātavyāya vā indrāya pacyasva yataḥ sautrāmaṇyā indrasya bhaiṣajyaṁ kartavyam asti* ।
>
> *Sutrāman* means one who protects well. *Sutrāmṇe* means for one, who protects well, or offers fine protection; or 'for one, who is to be well-protected', since by the performance of the *sautrāmaṇī* rite, a medical treatment is to be given to Indra.

The same verse occurs at *VājaS*, XIX.1 also, and commenting upon it, Mahīdhara reaffirms his first explanation, thus:

> *suṣṭhu trāyate rakṣati iti sutrāmā tasmai* ।
> *trāyateḥ āto manin* ।
> One who protects well is called *sutrāmā*. (It is) for him. The *manin* suffix is attached to the root *trai*. . . .

In connection with the explanation of the word, Weber[8] has rightly pointed out that the word *sutrāman* should mean 'one who protects well', but, in the context of the myth, it means, 'one, who is protected well'.

From the myth mentioned above it also becomes clear that the *sautrāmaṇī* was first performed as a medicinal rite to cure Indra. The faculties and the sensual powers, which he had lost after drinking *soma* were restored to him by the performance of this rite.

---

8. A. Weber, *op.cit.*, 101, f.n. 2.

Yet, this is not the only purpose attached to it. There are so many other purposes also attached to the *sautrāmaṇī* just as any other Vedic rite. In this connection Van Buitenen[9] has said,

> It is probably futile even to attempt a holistic explanation of any Vedic ritual. While single rites might have had single purposes and their meaning at one time have been explicable from this purpose, it is clear that in the course of the centuries, a tremendous conflation of ritual has taken place, so that no ritual, *agnihotra, iṣṭi*, etc. can be presumed to be in any sense unitary.

In some way, what Buitenen has stated is true. In the case of the *sautrāmaṇī* ritual also it is found that the rite is prescribed for the fulfilment of various purposes, starting from health to heaven.[10] Be this so, his view cannot be accepted fully. If the ritual is examined minutely and Vedic texts are studied closely, it is possible to form an opinion about the original form and purpose of a given rite and further, it is also possible to determine the earlier and the later layers in its development.[11]

To study the ritual of the *sautrāmaṇī* in this regard, it is necessary to decide which is the earlier form between the *caraka* and the *kaukilī*; and for that matter it will be useful to see first the general outline of the ritual of the two.

---

9. J.A.B. Van Buitenen, *The Pravargya*, p. 23.
10. Dr. V. Raghavan, in his book, *Festivals, Sports and Pastimes of India*, p. 15 has stated, while speaking about the festivals in the Vedic times that, 'The Sautrāmaṇī was marked by similar licentious behaviour in respect of unlimited drinking and offering of Surā and free talk with harlots.' In Vedic literature, however, we do not find any such description regarding *sautrāmaṇī*. The author might have perhaps been under such impression because of the description in the later text, called *Māṭhara Vṛtti*, where it is said, at II (7.23), *sautrāmaṇyāṁ surāpānaṁ raṇḍayā saha svecchālāpaś ca* ।
11. See F.W. Bodewitz, *The Daily Evening and Morning Offering (Agnihotra) According to the Brāhmaṇas*, Intr. pp. 1 and 2: and also, G.U. Thite, *Sacrifice in the Brāhmaṇa-texts*, pp. 16 ff.

Three days before the actual performance of the *caraka sautrāmaṇī* the ingredients of *surā* are mixed together and they are kept for fermentation. On the fourth day, three animal victims are offered to three deities namely the Aśvins, Sarasvatī and Indra Sutrāman. Three cups of *surā* are also offered to them. Then, a pitcher having a hundred holes is kept hanging on the southern fire and the remaining *surā* is poured into that pitcher. The *surā* thus poured trickles down into the fire and that is considered to be an offering to the fathers. At that time are uttered the verses which have the word *pitṛ* in them. Some of the remnants of *surā* is eaten by the sacrificer himself. Then the priests and the sacrificer, etc. go for the *avabhṛtha* bath.

The ritual of the *kaukilī* is not much different from that of the *caraka*. There are, nevertheless, certain additions in it. Thus, together with the cups of *surā*, three cups of milk are also offered to the Aśvins, Sarasvatī and Indra Sutrāman. On the first day a bull is offered to Indra and rice-pap is offered to Aditi. On the day of the actual performance of the rite, after the offerings of the three animals to the deities, there are thirtythree offerings of the fat of those animals and after that the sacrificer is anointed with the remnants of that fat. A *sāman* is sung at that time. Then the priests and the sacrificer, etc. take the *avabhṛtha* bath as in the *caraka*. After coming back from the *avabhṛtha* bath, rice-pap is again offered to Aditi and a bull is offered to Indra Vayodhas.

From the comparison of the ritual of these two forms of the *sautrāmaṇī*, it is evident that the ritual of the *caraka* is more simple, while that of the *kaukilī* is more elaborate. If the principle that, in a ritual the more simple precedes the more laborious and more elaborate is followed, then it becomes obvious that the *caraka* is the primary form of the rite and the *kaukilī* is the laterly developed form of it.[12] The insertion of the rite of the singing of the *sāman* in the *kaukilī* also leads to the same conclusion.

While examining the nature of the *caraka sautrāmaṇī* in the

---

12. J.A.B. Van Buitenen, *op.cit.*, p. 3.

light of Vedic texts, one does not fail to notice that many of the texts have described it at the end of the description of the *rājasūya* (cf. *VājaS*, X.31; *TaiS*, I.8.2, *TaiBrā*, I.8.5-6; *ŚatBrā*, V.5.4.1-35; *KātyŚS*, XV.9.22. to XV.10.24). From the sequence of the description it becomes apparent that the *caraka sautrāmaṇī* is a part of the *rājasūya*.

That, according to the *VājaS*, the *caraka* is considered to be a part of the *rājasūya* is further confirmed by the *Brāhmaṇa* and the *sūtra* text of the same recension, viz. the *ŚatBrā* and the *KātyŚS*. According to these texts, not only does the *caraka* form a part of the *rājasūya*, but also is a necessary complement of the latter.

It may be stated here in passing that, among the *Śrauta Sūtras*, the *KātyŚS*, gives the briefest description of the *sautrāmaṇī* and that description is, therefore, likely to be referring to the oldest phase of the *sautrāmaṇī* ritual.

In *TaiS*, I.8.21, there occurs at the end of the description of the *rājasūya*, only four *mantras* and a very brief *Brāhmaṇa* portion pertaining to the *caraka sautrāmaṇī*. There is no mention there of the purpose of the rite. Yet, its place in the *TaiBrā* clearly shows that it is to be performed as a part of the *rājasūya*. The *mantras* to be used in the *caraka* are collected in *TaiBrā*, at I.4.2.9-10, before the description of the *devasū* offerings in the *rājasūya*. The *Brāhmaṇa* portion occurs at I.8.5-6. It is preceded by the description of *prayujāṁ havīṁṣi* and followed by the rite of *agniṣṭoma* named *pavitra*. Both these rites are parts of the *rājasūya* ritual. Therefore, the *caraka sautrāmaṇī* also forms a part of the *rājasūya*, according to the *sandaṁśapatitanyāya* 'the rule regarding one, falling in between the two'.[13]

---

13. *Arthasaṅgraha* has explained the word *sandaṁśa* as — *ekāṅgānuvādena vidhīyamānayor aṅgayor antarāle vihitatvaṁ sandaṁśaḥ*. *Mīmāṁsākośa*, Vol.7, p. 4124 explains the word *sandaṁśapatitanyāya* as *sandaṁśaḥ 'sanāsī' iti yasya prasiddhiḥ* | *tadavayavayoḥ madhyapātinaḥ padārthasya yathāgrahaṇam evam pūrvottarayor grahaṇena tanmadhyapadārthasya grahaṇaṁ yatra vivakṣyate tatrāsya pravṛttiḥ* |

Moreover, it is specifically prescribed in Vedic texts that one, who has performed the *rājasūya* sacrifice, should subsequently perform the *sautrāmaṇī*, (cf. *MaiS*, II.4.2; *KāṭhS*, XII.10; *ŚatBrā*, V.5.4.14; *BaudhŚS*, XII.20; *ĀpaŚS*, XVIII.22.21; *HirŚS*, XIII.7.37; *MānŚS*, V.2.4.1; *VārāŚS*, III.2.7.1).

The *MaiS*, the *KāṭhS*, and the *ŚatBrā,* offer also the reason as to why the *sautrāmaṇī* should be performed after the *rājasūya*. Thus it is said in *ŚatBrā*, V.5.4.14:

> And as to why the performer of the Rājasūya performs this offering. He who performs the Rājasūya assuredly gains for himself all sacrificial rites, all offering even the spoon-full oblations; and instituted by the gods indeed is this offering, the Sautrāmaṇī: 'May offering be made by me with this one also! may I be consecrated by this one also!' thus (he thinks, and) therefore the performer of the Rājasūya performs this offering. (tr. by Eggeling)

The reason given in *MaiS*, II.4.1. and *KāṭhS*, XII.10 is however different. It is stated in these two Saṁhitās:

> The Adhvaryu should perform this sacrifice for one who wants to be consecrated by the *rājasūya*. One, who is consecrated by the *rājasūya* is deprived of strength and vigour. Since much strength and vigour have gone away from the sacrificer, the Adhvarya restores to him the same, by performing the *caraka sautrāmaṇī.*

It is clear from the explanation in these Saṁhitās that the *caraka sautrāmaṇī* is performed after the *rājasūya* as a curing and a redressing rite.

Secondly, the *caraka sautrāmaṇī* is prescribed after the *agnicayana* (*TaiS*, V.6.3.4; *TaiBrā*, III.12.5.33; *ĀpaŚS*, XVII.2.4.1; *BaudhŚS*, X.59; *MānŚS*, XI.2.6.27; *VārāŚS*, II.2.5.11).

The reason as to why it is to be performed after the *cayana* is given only in the *TaiS,* and the *TaiBrā*. It is stated in *TaiS*, 5.6.3.4:

sūyate vā eṣa yo'gniṁ cinute'gniṁ citvā sautrāmaṇyā yajete'ndriyam eva vīryaṁ sambhr̥tyā'tman dhatte ।

he who piles the fire is consecrated; having piled the fire, he should sacrifice with the Sautrāmaṇī, verily collecting power and strength, he places them in himself.
(tr. by Keith, Vol. 2, p. 457)

The reason given in *TaiBrā*, III.12.5.33 is similar to that stated in the *TaiS*. Thus, according to these two texts, the *sautrāmaṇī* performed after the *cayana* (viz. the *caraka*) is performed as a redressing rite.

The *caraka sautrāmaṇī* is prescribed also for a *somātipūta*, (cf. *MaiS*, II.4.1; *ŚatBrā*, V.5.4.13; *MānŚS*, V.2.4.1 and *KātyŚS*, XV.10.19). In the *ŚatBrā,* it is said,

he whom Soma purges is indeed emptied out of everything, for Soma is everything. He now causes him to be supplied with everything, for Soma is everything; and by offering he indeed becomes better: let him therefore cure thereby also one purged by Soma. (tr. by Eggeling, pt. III, p. 132)

The *MaiS* has given a different reason. According to it,

somenātipupuvānaṁ yājayed indriyeṇa vā eṣa vīryeṇa vyr̥dhyate yaṁ somo'tipavate yāvad eve'ndriyaṁ vīryam tad asminn āptvā dadhāti.

The *sautrāmaṇī* should be performed for one, who is excessively purged by *soma*, such a person is deprived of strength and vigour. The Adhvaryu performs this sacrifice and thereby reinstates that strength and vigour in him.

That it is to be performed for a *somātipūta* is not specifically mentioned in the *TaiBrā* and the *BaudhŚS*. However, it is suggested through the instruction of certain modification in the *mantra*s.

Thus in *TaiBrā*, I.8.6.4 it is first stated that *surā* should not be purified with the recitation of the *mantra*, *vāyuḥ pūtaḥ pavitreṇa* as it is lacking something. The *mantra*, *vāreṇa śaśvatā tanā* . . .

should be used for the purification. Afterwards this instruction is modified and it is told that it should be purified with the verse *vāyuḥ pūtaḥ pavitreṇa* . . . for one who is purged by *soma*. Similar injunction is found in *BaudhŚS*, XVII.34.

The *BaudhŚS* prescribes modification also in the *mantras* used for the consecration of the trickling *surā*. The *surā* remaining after the offerings of the cups is poured in a pot having a hundred holes and the trickling *surā* is consecrated with the eight verses beginning with the verse *pavamānaḥ suvarjanaḥ*. . . . But, if the sacrificer is a *somātipūta*, the *surā* at this time should be consecrated with the verses which are used as the *puronuvākyās* (invitatory verses) and the *yājyās* (offering verses) for the offerings to the Fathers, (*BaudhŚS*, XVII.36).

It is also mentioned that if the sacrificer is a *somātipūta,* a fourth animal should be immolated for Bṛhaspati (*TaiBrā,*I.8.6.4; *BaudhŚS*, XVII.36; *VaikhāŚS*, XI.3; *VārāŚS*, III.2.7.26; *HirŚS*, XIII.8.19; *ĀpaŚS*, XIX.2.1, 2).

In some of the *sūtra* texts, the *caraka* is prescribed for a *somavāmin* also together with the *somātipūta* (cf. *VārāŚS*, III.2.7.1; *ĀpaŚS*, XIX.4.11; *VaikhāŚS*, XI.1; *HirŚS*, XIII.8.44).

It is to be performed after the *vājapeya* (*ĀpaŚS*, XVIII.7.15; *VaikhāŚS*, XVII.18) and also in the rites which consist of the *abhiṣeka* ceremony (*ĀpaŚS*, XIX.4.13; *VaikhāŚS*, XI.1; *HirŚS*, XIII.8.44).

Besides these occasions, the *caraka* is prescribed for the fulfilment of certain desires also. It is prescribed for one who is desirous of prosperity '*bhūtikāma*' (*MānŚS*, V.2.4.1; *VārāŚS*, III.2.7.1; *HirŚS*, XIII.8.44; *VaikhāŚS*, XI.1) and also for one who is desirous of food and cattle '*paśukāma*' (*VārāŚS*, III.2.7.1 and *ĀpaŚS*, XIX.4.12) and who is desirous of progeny '*prajākāma*' (*ĀpaŚS*, XIX.4.12; *HirŚS*, XIII.8.44).

A king, who is deprived of his kingdom '*rājā aparuddhaḥ*' should perform this rite and also one who wants to perform black magic '*abhicaran*' or against whom black magic is performed '*abhicaryamāṇa*' (*ĀpaŚS*, XIX.4.11; *VaikhāŚS*, XI.1 and *HirŚS*, XIII.8.44).

Also it is prescribed for a brāhmaṇa or a kṣatrıya or a vaiśya, who is desirous of brilliance ('*tejaskāma*' *ĀpaŚS*, XIX.4.14). One who has an enemy '*bhrātṛvyavān*' should also perform it (*VārāŚS*, III.2.7.1). Also one who is desirous of acquiring a village '*grāmakāma*' should do so (*HirŚS*, XIII.8.44).

MaiS, II.4.1, *KāṭhS*, XII.10; *MānŚS*, V.2.4.1 and *VārāŚS*, III.2.7.1 prescribe the performance of the *caraka* also for one who is ill for a long time '*jyogāmayāvin*'.

In this connection the view of some other ritualists is quoted and rejected by the *MaiS*, and the *KāṭhS*. According to those ritualists, this rite is to be performed only for such a person as is suffering from something. Further, it is added that everybody can perform it since everybody is suffering (in some way or the other) and everybody wants to be better (i.e., strives for achieving something).[14]

The *kaukilī sautrāmaṇī* is prescribed for one, who has performed a *soma*-sacrifice (*ŚāṅkhāBrā*, XVI.10; *ŚatBrā*, XII.8.2.2). The reason is given in a myth in *ŚatBrā*, XII.8.2.1. It states,

> Prajāpati created the (Soma) sacrifice. He took it and performed it. When he had performed it, he felt like one emptied out. At that time, he saw[15] this sacrificial performace, the Sautrāmaṇī and performed it and then he was again replenished; and, indeed, he who performs the Soma-sacrifice is, as it were, emptied out, for his wealth, his prosperity is, as it were, taken from him.
>
> (tr. by Eggeling, pt. V, p. 239)

14. The actual word in the text is *bubhūṣati*. It seems to be a desiderative form of √*bhu* meaning 'wish to be' i.e., 'to wish to be better or to prosper'. For a detailed study of the word, See J. Gonda, *Four Studies in the Language of the Veda*, pp. 71 to 93.
15. For a discussion about gods and the creation of the sacrifice, see J. Gonda, "Vedic Gods and the Sacrifice" in *Numen*, Vol. XXX, Fasc. 1, July 1983, p. 30.

And, therefore, it is prescribed, in *ŚatBrā*, XII.2.2.2:

> Having performed a Soma-sacrifice, one ought to perform the Sautrāmaṇī: as a cow that has been milked would replenish again, even so, indeed, does he replenish himself, — he replenishes himself by offspring and cattle; and verily, he, who knowing this, performs the Sautrāmaṇī, or he, who (even) knows this, establishes himself in this world, and wins the heavenly world.
>
> (tr. by Eggeling, pt.V, p. 239)

According to *KātyŚS*, XIX.1.2 and *VaitāSū*, XXX.1, it is to be performed for one, who has performed a *soma*-sacrifice together with the *agnicayana*, i.e., who is a *sāgnicit somayājin.*

MānŚS, V.2.11.2 and *VārāŚS*, III.2.8.1 mention that the *kaukilī* is performed for all the purposes which are mentioned in connection with the *caraka*.

It is prescribed also for one, who has vomited *soma* (cf. *MānŚS*, V.2.11.2; *KātyŚS*, XIX.1.2; *ŚatBrā*, XII.8.2.2; *VaitāSū*, XXX.1).

While prescribing the *kaukilī* for a *somavāmin*, the *ŚatBrā*, mentions an objection raised by some people. Thus it is said in *ŚatBrā*, XII.7.2.2:

> *tad āhuḥ annaṁ vā etad brāhmaṇasya yat somo sa yo vā alam bhūtyai san bhūtiṁ na prāpnoti yo vā alam paśubhyaḥ san paśūn na vindate sa somavāmī paśavo hi soma iti.*

> As to this they say, 'Truly the Soma-juice is the Brāhmaṇa's food; and indeed it is not owing to Soma when a Brāhmaṇa vomits Soma. And he who vomits Soma is one, who, whilst being fit to (gain) prosperity, does not gain prosperity, and who, whilst being fit to (gain) cattle, does not gain cattle, for Soma is cattle. (tr. by Eggeling, pt. V, p. 217)

In the commentary on this passage it is said,

> The vomiting of *soma* is possible only in the case of the kṣatriyas and vaiśyas. Since *soma* is the food of the

> brāhmaṇas, he will not vomit it. But the kṣatriyas and vaiśyas are not entitled to the *soma*-drink; how then can it be said that they vomit it? The answer is: when they drink it, despite their not having a right to do so, that *soma*, drunk in an improper way can cause the vomiting.[16]

This passage in the *ŚatBrā* and the commentary upon it are very important. Two significant points are mentioned in them: (i) They reveal one important social fact that the kṣatriyas and the vaiśyas were not entitled to drink the *soma* (in the sacrifice) and (ii) The cause of the vomiting of *soma* as is suggested here is drinking the *soma* in an improper way.

That the *kaukilī* is to be performed for a *somavāmin* and a *somātipūta* is not specifically mentioned in the *ĀpaŚS,* and the *HirŚS*, but is suggested by certain modifications in the *mantra*s to be recited when the milk is purified for a sacrificer, who is a *somavāmin* or a *somātipūta.*

The *kaukilī* is performed also as a *kāmya* rite for the fulfilment of certain desires. It is performed for achieving prosperity (*KātyŚS*, XIX.1.1) and also for obtaining brilliance, vigour and strength (*VārāŚS*, III.2.8.1). One, who is desirous of obtaining heaven should also perform it (*ĀpaŚS*, XIX.10.14; *HirŚS*, XXIII.1.6.1). It is prescribed for a king, who is deprived of his kingdom and also for one, who does not possess cattle, even though he deserves to possess them (*KātyŚS*, XIX.1.4).

One, who is abandoned by fortune, and one, who desires to achieve preeminence should also perform this sacrifice, even if one

---

16. The relevant passage in the commentary on *ŚatBrā*, XII.8.2.2 reads —
tad āhur annam evai 'tat brāhmaṇasya yat somaḥ ǀ
nityatvād ity abhiprāyaḥ ǀ
brāhmaṇagrahaṇaṁ kṣatriyayor asomatvopapradarśanārtham ǀ
tat tū 'citam eva ǀ
anucitenā'pi somapānena somavāmī bhavati. . .

has not performed a *soma*-sacrifice (*VaitāSū*, XXX.2, 3).[17]

It is clear from the above details, that between the *caraka* and the *kaukilī*, the former is more brief and concise than the latter and, therefore, is the primary form of the same.

Further, the Vedic texts reveal that the *caraka sautrāmaṇī* is prescribed mainly:

(1) after the *rājasūya*,
(2) after the *agnicayana*
and also
(3) for a *somavāmin* and a *somātipūta*.

---

17. While translating this *sūtra* in his monograph *'Mantras of the . . . Sautrāmaṇī*, p. 66, Gonda seems to have read it as *na aniṣṭasomaḥ* instead of *nā aniṣṭasomaḥ* and has translated it as, 'one, who has not performed a *soma*-sacrifice, should not perform a *sautrāmaṇī* sacrifice.

In the commentary *akṣepānuvidhi*, however, it is commented on this *sūtra* that, the person (*nā*), who has not performed a *soma*-sacrifice can perform the *sautrāmaṇī iṣṭi* for the purposes mentioned in the second *sūtra*.

2

Rājasūya and Sautrāmaṇī

THE discussion in the previous chapter regarding the nature of the *sautrāmaṇī* has pointed out the relation between the *sautrāmaṇī* and the *rājasūya*. It has clearly shown that the *caraka sautrāmaṇī* — the primary form of the same — was performed as a redressing rite after the *rājasūya*. Yet, before entering into the discussion about the exact relation between the *rājasūya* and the *sautrāmaṇī*, it will be useful to take notice of a few significant features of the *rājasūya* and to see what necessitates the redressing rites after the *rājasūya*.

The *rājasūya* is one of the prominent sacrifices in ancient India. It is a *soma*-sacrifice to be performed by a kṣatriya king. To perform a *rājasūya* was always considered to be a point of honour for a king. In later literature, this sacrifice is many a time described as *mahākratu* (*Mbh*, II.11.55), *mahāyajña* (*Mbh*, II.13.17); *kratuśreṣṭha* (*Mbh*, II.42.46) etc. In *ŚatBrā*, V.5.4.14 it is said:

> *sarvān vā eṣa yajñakratūn avarundhe sarvā iṣṭīr api darvihomān yo rājsūyena yajate* ।
>
> He who performs the Rājasūya assuredly gains for himself all sacrificial rites, all offerings, even the spoonful-oblations.
> (tr. by Eggeling, pt. III, p. 132)

However, at the same time, one comes across such references also as, 'one, who performs the *rājasūya* becomes deprived of certain things, viz. sensual powers (*indriya*), vitality (*vīrya*), speech (*vāc*), milk (*payas*), etc.

Thus in *AV(Ś)*, IV.8.1. c, it is said: *tasya mṛtyuś carati rājasūyam*, 'Death attends his royal consecration'. In *ŚatBrā*, V.4.5.1 it is said, *varuṇād dha vā abhiṣiṣicānād bhago 'pacakrāma* 'When Varuṇa was consecrated, his lustre departed from him'. In *MaiS*, IV.4.9 it is stated, *vācā vā eṣa vyṛdhyate yo rājasūyenābhiṣiñcate* 'one, who gets himself a sacred bath by the *rājasūya*, becomes deprived of speech'. (cf. also *TaiBrā*, I.8.1.1; *ŚatBrā*, V.4.3.2; *PañcBrā*, XVIII.11.3. In *KāṭhS*, XII.10 and *MaiS*, II.4.1 it is said, *indriyeṇa vā eṣa vīryeṇa vyṛdhyate yo rājasūyenābhiṣiñcate* 'One, who gets himself a sacred bath by the *rājasūya* rite, becomes deprived of strength and vigour'.

Nevertheless, it is said nowhere in these texts that since a person, who performs the *rājasūya* becomes deprived of his strength and vigour, he should not perform that sacrifice. On the contrary, it is prescribed that the sacrificer should perform certain rites after the completion of the *rājasūya*, in order that he regains the strength and vigour and other things which have gone away from him and reinstates these in him and thus redresses himself. In *MaiS*, IV.4.9 and *PañcBrā*, XVIII.11.3 it is prescribed that the *yajñāyajñīya sāman* should be sung for one, who has performed the *rājasūya*. Thus the priest restores to the sacrificer the power and valour which had gone away from him, because the priest restored to Indra, these things which had gone away from him at the time he killed Vṛtra, by the singing of this *sāman*. The *vārāvantīya sāman* also is prescribed for this purpose (cf. *MaiS*, IV.4.9).

In *MaiS*, IV.3.1. it is said,

> Power and valour go away from him who performs the *rājasūya*. Therefore, a sacrificial cake is to be offered to Indra and Agni. Then these deities furnish him with power and valour.

The *sautrāmaṇī* rite also is prescribed for this purpose. Thus it is said,

> One, who is given a sacred bath by the *rājasūya* becomes deprived of the strength and vigour. Since much strength and vigour have gone away from one, the Adhvaryu reinstates

them in one by this rite. (cf. *MaiS*, II.4.1; *KāṭhS*, XII.10)

However, we do not find in any of these passages the reason as to why it is said that these things, i.e., the power, valour, strength, etc., go away from one, who has performed the *rājasūya* sacrifice. Discussion regarding this problem is not found in the works of Weber[1] and Heesterman[2] who have dealt with the ritual of the *rājasūya* in details.[3]

The *rājasūya* sacrifice is described in the *AitBrā*, also. *Adhyāya*s XXXIII to XXXIX deal with this sacrifice. The description of the ritual of the *rājasūya* found here is of a peculiar character. No exact parallel to it is found in any other ritual text.[4] The description contains the well-known legend of Śunaḥśepa, some preparatory rites to be performed by a kṣatriya sacrificer before the consecration ceremony (*dīkṣā*) and some rites to be performed after the completion of the sacrifice.

The discussion of the rites to be performed by a kṣatriya sacrificer before and after the sacrifice is of great significance in the present context. This discussion together with one on the position of a kṣatriya sacrificer in relation to the sacrifice and the priest, occurs in the *adhyāya*s XXXIV, XXXV, XXXVII and XXXIX.[5]

In the XXXVth *adhyāya* is described a preparatory rite to be performed by the kṣatriya sacrificer before the consecration. The name of the rite is *iṣṭāpūrtasyāparijyāni* offerings. It is in fact a set of offerings. The sacrificer offers four oblations of clarified butter before his consecration and similar four oblations he offers at the end of the sacrifice.

---

1. A. Weber, *Über die Königsweihe den Rājasūya.*
2. Heesterman, *The Ancient Indian Royal Consecration.*
3. G.U. Thite, has suggested a possible reason in "Antipathy to the Rājasūya", *Sambodhi*, Vol. I, Oct.1972, No. 3, pp. 43-58.
4. *See* A. Weber, *History of Indian Literature*, p. 44; also A.B. Keith, *Rigveda Brāhmaṇas*, Intr., p. 61.
5. *See* also, Manning, *Ancient and Medieval India*, Vol. 1, p. 99.

Sāyaṇa has explained the word *aparijyāni* as *vināśābhāvaḥ*, 'the absence of destruction'. The word *iṣṭa* means, the duties of the sacrificer to be performed according to his *varṇa* and *āśrama*, and *pūrta* means the benevolent acts such as the erection of water-reservoir, etc., performed by him. Therefore, the word *iṣṭāpūrtasyāparijyāni* would mean, 'the absense of the destruction of (the fruit acquired by) the duties and the benevolent acts (performed by the sacrificer)'.[6]

The verses to be recited at the time of making these offerings are very significant. At the time of making the offerings before the consecration the sacrificer recites the *mantra*, *punarno indro maghavā dadātu brahma punar iṣṭam pūrtaṁ dāt svāhā.* Thereby he prays,

> May Maghavan Indra give me back the holy power (*brahma*, as translated by Keith) and the *iṣṭa* and *pūrta* done by me. Therefore, I offer this offering.

The *mantra* to be recited after the completion of the sacrifice is, *punar no agnir jātavedā dadātu kṣatram punar iṣṭam pūrtaṁ dāt svāhā.* Thereby he prays,

> May Agni Jātavedas give me back the lordly power (*kṣatra*) and the *iṣṭa* and the *pūrta*. Therefore, I offer this offering.

---

6. The word *iṣṭāpūrta* is thus explained by the tradition:
   varnāśramānvayī dharma iṣṭam pūrtam athetarat |
   prapātaṭākādirūpaṁ tac ca sarvatra dṛśyate |
   also,
   smārtam pūrtaṁ śrautam iṣṭam iti kecid ihocire |
   Keith in his *Rigveda Brāhmaṇas,* p. 310, has translated the word as, 'Prevention of decay of the sacrifice and the gifts to the priests.'
   Haug, *Aitareya Brāhmaṇa of the Rigveda*, p. 324 has not translated the word, and has kept it as it is and has added its explanation in a footnote. 'Lit. the recompensation (*aparijyāni*) of what has been sacrificed (*iṣṭa*) and filled (*āpūrta*). *Iṣṭa* means only 'what is sacrificed' and *āpūrta* 'filled up to'. For, all sacrifices go up to heaven, and are stored up there to be taken possession of by the sacrificer on his arrival in heaven. (*see* *ṚV*, X.14.1).

The contents of these prayers make it clear that these offerings are given by the sacrificer for getting back the fruit of the *iṣṭa* and *pūrta* and also the *brahma* and the *kṣatra*. It can be said that the first offerings form a kind of a preparatory rite through which the sacrificer wants to acquire *brahma* and be consecrated, while the offerings after the completion form a kind of redressing rite by which he wants to acquire the *kṣatra* and be a kṣatriya again.

In the next sub-section, i.e., *AitBrā*, XXXIV.4, an option to these offerings is prescribed. These optional offerings are called *ajītapunarvaṇya* offerings. They are introduced by a *ṛṣi* called Saujāta Ārāḷhi. The name of the rite is explained by Sāyaṇa as follows: 'the thing lost is called *ajīta* and the instrument for getting it back is called *ajītapunarvaṇya*'.[7] These offerings are also given before the consecration and after the completion of the sacrifice.

The *mantra* to be recited at the time of making the offering before the sacrifice is *brahma prapdye brahma mā kṣatrād gopāyatu brahmaṇe svāhā*. He declares thereby,

> I go to *brahma* (i.e., the holy power). May *brahma* protect me from the *kṣatra* (the lordly power). Svāhā to *brahma*.

The reason as to why this *mantra* is to be recited is also given thus: One who approaches the sacrifice approaches the holy power. The sacrifice is the holy power. A person who is consecrated is as if born from the sacrifice. When he offers these offerings, the holy power, being pleased by them, protects him from the lordly power.

Then, again at the end of the sacrifice, he offers the oblations and recites the *mantra*:

> *kṣatram prapadye kṣatram mā brahmaṇo gopāyatu kṣatrāya svāhā* |
>
> I go to the *kṣatra*, the lordly power. May the lordly power

7. A.B. Keith, has given the meaning of this word as 'winning again of what has decayed' and Haug has translated it as: 'the recovering of what is not to be lost'.

> protect me from the holy power. These are the offerings to the lordly power.

The reason as to why this *mantra* is to be recited is given:

> A person, who approaches the kingship, approaches the lordly power; as the kingship is the lordly power. When he thus approaches the lordly power, the holy power does not oppress him. When he gives these offerings, the lordly power is pleased with him and protects him from the holy power.

The very name of these offerings suggests that these are the offerings given by the sacrificer for getting back something that has gone away from him. It is the *kṣatra* 'the lordly power' that has gone away from him.

Haug[8] has rightly pointed out, while explaining the word *ajītapunarvaṇya* that,

> This refers to the Kṣattra which the Kṣattriya first lost by his turning towards the Brahma, but subsequently regained it by embracing the Kṣattra which he cannot throw off, if he otherwise wish to retain his sovereignty.

But then the question arises as to why he has to approach the holy power before the consecration and again come to the lordly power after the performance?

To find an answer to this question, it is necessary to see the introduction pertaining to the prescription of both these offerings. For this purpose, the XXXIVth *adhyāya* cites a myth at its beginning. This myth is in brief as follows:

> Prajāpati created the sacrifice. After creating it, he created the people of two kinds: *hutāda* 'those who eat the sacrificial food' and *ahutāda* 'those who do not eat the sacrificial food'. The brāhmaṇas are those who eat it and kṣatriyas, the vaiśyas and the śūdras are those who do not eat it.

---

8. M. Haug, *op.cit.*, p. 325, f.n. 4.

> Once the sacrifice went away from them. The holy power and the lordly power both went to him with their respective weapons. The sacrifice was afraid of the weapons of the lordly power, viz. the horse, the chariot, the corslet, the bow and the arrow. Seeing his own weapons, viz. the sacrificial utensils, with the holy power he went to the holy power. Therefore, even now the sacrifice finds support in the holy power and in the brāhmaṇas. Then the lordly power went to the holy power and said, "You call me also in this sacrifice". The holy power agreed to do this and said, "Lay aside thine own weapons and with the weapons of the holy power with the form of the holy power, and (thus) becoming the holy power come to the sacrifice". Then the lordly power, having laid aside its own weapons, and taking with it the weapons of the holy power, assuming the form of the holy power and becoming (thus) the holy power (itself) went to the sacrifice. Therefore, now also the kṣatriya sacrificer puts away his own weapons, takes the weapons of the holy power, and appearing in the form of the holy power and becoming the holy power itself, goes to the sacrifice. (*AitBrā*, XXXIV.11)

This myth is very significant in that it tells us that the kṣatriya could perform sacrifice, but he had to become a brāhmaṇa before performing it. He had to put aside his qualities and duties of a kṣatriya and only then could he perform the sacrifice. Even the king was not an exception to this rule.

Therefore, before the consecration, the kṣatriya sacrificer has to offer certain oblations and announce, "I hereby become a brāhmaṇa". However, this *brāhmaṇatva* (= state of being a brāhmaṇa) was a temporary phase. After the sacrificial performance, he wanted to be a kṣatriya again and for this purpose, he had to offer oblations after the completion of the sacrifice also. Only then could he get back his lordly power.

This idea is more clearly expressed in *AitBrā*, XXXIV.5 thus:

> As a part of the *ajītapunarvaṇya* offerings, the kṣatriya has to pay homage to the *āhavanīya* fire. While praising this

> act, it is said in the *Brāhmaṇa*, "The kṣatriya has Indra as his deity, the *triṣṭubh* as his metre, the *pañcadaśastoma* as his *stoma*, *soma* as his kingdom, and the *rājanya* as his relatives. When such a kṣatriya is being consecrated for a sacrifice, he comes to assume the *brāhmaṇatva*. When he covers himself with the black-antelope-skin and observes the vows of the consecrated and when the other brāhmaṇas come around him, Indra takes away his sensual power, *triṣṭubh* his strength, the *pañcadaśa stoma* his life, the Soma his kingdom, and the fathers his fame and name, thinking, "he has become somewhat special, somewhat different from us. He has become the holy power."

Therefore, he pays homage to the *āhavanīya* fire and declares

> I am not going away from all these deities and, therefore, may all these presiding deities not take away my faculties. With all these qualities of a kṣatriya, I am approaching the holy power and the deity Agni, the metre *gāyatrī, trivṛt-stoma*, *soma* the king and thus becoming a brāhmaṇa.

When he thus pays homage to Agni, it is said that, these deities do not take away the respective faculties from him; but, though the faculties are not taken away, it seems that they are made inoperative. Otherwise, the necessity of making offerings for a second time would not have arisen. Thus, when he has performed the *udavasānīyā iṣṭi* he becomes a kṣatriya again and, therefore, in order to set all his faculties into action once again, he makes the after offerings and thereby declares, I become a kṣatriya by these offerings.

After offering these oblations, he pays homage to the *āhavanīya* fire. This act of his is also glorified in a significant way. Thus it is said,

> When the sacrificer has finished the sacrificial performance, the deities of the holy power think, 'now he has become a kṣatriya and has become someone different from us'. Therefore, they take away his splendour, valour, life, fame and name.

When the sacrificer pays homage to the *āhavanīya* fire, he announces by the *mantra*,

> Even if I am becoming a kṣatriya, I am not going away from all these deities of the holy power. Therefore, may they not take away from me all these things. With all these things, I am becoming a kṣatriya. May the merit of my acts remain with me. I am the same kṣatriya and, after the sacrificial performance, I will remain a kṣatriya.

Thus, by these offerings, the kṣatriya sacrificer regains his lordly power and sets it into operation again, without losing the fruit of the sacrificial performance.

Besides the *iṣṭāpūrtasyāparijyāni* and the *ajītapunarvanya* offerings, there is one more rite, viz. the *punarabhiṣeka* mentioned in the XXXVIIth *adhyāya* of the *AitBrā*. It is also intended for redressing the sacrificer, i.e., for bringing back to him his *kṣatriyatva* and to reinstall in him whatever has gone away from him. Since this rite has some striking similarities with the *sautrāmaṇī* ritual it will be dealt with in the subsequent chapter.

In the light of the above discussion, it becomes clear that the description of this ritual seems to point to the significance of such statements in the ritual texts as 'the strength, *indriya* or *vīrya*, *vāc* goes away from one, who performs the *rājasūya* sacrifice'; these statements refer to the inoperative stage of the qualities of the kṣatriya sacrificer during the time he is consecrated for the performance of the sacrifice. When the sacrificial performance is complete, some redressing rites are performed for the sacrificer by which his *kṣatriyatva* is set into operation once again and the (earlier consecrated) kṣatriya can act again as a kṣatriya without losing the fruit of the sacrifice.

Now two questions arise: (i) Why is not such discussion found in any other ritual texts? and (ii) Why is it that all the other texts, which merely mention that 'certain things have gone away from the sacrificer', prescribe some redressing rites and remain silent about the reason for it?

The answer to these questions may be the chronological position of the *AitBrā*, among the ritual texts.

The *AitBrā*, comprises of forty *adhyāya*s, the last ten of which are of peculiar character and have received special attention of many Vedic scholars.

According to Weber[9] these ten *adhyāya*s are a later addition to the *AitBrā*. However, this does not mean that their contents also are of later origin. In this regard, he agrees with Roth,[10] who is of the opinion that, regarding many of the legends in these chapters, it can be assumed that they had already gained a rounded and independent shape in tradition before they were incorporated into the *Brāhmaṇa* and of this there is ample evidence in the distinctly archaic character of their language, compared with that of the rest of the text.

Among these ten *adhyāya*s also, it can be observed, the first two are, in a way, a continuation of the discussion occurring in the previous chapters. As against this the last eight *adhyāya*s deal exclusively with the rites and duties to be performed by the kṣatriyas in general and a kṣatriya king in particular; they are not a continuation of any earlier topic.

It is evident that the discussion regarding the relation between the kṣatriya and the sacrifice, and between the kṣatriya and the priest, found in these eight *adhyāya*s of the *AitBrā*, is a discussion of very early times.

As we know, 'to perform a sacrifice' was considered to be a duty of the brāhmaṇas, but, in the course of time, the kṣatriyas also wanted to perform sacrifice. Or, it may be more probable that the kṣatriyas wanted their rites to be elevated to a higher status and to be included among the *śrauta* sacrificial ritual. Gradually, perhaps because of the growing influence of the kṣatriyas, the brāhmaṇas had to incorporate the rites of the kṣatriyas in their own sacrificial

9. A. Weber, *History of Indian Literature*, p. 44.
10. R. Roth, 'Die Sage Von Śunaḥśepa' (zweiter Artikel), *Indische Studien*, Vol. 2, pp. 112-23.

ritual and give the kṣatriyas the right to perform sacrifice.[11] The myth cited in *AitBrā*, XXXIV.1 also suggests that, at first, only the brāhmaṇas had the right to perform sacrifice, and the kṣatriyas were granted the privilege of performing it, only at a later period.[12]

This gave rise to some problems. First, if it is considered that to perform a sacrifice is a duty only of a brāhmaṇa, how could then a kṣatriya perform it? This problem was solved by making him a brāhmaṇa, at least temporarily! When a kṣatriya wanted to perform a sacrifice, he had to keep aside his *kṣatriyatva* — the differentiating qualities of a kṣatriya — and accept the *brāhmaṇatva* which was necessary for the performance of the sacrifice. Therefore, the offerings like the *iṣṭāpūrtasyāparijyāni* and *ajītapunarvaṇya* offerings were introduced into the ritual of the sacrifice. By offering these oblations before the consecration, the kṣatriya sacrificer announced that he thereby become a brāhmaṇa. The next difficulty was: where should his *kṣatriyatva* abide during that period? As a solution to this problem it was imagined that, when a kṣatriya was consecrated for a sacrifice, the faculties of a kṣatriya in him were taken away from him by the deities of those faculties. But this was not all. Since the *brāhmaṇatva* of the kṣatriya sacrificer was only a temporary phase and that he wanted to be a kṣatriya again, it was necessary to reinstall the kṣatriya qualities and faculties in him. Therefore, the after-offerings also were prescribed, after performing which he got back his *kṣatriyatva*.

In later literature, however, it seems to have become an accepted fact that a kṣatriya could perform a sacrifice and when he

---

11. M. Haug has suggested a possible reason in his Introduction to the translation of the *AitBrā*, p. xlvii; *see* also A. Weber, "Collectanea über die kasten verhältnisse in den Brāhmaṇa und Sūtra", *Indische Studien*, Vol.10, p. 17.

12. For a detailed discussion on the relation between the kṣatriyas and the brāhmaṇas, see the article mentioned above of Weber pp. 26 to 35 and also J. Muir, "On the Relations of the Priests to the Other Classes of Indian Society in the Vedic Age", *Journal of the Royal Asiatic Society of Great Britain and Ireland*, *N.S.* Vol. 2, pp. 257-302.
J. Muir, *Original Sanskrit Texts,* Vol. 1, Ch. IV, pp. 296 ff.;
J. Gonda, *The Ancient Indian Kingship in the Religious Point* of *View*.

was consecrated, he was born as a brāhmaṇa, the *brāhmaṇatva* abided in him up to the end of the sacrifice; and after the completion of the sacrifice, once again he became a kṣatriya as a matter of course and still could have retained with him the fruit of the sacrifice which he had performed as a brāhmaṇa (during that while).[13]

Thus in *ŚatBrā*, III.2.1.40 it is said,

> *tasmād api rājanyaṁ vā vaiśyaṁ vā brāhmaṇa ity eva brūyād brāhmaṇo hi jāyate yo yajñāj jāyate* ।
>
> Let him address even a Rājanya or a Vaiśya, as Brāhmaṇa, since he who is born of the sacrifice is born of the *Brahman* (and hence is a Brāhmaṇa). (tr. by Eggeling, pt. II. p.35)

Similar statements are found in the *KātyŚS* and the *ĀpaŚS* also. Thus it is said in *KātyŚS*, VII.4.11, 12:

> *anyo dīkṣito'yaṁ brāhmaṇa ity āha trir uccaiḥ* ।
> *brāhmaṇa ity eva vaiśyarājanyayor api* ।

and in *ĀpaŚS*, X.11.6:

> *brāhmaṇo vā eṣa jāyate yo dīkṣate tasmād rājanyavaiśyayor api brāhmaṇa ity eva āvedayati* ।

In *TaiS*, VI.1.4.3 also it is said,

> *adīkṣiṣṭāyam brāhmaṇaḥ iti trir upāṁśv āha.*

The *ŚatBrā* states a view of some that the *aśvamedha*, which is a sacrifice proper (only) to the *rājanya*s, should be begun in summer, which is the season of the *rājanya*s. This view is opposed by the *ŚatBrā*, and it is said in *ŚatBrā*, XIII.4.1.3

> *tad vai vasante eva abhyārabheta ya u vai kaś ca yajate brāhmaṇībhūya ivai'va yajate.*

---

13. For various other meanings of *dīkṣā see* G.U. Thite, "Significances of Dīkṣā", *ABORI*, Vol. LI, Poona, 1971, pp. 163-73.

> But let him rather begin it in spring: for spring is the Brāhmaṇa's season, and, truly, whosoever sacrifices, sacrifices after becoming as it were, a Brāhmaṇa: let him therefore by all means begin it in spring.
>
> (tr. by Eggeling, pt. V, pp. 347-8)

Thus, it is clear from these references that it is assumed later that a kṣatriya or a vaiśya, when he is consecrated, is considered a brāhmaṇa during the period of the performance of the sacrifice. It is natural therefore, that one does not come across any such discussions regarding the preparatory and the redressing rites anywhere else, except in the *AitBrā*.

The possible answer to the second question is: The later ritualists have seen that the *rājasūya* was performed together with the redressng rites. Though, the real significance had gone from such rites, they might have become a part of the *rājasūya* ritual. Devoid of such rites, the *rājasūya* could not have been considered as complete; and therefore, the later ritualists might have modified such rites (in some measure) and accepted them in their own ritual procedures.

3

The Punarabhiṣeka and the Sautrāmaṇī

It is mentioned before in the preceding chapter (p. 30) that there is besides the *ajītapunarvaṇya* and *iṣṭāpūrtasyāparijyāni* offerings, one more redressing rite viz. the *punarabhiṣeka*, which is described in the XXXVIIth *adhyāya* of the *AitBrā*. According to this rite, the kṣatriya sacrificer is given a sacred bath once again after he has taken the concluding bath, and has performed the offerings of the *anūbandhyā* cow and the *udavasānīyā iṣṭi* of the *rājasūya* sacrifice.

The paraphernalia of the ceremony is kept ready: a seat of *udumbara*-wood, a branch of *udumbara* tree and eight substances collected in a pot (this also made of *udumbara* wood). The eight substances are: curds, honey, clarified butter, rain waters fallen in sunshine, young sprouts of grass and barley, *surā*, and *dūrvā* grass.

The seat is placed near the altar. The tiger-skin is spread upon it. The sacrificer sits upon that skin. The priest then propitiates the waters. He holds the *udumbara* branch upon the sacrificer's head and sprinkles those substances upon him, reciting at that time three R̥gvedic verses and a *Yajus*-formula. Some prescribe the recitation of the *vyāhr̥ti*s also at this time. After that the priest gives an oblation of clarified butter as a part (*aṅga*) of this *abhiṣeka*, (*AitBrā*, XXXVII.1 to XXXVII.3).

The priest then gives the sacrificer a bowl of *surā* to drink. The remnants of the drink are given by the sacrificer to a person whom he thinks to be generous (*AitBrā*, XXXVII.4).

After that the sacrificer descends from the seat, puts a fire-stick into the fire and takes three steps in the north-east direction, paying homage to that direction with the *mantra*, *kḷptir asi* (*AitBrā*, XXXVII.5).

Then follows the description of a chariot drive. The sacrificer then goes back to the house reciting the *mantra*, *apa prāca indra* . . . (*Ṛ̥V*, X.131.1). Having gone to the house, he sits down behind the household fire and holds on to the priest who, at the end, offers three butter-libations to Indra, for freedom from distress, injury, loss and from danger. The priest then pronounces a prayer for progeny, oxen, horses and men.

The use of *surā* in the ritual is a remarkable feature of the *punarabhiṣeka*. The *sautrāmaṇī* also is a rite in which *surā* is drunk by the sacrificer. It is on the basis of this similarity that Bloomfield[1] has stated that the *punarabhiṣeka* is a form of the *sautrāmaṇī*. It is necessary, therefore, to compare the ritual of the *punarabhiṣeka* with that of the *sautrāmaṇī* and see the relation between the two. However, before turning to this comparison, it will be useful to see how *surā* came to be introduced in Vedic *śrauta* ritual.

Generally, it is found that *surā* is condemned in Vedic literature. It is considered as a cause of guilt and is grouped together with dice and ill-thoughts. Thus it is said in *Ṛ̥V*, VII.86.6.,

ná sá svó dákṣo varuṇa dhṛ̥́tiḥ sā́
súrā manyúr vibhídako ácittiḥ ।

In *KāṭhS*, XII.12 and *MaiS*, II.4.2, i.e., in the chapters on the *sautrāmaṇī*, *surā* is said to be 'foolishness and evil'. Thus it is said in *MaiS*, II.4.2:

ardhaṁ vai prajāpater ātmano dhairyam āsīt ardhan mālvyam . . . yan mālvyaṁ surā vai sā tato rājanyam asṛ̥jata tasmāj jyāyānśca kanīyānśca snuṣā ca śvaśuraś ca

---

1. Bloomfield, "Contributions to the Interpretation of the Veda", *JAOS*, Vol. 15, f.n. on p.152.

> *surāṁ pītvā vilālapanta āsate, mālvyaṁ hi tat, pāpmā vai mālvyam, tasmād brāhmaṇaḥ surāṁ na pibet pāpmanā'tmānaṁ net saṁsr̥jā iti.*

> Half of Prajāpati's self was courage and the other half was foolishness. That foolishness was *surā* itself. The kṣatriya was born from *surā*. Therefore, after drinking *surā* the elder one and the younger one, the daughter-in-law and the father-in-law go on chattering. And that is foolishness, and this foolishness is evil. Therefore, a brāhmaṇa should not drink *surā*, otherwise, he would unite himself with evil.

Even though, *surā* is condemned in such a harsh way, it is noticed to have been used in the Vedic ritual. In the *AitBrā*, it is used in the *rājasūya* ritual, at the end of the *abhiṣeka*-ceremony. After getting the sacrificial gifts, the priest hands over a bronze bowl of *surā* to the kṣatriya sacrificer. The purpose of this act is not given. But the drinking of *surā* is glorified and it is stated that as a wife or a son gives pleasure and peace to a person all through his life, in the same way, *surā* or *soma* or food in general, gives pleasure and peace to the kṣatriya sacrificer (cf *AitBrā*, XXXIX.6).

In this respect, what Weber has stated seems to be correct. Regarding the *rājasūya* ritual he has remarked,

> The Rājasūya sacrifice is basically a kṣatriya ritual and only secondarily it has been accepted in the holy Vedic Śrauta ritual, just like the Vājapeya, the Aśvamedha or the Puruṣamedha. The purpose was to bring these important and popular ceremonies under the control of the priests. Originally they were a part of the popular ritual.[2]

Similar view is expressed by Heesterman also. He has stated.

> The Rājasūya is one of those Śrauta sacrifices in which the royal rites and cults, probably of diverse origin, were

---

2. Weber, *Über die Königsweihe den Rājasūya*, p. 98; J. Gonda, also has expressed similar opinion in *Die Religionen Indiens*, p. 173.

> preserved. Thus there will have existed also other royal rites (notably unction-ceremonies, *abhiṣeka*) of varying form which have left traces in the *abhiṣeka*s described in the seventh book of the Aitareya Brāhmaṇa.[3]

It is very much probable, thus, that, even before the Vedic *rājasūya*, the consecration ceremony was performed for a king. Afterwards, perhaps because of the growing influence of the kṣatriyas, the priests had to accept these rites in the *śrauta* ritual. The kṣatriyas might have desired and attempted to get these rites included in the *śrauta* ritual, to elevate their status and firmly establish them; and further to have for themselves a right of performing a *śrauta* sacrifice.

The drinking of *surā* also seems to be some such kṣatriya practice. It seems that this was a drink special and favourite especially to the kṣatriyas. It is noteworthy, that while glorifying the sprinkling materials, *surā* is called the *kṣatra* in the *punarabhiṣeka* (*AitBrā*, XXXVII.4).[4] Also remarkable is the glorification of it in the *rājasūya* in the *AitBrā*, where it is said that *surā* gives, just like *soma* or any other food, pleasure and peace especially to a kṣatriya sacrificer (*AitBrā*, XXXIX.6).

In this regard, the passage in *MaiS*, II.4.2 is also very important. Just after the condemnation of *surā*, it is said,

> *tad u etad rāṣṭrīyāya brāhmaṇam brūyād tad ya evaṁ vidvān surām pibati na hai'nam drūṇāty eṣā vai prajāpateḥ vīryavatī tanūr vīryam prajāpatiḥ vīryam asmin dadhāti*
>
> This portion of the brāhmaṇa should be told to the *rāṣṭrīya* (i.e., a king, *rājanya*). When one knowing this, drinks *surā* it does not harm the one. This is the body of Prajāpati possessing valour. Valour is Prajāpati. He thus, places valour in him.

The word *brāhmaṇa* refers to the mythical portion which has just

3. Heesterman, *Ancient Indian Royal Consecration*, Intr. pp. 3ff.
4. G.U. Thite, *Sacrifice in Brāhmaṇa Texts*, pp. 49ff.

preceded this statement, wherein it is told that the *rājanya* was born from *surā* and *surā* had its origin in Prajāpati himself. And, therefore, even if a brāhmaṇa is not allowed to drink *surā*, the kṣatriya sacrificer can drink it without any harm, since *surā* is valour and by that, the valour is established in that sacrificer.

There is one more remarkable point about the ritual of *surā*. Generally in the *śrauta* ritual, earthen or wooden pots are used. The use of metal is conspicuously absent in it. According to the *AitBrā* however, the sacrificer is given *surā* in a bronze bowl both in the *rājasūya* and in the *punarabhiṣeka*.

While giving the bowl of *surā* to the sacrificer king, the priest recites the *mantra* —

svādiṣṭhayā madiṣṭhayā
pavasva soma dhārayā
indrāya pātave sutaḥ I —*AitBrā*, XXXIX.6

'With thy sweetest, most intoxicating stream be thou purified, O Soma, pressed for Indra to drink.
(tr. by Keith, p. 335)

The sacrificer drinks it with the *mantra* —

yad atra śiṣṭaṁ rasinaḥ sutasya
yad indro apibac chacībhiḥ
ahaṁ tad asya manasā śivena
somaṁ rājānaṁ iha bhakṣayāmi —*AitBrā*

That which is left over of the pressed
juice, rich in sap
which Indra drank mightily
Here with auspicious mind this of him,
I partake of Soma, the king.
To thee, O bull (the *soma*) being pressed,
I offer the pressed juice to drink;
Rejoice and make thyself glad: (tr. by Keith, p. 335)

While glorifying this act of drinking *surā*, it is stated,

The *soma* drink which is in *surā* is what is drunk by the

kṣatriya when he is sprinkled by the great *abhiṣeka* of Indra and not Surā.

The comparison of *surā* with *soma* is a means of elevating the drink in prestige and accepting it in the Vedic *śrauta* ritual.[5] This tendency is further found in the *ŚatBrā* also. In *ŚatBrā*, XII.8.2.3 to 15 everything used in the *sautrāmaṇī* is compared with the things used in a *soma*-sacrifice. This can be considered as a deliberate attempt of the author of the *Brāhmaṇa* text to establish the *sautrāmaṇī* as a separate *iṣṭi*.

There is one more possible reason as to why these *mantra*s which are addressed to *soma* might have been used for *surā*.

According to the *AitBrā*, in the *rājasūya* sacrifice the kṣatriya is not entitled to partake of the remnants of the oblations, i.e., *soma*. He is an *ahutāda* as is mentioned in the myth in (*AitBrā*, XXXIV.1). The purpose behind excluding the kṣatriya in this way from the partaking of *soma* is of course to maintain the superiority and the speciality of the brāhmaṇa class. Therefore, instead of *soma*, the sacrificer is given a different drink. He is given the juice of the fruits of *udumbara*, *plakṣa* and *aśvattha* and the juice of the roots of the banyan tree. While glorifying this drink, it is stated, 'This is his own drink. It belongs to the kṣatriya.' The sacrificer king partakes of the juice with the *mantra*,

yad atra riptam . . . bhakṣayāmi

By the recitation of this *mantra*, the drink special to the kṣatriya king is called *soma*.

After partaking of that drink, the sacrificer king touches himself with the recitation of the *mantra* —

śaṁ na edhi hr̥de pītaḥ pra ṇa
āyur jīvase soma tārīḥ —*AitBrā*, XXXV.8

5. D.J. Hoens, *Śānti—A Contribution to Ancient Religious Terminology*, p. 146.

Be thou kindly to our heart when
drunk, do thou extend our life,
to live long, O Soma. (tr. by Keith, p. 317)

The drink is again referred to as *soma* by the recitation of this *mantra*.

In this particular context, the kṣatriya sacrificer is given the drink as a substitute for *soma*. When the priests are partaking of the *soma*-juice, the sacrificer is given this special drink. It is, therefore, only natural that the *mantra*s addressed to *soma* are employed to consecrate — *abhimantraṇa* — the act of drinking.

Later, the sacrificer is given the *surā*-drink, which is a drink special to the kṣatriyas. It is no wonder then, that the *mantra*s, previously used in connection with a drink which belongs to the kṣatriya himself, are employed in respect of *surā* also.

Since, the *surā*-drink is thus a special drink of the kṣatriyas, it is but natural that it is found used in the *punarabhiṣeka* ritual, which is performed, as will be seen, to redress the sacrificer and to set his *kṣatriyatva* into operation again, which was made inoperative during the sacrificial performance.

There is yet another possibility as to why *surā* might have been used in the *punarabhiṣeka*.

It is probable that there had been a popular practice of reestablishing by means of *surā*, the strength and sense-power lost by excessive purging or by vomiting of *soma*. This medical, or magico-medical quality of *surā* could have been observed by the Vedic ritualists; and, therefore, this practice was accepted by them in the Vedic *śrauta* ritual, with a view to restoring to the kṣatriya sacrificer the vigour, *kṣatra*, sensual-power, etc. which had gone away from him.

While accompanying this *surā*-ritual in the *punarabhiṣeka* with the *mantra*s, it is only natural that the *mantra*s used in connection with *surā* in the *rājasūya* in the *AitBrā*, are used here also. Thus when the priest hands over the bowl of *surā* to the sacrificer, he (the priest) recites the *mantra, svādiṣṭhayā madiṣṭhayā*

. . . and while accepting it, the sacrificer recites the *mantra*,

> *nānā hi vāṁ devahitaṁ sadaskṛtaṁ*
> *mā saṁsṛkṣāthām parame vyoman* |
> *surā tvam asi śuṣmiṇī soma eṣaḥ*
> *mā mā hiṁsīḥ svāṁ yonim āviśan* ||

> Separate for you is the place made by the gods, Be ye not united in the highest heaven, *surā* thou art, the impetuous; he is king *soma*; Harm him not, when entering your own place of birth. (tr. by Keith, p. 325)

The *mantra* used for the propitiation of *surā* in the *punarabhiṣeka* is different from that used in the *rājasūya*. But both these *mantra*s are found to have been used in the *sautrāmaṇī* ritual also.

In the *caraka sautrāmaṇī*, after the offerings of *surā* are made the remnants of the oblation material are partaken by the sacrificer himself. At that time he recites these two *mantra*s (*ĀpaŚS*, XIX.3.4; *VaikhāŚS*, XI.5).

Sometimes a brāhmaṇa is hired for partaking these instead of the sacrificer himself. In that case, the brāhmaṇa partakes of it, reciting these two *mantra*s (*BaudhŚS*, XVII.36).

According to *MānŚS*, V.2.4.29, the sacrificer himself partakes of it, with the recitation of only one *mantra*, viz. *nānā hi vām*. . . whereas *HirŚS*, XIII.8.28 prescribes the *mantra, yadatra śiṣṭam* . . . for the same purpose. It is the Hotṛ and the Adhvaryu, who partake of the remnants of the oblation material with the recitation of this *mantra*, as is mentioned in *VārāŚS*, III.2.7.31.

It is mainly on the basis of these *mantra*s common to the *surā*-ritual of the *punarabhiṣeka* and that of the *sautrāmaṇī* that Hoens has identified the *punarabhiṣeka* with the *sautrāmaṇī*.

However, there are in *sautrāmaṇī* animal-offerings made to the Aśvins, Sarasvatī and Sutrāman Indra. *Surā* also is offered to these deities. In the *kaukilī*, together with the animal-offerings and the offerings of *surā*, milk also is offered to these three deities. There is no such offering in the *punarabhiṣeka* except those of clarified butter offered after the *abhiṣeka* ceremony. It is difficult, therefore, to agree with Hoens and identify the *punarabhiṣeka* with the *sautrāmaṇī*.

Nevertheless, there are some important similarities between the ritual of the *punarabhiṣeka* and that of the *sautrāmaṇī*.

1. Just like the *sautrāmaṇī*, the *punarabhiṣeka* also is performed at the end of the *rājasūya*, even though its description occurs in the *AitBrā*, before the description of the *abhiṣeka* in the *rājasūya*, i.e., *AitBrā*, XXXVII.1 where it is stated that the kṣatriya sacrificer is sprinkled over again after he has taken the concluding bath and has performed the animal-sacrifice of the *anūbandhyā* cow and the *udavasānīyā iṣṭi*.

2. The *punarabhiṣeka* also is a redressing rite. The purpose of the rite is stated at the beginning of the description of the rite. Thus it is said in *AitBrā*, XXXVII.1,

   sūyate ha vā asya kṣatraṁ yo dīkṣate kṣatriyaḥ san I. . . *athainam . . . punarabhiṣiñcanti* I

   The first sentence is translated variously by scholars.

   Keith has translated it, "His lordly power is consecrated, who being a Kṣatriya consecrates himself", p. 332. It is apparent that he has translated the word *sūyate* as 'is consecrated', which is not satisfactory. Thomas has translated it as "His royal power is quickened by it",[6] but this also does not seem to make the sense of the passage clear.

   Haug has translated it as, "Now follows (the rule) of Punarabhiseka of the Kṣatriya who is inaugurated as a sacrificer, and whose Kṣattram is in (such a way) new born" p. 345 He has translated the word *sūyate* as 'new born'.[7] This meaning seems

---

6. F.W. Thomas, in Hasting's *ERE*, Vol. 1, Article "Abhiṣeka" pp. 20-4
7. For a detailed discussion on the root *sū* (or *sū*) *see* Heesterman, *op.cit.*, pp. 72 ff.

to be acceptable. The *kṣatra*, i.e., the *kṣatriyatva* of the sacrificer is new born, i.e., it is born newly as *brahma*. He has become a brāhmaṇa since he is consecrated (*dīkṣita*). It is already seen in the previous chapter that this idea is stated explicitly in the other ritual texts.

Since the kṣatriya sacrificer has become a brāhmaṇa for the sacrificial performance, it is necessary that he should again become a kṣatriya after the completion of the sacrifice. And therefore, he is once again sprinkled over so that his *kṣatriyatva* is restored to him and that he is redressed as a kṣatriya.

There are some other acts to be performed in this rite with the same purpose of redressing the sacrificer and of restoring to him the faculties which have gone away from him, e.g., as a part of this sprinkling, two oblations of clarified butter are offered in the fire after the sprinkling. Regarding these oblations, it is stated,

> These things have departed from a Kṣatriya who has sacrificed; the holy power and the lordly power, strength, the eating of food, the sap of the plants and the waters, splendour, refreshment, growth and propagation; moreover, as this is a symbol of the lordly power, the sap of food, the lordly power of the plants and support. In that he offers beforehand these two liabtions, thus he confers on him the holy power and the lordly power.
>
> —*AitBrā*, XXVII.3 (tr. by Keith, p. 324)

While glorifying the different materials used for the sprinkling, it is stated that the *udumbara* is the strength, the grass and green barley are a symbol of refreshment and growth, etc. Further, in connection with this rite, *surā* is said to be the symbol of the lordly power (*kṣatra*) and also the sap of food. As the Adhvaryu sprinkles the sacrificer with *surā*, he confers upon him the symbol of the lordly power and also the sap of food.

After these things are separately glorified, it is said further, *etāni ha vai yāny'asmād ījānād vyutkrāntāni bhavanti tanye'vā 'smins tad dadhāti tair evai 'naṁ tat samardhayati*

all these things, viz. the lordly power, the sap of food, the brilliance and the splendour, etc., have gone away from the sacrificer who is consecrated for the sacrifice, even though he is a kṣatriya. When he sprinkles the sacrificer with all these materials, he thereby confers upon the sacrificer those that have gone away from him.

—*AitBrā*, XXXVII.4

The redressing nature of the rite becomes sufficiently clear from these passages. Thomas also has pointed this out when he has stated, "the object of the rite was probably to reinforce his vigour as such".[8]

3. In the texts other than the *AitBrā*, the *sautrāmaṇī* is the only rite in which the sacrificer is given the *surā*-drink. True, in the *rājasūya* of the *AitBrā*, also, *surā* is drunk by the sacrificer, but that is done for some different purpose. In that context it is said that as the sacrificer drinks *surā*, it secures for him peace and comfort all throughout his life. *Surā* is said to be nourishing and pleasant, just like any other food, *soma*, etc. (*AitBrā*, XXXIX.6).

These are the similarities between the two rites, in respect of their nature. There are, again, some other ritual peculiarities also found in both these rites. In the *kaukilī sautrāmaṇī*, the sacrificer is given a sacred bath (*abhiṣeka*) after the animal-offerings. It is observed that some of the features of this rite are strikingly similar to those of the *punarabhiṣeka*.

1. In the *punarabhiṣeka* ceremony, while placing a stool for the sacrificer, it is put in such a way that two of its legs are within the altar and the remaining two are outside it (*AitBrā*, XXXVII.1).

Similarly, while placing a stool for the sacrificer at the time of

8. F.W. Thomas , *op.cit.*, pp. 20-4.

the sacred bath in the *kaukilī sautrāmaṇī*, the seat is put in such a way that two of its legs are on the northern altar and the other two are on the southern one (*ŚatBrā*, XII.8.3.6 and *KātyŚS*, XIX.4.7).

2. In *AitBrā*, XXXVII.3, it is stated that the sacrificer is sprinkled over optionally with the *vyāhṛtis* also. This view is referred to by the *ŚatBrā*. In *ŚatBrā*, XII.8.3.18 it is mentioned that, according to some, the sacrificer is given the sacred bath with the *vyāhṛtis* also. But this view is not accepted by the brāhmaṇa and it is further stated there that the sacrificer should be given the sacred bath only with the recitation of the *yajus*-formula. The passage in the *ŚatBrā*, reads:

   taṁ hai'ke etābhiśca devatābhir abhiṣiñcanti ǀ
   bhūr bhuvaḥ svar ity etābhir u ca vyāhṛtibhiḥ ǀ
   etā vai vyāhṛtaya idaṁ sarvaṁ ǀ
   tad enam anena sarveṇā' bhiṣiñcāma iti ǀ
   na tathā kuryāt ǀ
   etābhir evai'naṁ devatābhir abhiṣiñcet ǀ
   etā u hye'va devatā idaṁ sarvaṁ ǀ

   KātyŚS, XIX.4.16 also states this option.

3. In the *kaukilī sutrāmaṇī* a *sāman* is sung after the *abhiṣeka*, according to the tradition of the *Śukla Yajurveda*. It is called the *saṁśāna sāman*. In the *ŚatBrā*, the final parts of the *sāman* (the *nidhanas*) are prescribed as *saṁśravase*, *viśravase*, and *satyaśravase*. In *KātyŚS*, XIX.5.3.5, however, a distinction is made and separate *nidhanas* are prescribed for a brāhmaṇa, a kṣatriya and a vaiśya. The *nidhanas* prescribed for a kṣatriya are *jityai* 'for conquest', *satyajityai* 'for victory', *vijityai* 'for winning' and *saṁjityai* 'for success'. It seems that these *nidhanas* also have some connection with the *punarabhiṣeka* ritual for, at the end of the *abhiṣeka* in it, the sacrificer salutes the *brahman* 'holy power' thrice and releases his speech, saying, 'I give a boon for *jiti, abhijiti, vijiti* and *saṁjiti*'.

It seems that the *KātyŚS* has accepted these terms from the *AitBrā*, with just a little variation, viz. *satyajityai* instead of *abhijityai* and has employed them in connection with a kṣatriya sacrificer. It should be noted in this context that no other employment of these four terms together could be traced in any other ritual text.

Because of these striking and important similarities, it can be safely said without being wrong, that the *punarabhiṣeka* is the precursor of *sautrāmaṇī* and that it is the rudimentary form of the latter.

To see how the *sautrāmaṇī* is developed and is elaborated on the basis of the *punarabhiṣeka*, it is necessary to compare the *rājasūya* of the *AitBrā* together with the rite of the *punarabhiṣeka*, with the *rājasūya* in other ritual texts together with the rite of the *sautrāmaṇī*.

While constructing an elaborate Vedic ritual around the practice of *surā*-drinking, the other texts seem to have mingled together the rites mentioned in the *rājasūya* of the *AitBrā* and the *punarabhiṣeka*. Further, they have modified and rearranged them in the ritual of the *rājasūya* and the *sautrāmaṇī*.

Thus, whereas in the *AitBrā*, the *abhiṣeka* is prescribed twice, the second *abhiṣeka* is omitted from the *caraka sautrāmaṇī* and only the *surā*-ritual is elaborated in it. The rite of king's symbolical victory over the enemy, which forms a part of the *punarabhiṣeka*, is excluded from the *sautrāmaṇī* and is included in the ritual of the *rājasūya* in the other texts.

Just in the same way, *surā*-drinking is excluded from the *rājasūya* in texts other than the *AitBrā*,[9] and it is prescribed

9. According to *TaiBrā*, I.7.6.5; *ĀpaŚS*, XVIII.14.7; *HirŚS*, XIII.5.22 and *BaudhŚS*, XII.9, in the ritual of the *rājasūya* the sacrificer king is given curds, juice of *udumbara* fruit and sprouted barley or paddy (*śaṣpa* or *tokma*). *TaiBrā*, I.7.6.5 declares that by being made to eat the barley sprouts, he is made the recipient of a *surā*-offering.

In this regard, Heesterman has remarked in his book *op.cit.*, p. 94, f.n. 17, that 'The young barley shoots (*śaṣpāṇi*) apparently belong to the sphere of the *surā* cult, as they are the basic material for the preparation of the *surā* beverage."

However, this rite takes place before the sacred bath in the *rājasūya* and not after it.

exclusively in the *sautrāmaṇī*. While doing so, these texts have adopted the *mantras* accompanying the *surā*-ritual, viz., *nānā hi vām devatitam* . . . and *yadatra śiṣṭaṁ rasinaḥ sutasya* . . . in the *sautrāmaṇī* ritual.

That the *sautrāmaṇī* is modelled on the *punarabhiṣeka* is evident, as is thus seen from the ritual similarities in the *kaukilī* ritual.

The myth about the origin of the *sautrāmaṇī* is also adopted from the *rājasūya* ritual of the *AitBrā*.

It is seen in the previous chapter that, because of the growing influence of the kṣatriyas, the priests had to allow them to perform a sacrifice. However, while allowing them to do so, the priests took due care that the kṣatriya would always hold a subordinate position in the sacrifice.[10] There are various instances of that, e.g. *see AitBrā*, XXXVII.6; XXXIX.6. Thus, as a device of maintaining the superiority of the priestly class, they pilfered the part of the kṣatriya of the remnants of the oblations of *soma* in that sacrifice. With a view to justifying this behaviour of theirs they created a myth. The myth is cited in *AitBrā*. XXXV.2. It reads:

yatre'ndraṁ devatāḥ paryavr̥ñjan viśvarūpaṁ tvāṣṭram abhyamaṁsta vr̥tram astr̥ta yatīn sālāvr̥kebhyaḥ prādād arurmaghān avadhīd br̥haspateḥ pratyavadhīd iti tatre 'ndraḥ somapīthena vyārdhyate'ndrasyā'nu vyr̥ddhiṁ kṣatraṁ somapīthena vyārdhyatā'pīndraḥ somapīthe 'bhavat tvaṣṭur āmuṣya somaṁ tad vyr̥ddam evā'dyāpi kṣatraṁ somapīthena ।

When the gods excluded Indra (saying) 'He hath misused Viśvarūpa, son of Tvaṣṭr̥, he hath laid low Vr̥tra, he hath

10. Manning, in *Ancient and Medieval India*, p. 103, has noted in this regard, "The concluding chapters of the Aitareya Brāhmaṇa show, by historical example, how the prosperity of kings depended upon the due performance of religious ceremonies and the liberality with which these officiating priests were afterwards rewarded."

> given the Yatis to the hyaenas, he hath killed the Arurmaghas, he hath contended with Bṛhaspati', then as a punishment for all these sins Indra was deprived of the Soma drinking, and in accordance with the deprivation of Indra the lordly power was deprived of the Soma drinking. Indra obtained later a share in the Soma drinking, having stolen the soma of Tvaṣṭṛ, but to day even the lordly power is deprived of Soma drinking. (tr. by Keith, p. 314)

This myth is further expanded and modified to serve the purpose of the *sautrāmaṇī.*[11] Thus, in the myth regarding the *sautrāmaṇī*, it is further stated that, though Indra drank that *soma*, it came out of his body. Therefore one, who is not invited to drink *soma*, should not drink it. At that time, Indra was cured by Aśvins and Sarasvatī by means of the *sautrāmaṇī*. Hence, it should be performed also for one, who is excessively purged by *soma*, or has vomited *soma*.

In this way, the discussion of the *rājasūya* in the *AitBrā*, leads us to the origin of the rite *sautrāmaṇī*. It informs us that the kṣatriya sacrificer who was consecrated for a sacrifice had to perform certain redressing rites after the performance of the sacrifice. The *punarabhiṣeka* was also one of the redressing rites, which the kṣatriya sacrificer performed to restore to himself the *kṣatra* which had temporarily gone away from him. The comparison of the ritual of the *punarabhiṣeka* and that of the *sautrāmaṇī* brings it into light that the *punarabhiṣeka* is the precursor of the *sautrāmaṇī* and that the *surā*-ritual described in the *AitBrā*, is further elaborated by the ritualists and the *sautrāmaṇī* is formed as a separate rite.

---

11. All the primordial myths in connection with the *sautrāmaṇī* are going to be dealt with in a separate chapter.

4

Sautrāmaṇī as a Medicinal Rite

THE *sautrāmaṇī* rite is prescribed for one who has vomited *soma* (*somavāmin*) or who has evacuated *soma* (*somātipūta*); (*MaiS*, II.4.1; *KāṭhS*, XII.10; *ŚatBrā*, V.4.6.13; *ĀpaŚS*, XIX.4.11; *MānŚS*, V.2.4.1; *VaikhāŚS*, XII.1; *HirŚS*, XIII.8.44; *VārāŚS*, III.2.7.1). It is stated that a person who vomits *soma* becomes deprived of strength and vigour. When the priest performs this sacrifice for such a person, he restores that strength and vigour in him, (*MaiS*, II.4.1; *KāṭhS*, XII.10). It is thus a curing rite.

Certain other rites also are prescribed for the same purpose. Besides the performance of the *sautrāmaṇī*, offering of *caru* (rice) prepared of millet is prescribed for a *somavāmin*, (*TaiS*, II.3.6.7; *KāṭhS*, XI.1 and *ĀpaŚS*, XIV.30.17). According to the *PañcBrā*, XXVIII.5.3; *LāṭyāŚS*, VIII.10.7 and *KātyŚS*, XXII.9.5, a one-day *soma*-sacrifice called *tīvrasoma* or *tīvrasut* should be performed for such a person. While dealing with *KauśiSū*, XXV.20 and 21 Keśava has stated an additional employment of the verse *vāyoḥ pūtaḥ pavitreṇa* (*AV*(*Ś*), VI.51.1). According to him, with the recitation of this verse, fire-sticks of *palāśa* tree should be offered on the fire, after they have been anointed with the *soma*-juice, for a *somavāmin* or a *somātipūta*.

One becomes curious, therefore, about the reason of the vomiting of *soma* and about why the *surā*-ritual came to be prescribed for it.

Regarding the cause of the vomiting or purging of *soma*, some scholars have stated that it was due to excessive *soma*-drinking.

According to them the *soma*-juice was an intoxicating beverage and the vomiting was a disease like the hangover caused by drinking excessively.[1]

However, in the Vedic texts, there is no reference whatsoever to the excessive *soma*-drinking. A myth is cited while mentioning the cause of vomiting. The myth is:

> Indra killed the son of Tvaṣṭṛ. Tvaṣṭṛ became angry and performed a *soma*-sacrifice, to which Indra was not invited. Even though he was not invited, Indra created nuisance to the sacrifice and drank the *soma*-juice per force. But he became deprived of that *soma*-juice. It came out of his body.

It is added further,

> therefore a person should not drink *soma*, when he is not invited. Otherwise he also becomes deprived of the *soma*-drink. —*MaiS*, II.4.1; *KāṭhS*, XII.9 and XII.1.

In *ŚatBrā*, XII.7.1.1 and *GopBrā*, II.5.6 it is stated that Tvaṣṭṛ performed the *soma*-sacrifice as a means of performing black magic or exorcism against Indra.

It is clear from these references that the explanation of the causes of the vomiting given by the Vedic texts is not at all a medical one. The vomiting was a result, according to them, of a sin caused by a breach of taboo and of exorcism.

One will not be surprised by this explanation when one takes into account the general concept about the causation of disease in the primitive medicine.[2]

---

1. *See* J. Eggeling, *Śatapatha Brāhmaṇa*, part III, p. 129, f.n. 1; also H. Oldenberg, "Indra und Namuci", *Kleine Schriften*, Teil 1, p. 639, and also R. Griffith, *Śukla Yajurveda*, p. 102.
2. For detailed discussion on this subject see, William George Black, *Folk-Medicine*, pp. 1-33; G.J. Frazer, *Golden Bough* (abridged), pp. 196, 542, etc.

   Siegerist, *History of Medicine*, Vol. 1. pp. 125-39

   J. John Collins, *Primitive Religion*, pp. 106-7.

   Jayne, *Healing Gods of Ancient Civilization*, p. 145.

The concepts about disease and its treatment among the primitive people are very much different from those in the modern times. According to primitive man, medicine is closely connected with magic and religion. Disease is not regarded as a normal thing and a physical or a mental disorder. It is regarded as a normal thing caused by supernatural powers or practices, which are other than the properly medical ones. Medical ritual in primitive religion included supernatural practices or beliefs used either to cause illnesses or to cure them. It is a set of practices intended to protect a person against evil forces and to bring him good luck.

Concepts about disease prevalent among the primitive people are classified in four major categories (1) sorcery, (2) breach of taboo, (3) disease object intrusion, (4) spirit intrusion.[3]

In ancient Indian texts also, it is observed, that diseases are supposed to be caused by (1) evil beings, (2) sins, (3) heresy, (4) absence of proper religious behaviour, (5) black magic practised by others, etc.[4] Even if breaking a taboo is not mentioned separately, it can be included among sins.

One, or more than one of these causes can be present in some given illness.

It would not be out of place to note here the exact nature of the reasons mentioned in the Vedic texts in the present connection.

1. *Breach of a taboo*: A human illness is supposed to be caused by violation of some taboo. A taboo is a kind of supernatural no-no. A person is told not to do something. If he violates that taboo, it leads to retaliation, and the important thing is: even if the person himself might not be knowing the taboo, he gets punished if he violates this taboo knowingly or unknowingly and gets punished for it.

2. *Sorcery or exorcism*: Illnesses are believed to be caused by persons having the powers of sorcery or exorcism. These powers

3. J. John Collins, *Primitive Religion*, pp. 107ff.
4. For a detailed discussion see G.U. Thite, *Medicine, Its magico-religions Aspects*, pp. 4-38.

are supposed to have been inherent in them right from their birth or they might have acquired them with the help of ritual manipulations.

In the present case it is said that Tvaṣṭṛ performed the *soma*-sacrifice as a means to perform black magic or exorcism against Indra. At the time of the actual performance of that sacrifice, he kept *soma* — the oblation material — directly on the ground. In a ritual performace, generally the material to be used in the sacrifice is not put directly on the ground. Something, most of the times, the *darbha* blades are put inbetween. Thus the lack of proper ritual procedure also seems to be a means of performing black magic.

After learning about the disease concepts and the magico-medical or supernatural elements in the healing ritual of the primitive religion, one might naturally be curious about the efficacy and success of these curing rituals. One thing, however, must be made clear here. If the curing ritual was not successful nobody was likely to question the effectiveness of the cures themselves. Generally, the reasons for the failure were considered to be counter-magic, lack of correctness in the ritual procedure, omission of some rites, etc. It was not the efficacy of the cure but the means of its application that was called in question.[5]

It is, nevertheless, fairly certain that some cures worked because the treatment involved some certain — sometimes unconsciously — rational, i.e., medically effective elements. The use of massage, hot baths, physical shocks and potions might be of actual therapeutic value to the patient. It is possible that a few plant derivatives used in primitive curing are 'objectively active' and do have advantageous effects even in our medical pharmacopoeia. The *Atharvan Materia Medica* also contains many substances, some of which are of recognised intrinsic virtue.

But the medical power of these substances was not of much

---

5. J. John Collins, *Primitive Religion,* p. 108. Siegerist, *History of Medicine.* p. 138.

importance to the primitive man. The remedies were conceived as having magical powers that could cure diseases and they were given in connection with *mantras* — 'spoken charms or spells' in metrical forms.[6]

In the Vedic religion also these *mantras* have much importance. In it man sought to gain the favour of the gods and the divinities with the help of hymns, prayers and sacrifice and tried thereby to receive benefits according to his desires.[7]

Regarding the *sautrāmaṇī* also it is stated that it was basically a popular rite, performed for medical purposes.[8] However, the reason why this is to be considered as a popular rite is not stated. When the ritual of the *sautrāmaṇī* is studied in the light of the above discussion, some popular features can be noticed in it.

The use of the eagle-wing feathers is one of such peculiarities. In curing rituals, it is observed, that the treatment consists of brushing away the evil influences with eagle-wing feathers.[9] In the *sautrāmaṇī* ritual also the eagle-wing feathers are used. According to one tradition the sacrificer himself is purified with the feathers, (*MānŚS*, V.2.11.20; *ŚatBrā*, XII.7.3.22); while according to some other texts, the bowls filled with *surā* are wiped with these feathers and are thereby purified (*BaudhŚS*, XVII.34; *ĀpaŚS*, XIX.2.12). I have not come across any other reference in the Vedic texts to the ritual use of the eagle-wing feathers.

The magico-medical use of *surā* is another important feature in this regard. In connection with the use of *surā* and some such other substances Gonda has observed that "uncommon sacrificial material is often prescribed in the magic and curative rites (the reason is not always obvious)".[10] It will be interesting to see if we can find any

6. J. John Collins, *Primitive Religion*, pp. 116ff.
7. Siegerist, *op.cit.*, p. 198.
8. Jayne, *Healing Gods*, p. 157.
9. A. Weber, *Über die Königsweihe, den Rājasūya*, pp. 5 and 98; A Hillebrandt, *Ritualliteratur, Vedische Opfer und Zauber*, p. 159; G.U. Thite, *Sacrifice in the Brāhmaṇa-texts,* pp. 85, 86.
10. J. John Collins, *Primitive Religion*, p. 115.

reason for the use of *surā*.

In the curing rituals of the folk-medicine, it is stated, some rites are performed basically to strengthen and purify the patient. At times the patient is given some medicine to drink.. Sometimes he is bathed also with the medicine. Special offerings are offered or are deposited at shrines for the recovery of the patient.[11]

In the Indian medicinal texts it is stated that *surā* does possess some medicinal qualities. Thus, in *Mādhava Nidāna* (XVIII.2-7) it is said, "*Surā* by its nature is just like any other food. If it is consumed in a wrong way, it causes diseases but used in the right way, it is just like *amṛta*". In *Aṣṭāṅga Hṛdaya,* I.8.48, it is stated, "*Surā* is a tonic for the weak ones". In *Bhela Saṁhitā*, I.19 it is noted that "if *surā* is drunk in right measure it creates joy, strength, energy and brilliance in a person".

It is possible that the person was given the *surā* drink because of such nourishment value of it. Besides the nourishing nature, *surā* is prescribed as a remedy for vomiting and diorrhea also. *Surā* is described as causing constipation, (*viṣṭambhinī*, *Suśruta Saṁhitā* I.45.179). *Surā* prepared from barley is also of this nature. It is also described as *viṣṭambhinī* in *Aṣṭāṅga Saṁhitā*, I.6.27). According to *Suśruta Saṁhitā*, I.45.176, *surā* is a medicine in the case of vomiting also. First, the method of the preparation of *surā* is described in it and in the end it is said that the same method of preparing *surā* is prescribed in the case of vomiting also, (*eṣa eva surākalpaḥ vamaneṣvapi kīrtitaḥ*).[12]

Therefore, it seems that *surā* was used in popular medicinal rites. It was used as a remedy for vomiting and evacuation. When the rites of the kṣatriyas were accepted in the Vedic ritual, *surā* was also included in it. Once it was admitted in the Vedic hieratic religion, the other qualities of that drink were also taken notice of and the *surā*-ritual came to be prescribed for a *somavāmin* and a *somātipūta*.

---

11. J. Gonda, *Vedic Ritual — The Non-Solemn Rites*, p. 186.
12. J. John Collins, *Primitive Religion*, p. 115.

5

Relation between the Agnicayana and the Sautrāmaṇī

In the previous chapters we have seen as to why the *sautrāmaṇī* was performed after the *rājasūya* and also as a redressing rite for one who has vomited or evacuated *soma*. It is prescribed to be performed after the *agnicayana* also[1] (cf. *TaiS*, V.6.3.4; *TaiBrā*, III.12.5.33; *ĀpaŚS*, XVII.24.1; *BaudhŚS*, X.59; *KātyŚS*, XIX.1.2; and *VaitāSū*, XXX.1).

In Vedic literature, however, we do not find any discussion regarding the exact nature of the relation between the *agnicayana* and the *sautrāmaṇī*. It does not become clear whether the *sautrāmaṇī* is a part of the *agnicayana*, without which the rite of the *agnicayana* cannot be complete, or whether it means that one is eligible to perform the *sautrāmaṇī* when one has performed the *agnicayana*.

When one looks into the Vedic texts in this regard, one finds that the relation between the *agnicayana* and the *sautrāmaṇī* is of varied nature. The *TaiS*, V.6.3.4 and the texts which follow it, viz. the *TaiBrā*, the *ĀpaŚS*, and *BaudhŚS* prescribe the *caraka sautrāmaṇī* after the *agnicayana*. The *KātyŚS*, and the *VaitāSū*, on the other hand, prescribe instead of the *caraka*, the *kaukilī*

---

1. *See* J. Gonda, *Mantras of the Agnyupasthāna and the Sautrāmaṇī*, p. 63; *Śrautakośa*, ed. by C.G. Kasikar, *et al.*, Skt. Section, Vol. 1, p. 698; and also A. Hillebrandt, *Ritualliteratur,* pp. 159ff.

sautrāmaṇī to be performed after the *agnicayana*.

It becomes necessary, therefore, to see what could be the exact relation between the *agnicayana* and *sautrāmaṇī* and to try to find the reason as to why there is a difference in the prescription of various Vedic texts.

In all likelihood, it is in *TaiS*, V.6.3.4 *agniṁ citvā sautrāmaṇyā yajeta*, where the first mention of the *sautrāmaṇī* in relation to the *agnicayana* has occurred. To understand the real significance of this sentence, it is necessary to see the context in which it has occurred.

In the ritual procedure of the *agnicayana*, there is a certain rite, according to which the sacrificer is given a sacred bath. After the description of the rite, it is said,

> *tad vai rājasūyasya rūpaṁ | ya evaṁ vidvān agniṁ cinuta ubhāv eva lokāv abhijayati yaś ca rājasūyenejānasya yaś cāgnicitaḥ | indrasya suṣuvāṇasya daśadhā indriyaṁ vīryam parāpatat | tad devāḥ sautrāmaṇyā samabharan | sūyate vā eṣa yo'gnim cinute'gniṁ citvā sautrāmaṇyā yajete'ndriyam eva vīryaṁ sambhṛtyā'tman dhatte |*
>
> That is the form of the royal consecration. He, who knowing thus, piles the fire, conquers both the worlds, that of him who has offered royal consecration and that of the piler of the fire. When Indra had been consecrated, his power and strength fell away in ten places; the gods brought it together with the Sautrāmaṇī; he who piles the fire is consecrated; having piled the fire, he should sacrifice with the Sautrāmaṇī, verily collecting power and strength, he places them in himself. (tr.by Keith, p. 457)

It is evident from this passage that the rite of the *abhiṣeka* in the *agnicayana* is compared to the *rājasūya*, obviously for glorifying it. To establish the importance of this rite, it is added, that one, who knowing thus piles the fire-altar, wins both the worlds, that of the piler of the fire-altar and that of the sacrificer of the *rājasūya*.

The author of the *Taittirīya Saṁhitā* is, however, not contented with the mere identification of this *abhiṣeka*-rite with the *rājasūya*. He extends the comparison further and adds that Indra, when the *abhiṣeka* was performed for him (in the *rājasūya*) lost his strength and valour and the gods got them back for him with the help of the *sautrāmaṇī*. One, who has piled the fire-altar, is also given the sacred bath. Therefore, after having piled the fire-altar, one should perform the *sautrāmaṇī* also, and place in oneself that power and strength.

In this passage, it is noticeable that, together with the rite of the *abhiṣeka* in the *agnicayana*, the *sautrāmaṇī* also is elevated by this injunction. It is commonly observed that in Vedic texts, efforts are always made to elevate a certain sacrificial rite by showing that the concerned rite has some connection with the *soma*-ritual. The *sautrāmaṇī* is a part of a *soma*-sacrifice, viz., the *rājasūya*; it is nevertheless performed exclusively for the kṣatriyas. Now, the injunction *agniṁ citvā* . . . connects the *sautrāmaṇī* with the *agnicayana* and hence a person, who performs a *soma*-sacrifice together with the *agnicayana*, is also considered to be eligible for performing the *sautrāmaṇī*. Thus, the sentence does not mean that the *sautrāmaṇī* is a part of the *agnicayana*. It means that one, who has piled the fire-altar, can perform the *sautrāmaṇī*. The commentary of Sāyaṇa on this passage is noteworthy in this respect; it reads:

> *sautrāmaṇyāḥ cayanāṅgatvaṁ na bodhyate kintu kālavidhir ayaṁ tasmād idaṁ vākyam prakaraṇād utkarṣṭavyaṁ* ।
>
> This does not mean that the *sautrāmaṇī* is a part of the *cayana*. It is an injunction denoting the time (of its performance). Therefore, this sentence should be removed from this chapter.

As there is no specific mention in this passage either of the *caraka* or of the *kaukilī*, one becomes curious about which form of the *sautrāmaṇī* is intended in it.

One may remember here that there does not at all occur in the

TaiS, the description of the *kaukilī sautrāmaṇī*. It is only the *caraka sautrāmaṇī* which is described at *TaiS*, I.8.21. It follows, therefore, that in the above-quoted passage, reference is made to the *caraka sautrāmaṇī*.

There is one more reason for holding this view. In order to glorify the rite of the *agnicayana*, the rite of the *abhiṣeka* in it is compared with the *abhiṣeka* in the *rājasūya*. Further, to make the comparison perfect, the *sautrāmaṇī* is prescribed after the *agnicayana*. The *sautrāmaṇī* which is performed as a part of the *rājasūya*, is the *caraka sautrāmaṇī*. Therefore, the *sautrāmaṇī*, which is connected with the *agnicayana* in this context is also the *caraka sautrāmaṇī*.

The statement about the *sautrāmaṇī* in connection with the *cayana* occurs in *TaiBrā*, III.12.5.33,

> *satejasam evāgniṁ cinute* ।
> *agniṁ citvā sautrāmaṇyā yajeta maitrāvaruṇyā vāmikṣayā* ।
> *vīryeṇa vā eṣa vyṛdhyate yo'gniṁ cinute* ।
> *yāvad eva vīryaṁ tad asmin dadhāti* ।
>
> He piles the fire-altar with brilliance. After having piled it, he sacrifices with the *sautrāmaṇī* or with the *maitrāvaruṇī āmikṣā*. One, who piles the fire-altar is deprived of one's strength. That much strength one places in oneself.

It is evident from this passage that the *sautrāmaṇī* is introudced in the ritual of the *agnicayana* only abruptly. There is no connection whatsoever between the preceding sentence and the one under reference. The *sautrāmaṇī* is optionally prescribed here after the *agnicayana*. The myth related to Indra, referred to at *TaiS*, V.6.3.4, occurs in the *TaiBrā*, also and it is further added there that one, who piles the fire-altar is deprived of strength and it is again placed in oneself by the performance of the *sautrāmaṇī*.

Among the *sūtra*-texts of the *Taittirīya* recension, the *ĀpaŚS*, and the *BaudhŚS*, prescribe the *sautrāmaṇī* after the *agnicayana*. The reference to it occurs not in the chapter on the *sautrāmaṇī* but at the end of the chapter which deals with the *agnicayana*. Thus

ĀpaŚS, XVII.24.1 reads:

> *agniṁ citvā sautrāmaṇyā yajeta maitrāvaruṇyā vāmikṣayā*
>
> After having piled the fire-altar, one should sacrifice with the *sautrāmaṇī* or with the *maitrāvaruṇī āmikṣā*.

It seems that Āpastamba has followed the *TaiBrā*. *BaudhŚS*, 10.59 reads:

> *atha devikāhavirbhir yajate'tha traidhātavīyayā yajate 'tha sautrāmaṇyā yajate.*
>
> Then (i.e. after the *agnicayana*) he sacrifices with the *devikā*-offerings, then with the *traidhātavī* offering and then he performs the *sautrāmaṇī*.

Both Āpastamba and Bodhāyana seem to have just quoted the statement occurring in the Saṁhitā or the *Brāhmaṇa* text. They have not entered into discussion about the exact relation between the *agnicayana* and the *sautrāmaṇī*.

The *MaiS*; the *KāṭhS*; the *MānŚS* and the *VārāŚS*, also have just quoted the sentence *agniṁ citvā*. . . at the end of the chapter dealing with the *agnicayana*. There is no reference, however, to the relation between the *agnicayana* and the *sautrāmaṇī*.

In the *VājaS*, the *mantra*s of the *kaukilī sautrāmaṇī* are cited after those of the *agnicayana*. The *ŚatBrā* has not referred to any kind of connection between the two. The *KātyŚS* has, however, connected the *kaukilī sautrāmaṇī* with the *agnicayana*. It reads at XIX.1.2,

> *agnicitsomayājisomātipūtasomavāminām*
>
> The (*kaukilī*) *sautrāmaṇī* (is to be performed) for one, who has piled the fire-altar, or has performed a *soma*-sacrifice, or who is excessively purged by *soma*, or has vomited *soma*.

(According to the commentary of Karkācārya, it is to be performed for one, who has performed a *soma*-sacrifice with the rite of the piling of the fire-altar. . .). Thus according to the *KātyŚS* the *kaukilī sautrāmaṇī* is *naimittika*. Whenever one has performed the *cayana*, one has to perform the *sautrāmaṇī*.

There is one more *Śrauta Sūtra* which prescribes the *kaukilī* after the *agnicayana*. Thus, *VaitāSū*, XXX.1 prescribes,

> *agnicit somātipūtaḥ somavāmī sautrāmaṇyā'bhiṣicyate*
> One, who has piled the fire-altar, or is excessively purged by *soma*, or has vomited *soma*, is given a sacred bath with the *sautrāmaṇī*.

It is necessary, therefore, to find the reason as to why there is such variation in the *KātyŚS*, and the *VaitāSū*.

From a careful study of the *KātyŚS*, it is evident that, Kātyāyana was deeply influenced by the method of discussion of the Mīmāṁsā school of thought.[2]

His work contains many technical terms of the Pūrva Mīmāṁsā. Unlike the other *Śrauta Sūtras*, the *KātyŚS*, enters into a discussion, giving the pros and cons of a number of topics related to the sacrificial performance.

Moreover, the *KātyŚS* contains the largest number of *sūtra*s that have their counterparts in the *Pūrva Mīmāṁsā Sūtra*s. There are certain instances, where the *KātyŚS* seems to have compressed into one *sūtra* a number of corresponding *sūtra*s from the *Pūrva Mīmāṁsā Sūtra*s.

It is essential, therefore, to see the discussion in the *Mīmāṁsā sūtra*s regarding the *agnicayana* and the *sautrāmaṇī*.

The *mīmāṁsaka*s, while interpreting the sentence *agniṁ citvā* . . . have stated that the *sautrāmaṇī* is a part of the *agnicayana*, (*see MīmāSū*, IV.3.29 to 31). It is discussed there: If the sentence is considered to be a statement regarding time, there will be no connection between the *agnicayana* and the *sautrāmaṇī*, and

2. For a detailed discussion, see D.V. Garge, *Citations in the Śābara Bhāsya*, pp. 16, 17; also J. Gonda, *History of Indian Literature*, Vol. 1, fasc. 2, *The Ritual Sūtras*, p. 529.

the 'indication of the context' *lakṣaṇā* will be rejected, because when the *sautrāmaṇī* is laid down in the same context as that of the *agnicayana*, it is understood that the *sautrāmaṇī* is a part of the *agnicayana*.

The relation between the two is established here, as we see, not upon the meaning of the actual words in the *Śruti*, but on the basis of the context of their occurrence.

The opponent then rightly remarks: the time for the subsidiaries is the same as that for their primaries; as a matter of fact, there is only one time for the primaries and their subsidiaries, as is going to be explained under *MīmāSū*, XI.2.7. Therefore, after having piled the fire-altar, one should immediately proceed with the performance of the other sacrifice, viz. the *sautrāmaṇī*.

However, the practice is different. The *agnicayana* is not an independent sacrifice. It is a rite, which is performed as a part of a *soma*-sacrifice. It is, moreover, a subsidiary rite and is to be performed before a *soma*-sacrifice, not after it. Hence, the *sautrāmaṇī*, even though it is enjoined to be performed after the *agnicayana*, is performed actually after the *soma*-sacrifice.

Therefore, once they have asserted that the *sautrāmaṇī* is a part of the *agnicayana*, the *mīmāṁsaka*s had to attempt all kinds of verbal acrobatics to put their theory in accordance with the practice.

Thus it is stated in *MīmāSū*, IV.3.41:

> As a matter of fact the rite in question, i.e., the *sautrāmaṇī* is enjoined to be performed after the completion of the other rite. Hence, on account of the general injunction, it should be performed at its own proper time.[3]

(It is to be noted here that the *mīmāṁsaka*s, while determining the relation between the *agnicayana* and the *sautrāmaṇī* have rejected this meaning; and at that time the reason given by them is: this is

---

3. The summary of the discussion of the *Mīmāṁsā sūtra*s is given here with the help of the English translation of the same by Ganganath Jha.

not the direct meaning of the sentence, but one derived indirectly by indication (*lakṣaṇā*) to be understood in the text.)

The commentary on this *sūtra* reads:

> The other rite has been enjoined to be performed after the completion of the primary sacrifice. A sacrifice is taken to be complete only when all the subsequent rites also have been performed. This is suggested by the phrase *agniṁ citvā*. Therefore, the *sautrāmaṇī* is to be performed, at its own time after the *agnicayana*.

Upon this is raised an objection by the opponent. He has observed, the phrase *agnim citvā* in the sentence means, 'having completed the rite of the *agnicayana*' only, and hence it does not mean 'having completed the *soma*-sacrifice' also, which follows the *agnicayana*.

The answer given to this objection is: 'That is not so'. The words of the text are *agniṁ citvā* which mean 'having embellished the fire, by means of the *cayana* rite'. But merely placing the fire upon the ground does not confer any benefit upon the fire. If a sacrifice is performed in that fire, then only that *agnicayana* (together with that sacrifice) could be regarded as conferring sanctity upon the fire; and hence the phrase 'having completed the *agnicayana*' must mean 'after having performed the sacrifice in the fire which is placed upon the ground'. The benefit conferred on Agni, whereby it helps the sacrificer, does not consist in merely placing it on the ground, but also in performing a sacrifice on that fire. Hence, the phrase 'completing the *agnicayana*' must mean, 'after having performed the sacrifice'.

Thus it is in the *Mīmāṁsā sūtra*s, that, with so many efforts, the *mīmāṁsaka*s have come to the conclusion that,

> the *sautrāmaṇī* is considered to be a part of the *agnicayana*, and it is to be performed at its own proper time, not after the *agnicayana*, but after the *soma*-sacrifice, of which the *agnicayana* forms a part.

As we have seen, Kātyāyana was very much influenced by the

mīmāṁsakas; and it is due to the influence of that school that he has connected the *sautrāmaṇī* with the *agnicayana* and has considered it as a part of the *agnicayana*.

Still the question remains unsolved as to why Kātyāyana has connected the *kaukilī* with the *agnicayana* and not the *caraka* like the other texts.

A possible explanation is: *MīmāSū*, IV.3.41 reads,

apavṛtte tu codanā syāt tatsāmānyāt svakāle ।

> As a matter of fact, the sacrifice in question is enjoined to be performed on the completion of the other sacrifice. Hence, on account of the general injunction, it should be performed at its own proper time.

The *caraka sautrāmaṇī* is not an independent rite. It is performed either as a part of the *rājasūya*, or occasionally after vomiting or purging the *soma*. Hence, it cannot have its own time for performance. The *sautrāmaṇī* which is included in the seven *havis*-sacrifices, as an independent rite, is the *kaukilī sautrāmaṇī*. It is probable, therefore, that due to the influence of this *sūtra*, Kātyāyana has connected the *kaukilī sautrāmaṇī* — the independent rite — with the *agnicayana*.

Besides the *KātyŚS*, we have observed, the *VaitāSū* also connects the *kaukilī sautrāmaṇī* with the *agnicayana*. Since the author of the *VaitāSū* was very much under the influence of the *Śukla YV*,[4] it is no wonder that while modelling its ritual on the basis of the *KātyŚS*, he also has connected the *kaukilī sautrāmaṇī* with the *agnicayana*.

To sum up the discussion, we can say,

1. In the *TaiS* the *sautrāmaṇī* is connected with the *agnicayana* with the intention of elevating the rite of the *abhiṣeka* in the *agnicayana* and also the rite *sautrāmaṇī* as well.

---

4. *See* C.G. Kashikar, *A Survey of the Śrauta Sūtras*, p. 101.

2. It is evident from the comparison of the *agnicayana* to the *rājasūya* that the *sautrāmaṇī* which is connected with the *agnicayana* in the *TaiS*, is the *caraka sautrāmaṇī*.
3. The *mīmāṁsaka*s have stated that the *sautrāmaṇī* is a part of the *agnicayana* and it is to be performed after the *soma*-sacrifice, of which the *agnicayana* forms a part.
4. In all likelihood, it is due to the influence of the Mīmāṁsā school that in the *KātyŚS*, the *kaukilī sautrāmaṇī* is connected with the *agnicayana*.

6

Primordial Myths in Connection with the Sautrāmaṇī

EVER since man began to think scientifically, mythological literature was considered as 'a product of superstitions and primitive minds'. It was held to be meaningless and looked down upon as 'a mere chaos and a shapeless mass of incoherent ideas'.[1] It was neglected by scholars as only a tell-tale matter.

But only very recently, scholars, particularly anthropologists, have begun to take interest in mythology and have started to look at it with a different viewpoint.

The word 'myth' is derived from the Greek word *Mythos* which itself means something uttered, be it a statement or a story, and thus it consisted mainly in oral literature that passed over from generation to generation; while it so passed over a long period and through a continued chain of people, it could not remain unaffected by the impact of their civilisation. And, therefore, mythology is in a way a mirror of beliefs and behaviour of the people and also represents the social and cultural background of a particular community. Thus the study of mythology is now accepted as important for the understanding of various civilisations.

In a way, it can be said that there is not much difference between the origin of science and that of mythology. Man's incessant

---

1. Ernst Cassirer, *An Essay on Man*, p. 72; and Claude Levi Strauss, *Myth and Meaning*, intr. p.v.

quest for 'how' and 'why' in nature as well as in society is the fountainhead of both. The difference lies in the means used to answer these questions. The substratum of science is thought and logic, whereas that of mythology is feeling and fantasy.

It will not be out of place to note here the remark of Levi Strauss,

> There is not really a kind of divorce between mythology and science. It is only the present state of scientific thought that gives us ability to understand what is in this myth, to which we remained completely blind before the idea of binary operations became familiar to us.[2]

It is said that "myth is an extremely complex cultural reality which can be approached and interpreted from various and complementary viewpoints".[3] However, it deals mainly with something, which was produced, which originated (in thought) or which just began to be; it tries to find out how things came into existence. It gives an account of how a particular thing — may it be an island, a plant, a particular rite, a sort of human behaviour or that the world itself came into existence. It is but natural, therefore, that a considerable number of myths are cosmogonical.

Myths play a significant role in connection with ritual also.[4] Myth is a system of word symbols, while the ritual is a system of object and act symbols. In other words, myth is the *legomenon* 'the thing said' and ritual is the corresponding *dromenon* 'the thing

---

2. Levi Strauss, *op.cit.*, p. 23.
3. *Myths, Rites and Symbols,* a Mircea Eliade Reader, ed. C. Beane Wendell and G. Doty William, Vol. 1, p. 3.

   For various theories about nature-myths, *see* Jan De Vries, *Perspectives in the History of Religions*, tr. by Kees W. Bolle, pp. 80-90.
4. For an elaborate discussion regarding the relation between myth and ritual *see*, Clyde Kluckhohn, "Myths and Rituals: A General Theory", *The Bobbs Merrill Reprint Series in the Social Sciences* — S. 1146, Pam. 156, pp. 45-79; G.S. Kirk, *Myth — Its Meaning and Functions in Ancient and Other Cultures*, pp.8-31; and E.O. James, *Comparative Religion*, pp. 99-118.

performed'. They are thus mutually dependent. Nothing can be said with certainty about the primacy of one between these two. After a long discussion in this regard, Klukhohn has come to a conclusion that, "To a considerable degree, the whole question of the primacy of ceremonial or mythology is as meaningless as all questions of 'the hen or the egg' form."[5]

In Vedic texts also, one comes across so many myths. They are of manifold nature. The cosmogonical myths are found especially in the *Ṛgveda* while in the texts of the *Yajurveda* are found such myths as tell about the origin of a certain rite. These myths are regarded as a 'sacred tradition, primordial revelation or an exemplary model'.[6]

Regarding the *sautrāmaṇī* also such myths are cited; in them is narrated the origin of the rite and also the information as to who performed it first, why and in what way.

These myths begin with the narration of the quarrel between Indra and Tvāṣṭra, the son of Tvaṣṭṛ.

> Tvaṣṭṛ had a three-headed[7] six-eyed son. He had three mouths; and because he was thus shapen, he was called Viśvarūpa[8] ('All-shape'). One of his mouths was *soma*-drinking, one spirit-drinking, and one for other food. Indra hated him, and cut off those heads of his.
>
> — *ŚatBrā*, V.5.4.2-3, tr. by Eggeling, pt. III, p.130.

In the *ŚatBrā*, the reason why Indra hated Viśvarūpa is not mentioned. That is suggested in a myth in the *MaiS*, II.4.1 and also

5. Clyde Kluckhohn, *op.cit.*, p. 54.
6. Mircea Eliade, *Myth and Reality*, p.1.
7. About the three-headed god, *see* Buddha Prakash, *Ṛgveda and the Indus Valley Civilization,* and also, K. Ostergaard, "Three headed God", *Kuml*, 1954 (1955, Denmark) pp. 55-77; also Willibald Kirfel, *Die Dreiköpfige Gottheit*.
8. For various interpretations of Viśvarūpa see Narayan Aiyangar, *Essays on the Indo-Aryan Mythology*, Madras, 1901, part I, pp. 168ff and art II pp. 167ff; also Max Müller, *Contributions to the Science of Mythology*, p. 794.

in the *KāṭhS*, XII.9. These two latter texts give some more information about Viśvarūpa:

> He was indeed a son of Tvaṣṭṛ, but he was (and perhaps it was the important reason of the hatred) a nephew of the *asuras* — his mother was a sister of the *asuras*. Indra thought that Viśvarūpa would be **this**. The meaning of **this** is however not explained here; but it suggests that there was a kind of rivalry between Indra and Viśvarūpa for **this**.

According to the account in the *MaiS* and the *KāṭhS*, Indra himself did not kill Viśvarūpa. He wrestled with him and in the course of the bout both of them fell down. At that time, Takṣan was standing near them. Indra asked him to cut down Viśvarūpa's heads. At this Takṣan jumped upon Viśvarūpa and cut down his head with an axe (*paraśu*).

From that mouth of Viśvarūpa, by which he drank *soma*, a hazel-cock sprang forth, from that, by which he drank *surā*, a sparrow sprang forth and from that, by which he ate food, a partridge (*tittirī*) sprang forth (cf. *MaiS*, II.4.1. and *KāṭhS*, XII.9). The *ŚatBrā* states the reasons why these specific birds are connected with *soma*, *surā* and food.

> From the one which was 'Soma-drinking', a hazel-cock sprang forth; whence the latter is of brownish colour, for king Soma is brown, and from the one which was 'spirit-drinking', a sparrow sprang; whence the latter talks like one who is joyful, for when one has drunk spirits, one talks as one who enjoys himself. And from the one which was for other (kinds of) food, a partridge sprang whence the latter is exceedingly variegated: ghee drops indeed have, as it were, dropped on his wings in one place, and honey-drops, as it were, in another; for suchlike was the food he consumed with that (mouth). (tr. by Eggeling, pt.III, p.130)

While citing the myth in connection with the *kaukilī*, all this portion is omitted in the *ŚatBrā* and the myth in *ŚatBrā*, XII.7.1.1 begins with the sentence: 'Indra killed the son of Tvaṣṭṛ'.

When Tvaṣṭṛ came to know this, he became furious. He brought *soma* to perform a sacrifice. He did not invite Indra to it. He pressed that *soma* in a pot having a hundred or a thousand thorns around it. He put that pot down on the ground, i.e., without putting anything in between the *soma* and the ground. (Generally, all sacrificial material is kept *anadhaḥ*, 'not directly on the ground'. Mostly, blades of *darbha*-grass are first put on the ground and then the material of offering is put upon the same; this sanctifies the material and makes it sacrificial).

Indra wanted a share in that sacrifice, but, as he had no invitation he could not get it and so he created nuisance to that sacrifice. He drank *soma* per force. In the *KāṭhS* and the *MaiS* it is added that he drank that *soma*, using a straw (*nāḍī*), since the pot had a hundred thorns around it. The *soma*-juice he had drunk came out of his body. He became devoid of that *soma*-juice. Therefore, a person should not drink *soma*, when he is not invited to drink it. If he did so, he would also become deprived of that *soma*-juice.

It is clear from this myth that Indra broke the taboo that *soma* should not be drunk, by the one, who is not invited to drink it, and then, as a result of the breach of the taboo, he got punished. In *ŚatBrā*, XII.7.1.1 and *GopBrā*, II.5.6, it is added that Tvaṣṭṛ had performed that *soma*-sacrifice as a means of exorcism. He wanted to perform black magic against Indra. This is not explicitly mentioned in the *KāṭhS* and the *MaiS*; however, the reference to Tvaṣṭṛ putting *soma* directly on the ground implies his intention of performing exorcism since it is well-known that lack of proper ritual procedure also was considered as what could create ill-effects on the person concerned.

When Indra drank that *soma*, it came out from various parts of his body. While describing this state of his it is said at *ŚatBrā*, V.5.4.8.

> It flowed in all directions from (the openings of) his vital airs; only from his mouth it did not flow. Hence there was an atonement; but had it flown also from his mouth, then indeed there would have been no atonement.
>
> (tr. by Eggeling, pt. III, p. 131.)

Further, in *ŚatBrā*, V.5.4.9, the reason is given as,

> For there are four castes, the Brāhmaṇa, the Rājanya, the Vaiśya and the Śūdra; but there is not one of them that vomits Soma; but were there any of them, then indeed there would be atonement.[9]
>
> (tr. by Eggeling, pt. III, p. 131)

It is narrated in *KāṭhS*, XII.9 and *MaiS*, II.4.1 as to how the *soma* thus flown out from Indra's body took various forms; viz. that which came from Indra's nose became two lions; that which flowed from his ears became two wolves; that from his eyes became two tigers; and that which flowed from the lower part became the *sautrāmaṇī*.

The description in the *ŚatBrā* is slightly different. Thus, in *ŚatBrā*, V.5.4.10, it is stated,

> from what flowed from the nose a lion sprang; and from what flowed from the ears a wolf sprang; and from what flowed from the lower opening wild beasts sprang, with the tiger as their foremost; and what flowed from the upper opening that was the foaming spirit (*parisrut*). And thrice he spit out; thence were produced the (fruits called) 'Kuvala, karkandhu, or badara, 'He (Indra) became emptied out of everything, for Soma is everything.'
>
> (tr. by Eggeling pt. III, p. 131)

In this way, the texts tell us about the origin of the various material used in the *sautrāmaṇī*, especially in connection with *surā*. *Surā* is of course the main offering material of the *sautrāmaṇī* sacrifice. The hairs of the wild beasts, which are mentioned above are put either in *surā* or on the cuttings of the animals. If the hairs are not used, then the priests meditate upon the animals. The powder of the three berries is also poured into the *surā* at the time of offering.

ŚatBrā, XII.7.1.2-9 gives a long list of all the sacrificial material used in the *sautrāmaṇī* and connects the origin of that material

---

9. The significance of this passage is not clear to me.

with Indra's faculties which went away from him at this time. For example, in *ŚatBrā*, XII.7.1.2 it is stated,

> From his eyes his fiery spirit flowed, and became that grey (smoke-coloured) animal — the he-goat; and what (flowed) from his eye-lashes became wheat, and what (flowed) from his tears became the kuvala — fruit.
>
> (tr. by Eggeling pt. V, p. 214)

The myth cited in this connection in *TaiBrā*, I.8.5.1 is altogether different from those in the texts mentioned above. It is very brief and does not have any reference to Viśvarūpa or anybody else as Indra's foe. The myth reads; when Indra was about to perform a *soma*-sacrifice, his valour went away from him in ten-fold way; what he spat out first became the berries named *kuvala*, what he spat out on a second occasion became *badara*, and what on the third occasion became *karkandhu*. What came out from his nose became a lion. That which came out from the ears became a wolf, and that which came out from the eyes became a tiger, what came from the upper side became *soma* and that which flowed from the lower side became *surā*.

After telling about the origin of the sacrificial material, the origin of the *sautrāmaṇī* sacrifice itself is narrated in the texts.

> Being thus purged by Soma, he walked about as one tottering. The Aśvins cured him by this (offering) and caused him to be supplied with everything, for Soma is everything. By offering he indeed became better!
> (*ŚatBrā*, V.5.4.11, tr. by Eggeling pt. III, p. 131; cf. also *MaiS*, II.4.1. and *KāṭhS*, XII.9)

Further, the name of the rite is explained in *ŚatBrā*, V.5.4.12. Thus it is stated,

> The gods spake, 'Aha! these two have saved him, the well-saved (sutrāta): 'hence the name sautrāmaṇī'.
>
> (tr. Eggeling pt. III, p. 131).

After telling about the origin of the various material, a very different version of the myth is given in *ŚatBrā*, XII.7.1.10ff. But, before turning to it, it will be worthwhile to see whether a myth, similar to that described above, is found elsewhere and whether it is useful for the interpretation of it.

The same myth occurs in *ŚatBrā*, I.6.3.1 in connection with an offering of an eleven-potsherd cake for Agni and Soma in the *darśapūrṇamāseṣṭi*, and in *TaiS*, II.4.12 in connection with the *traidhātavī iṣṭi*. However, that does not offer any further help for the interpretation of the myth under discussion.

Similar story is found in *TaiS*, II.5.1 in connection with the offering of an eleven-potsherd cake for Agni and Soma, in the *darśapūrṇamāseṣṭi*. The story reads:

> Viśvarūpa, the son of Tvaṣṭṛ was the domestic priest of the gods, and the sister's son of the asuras. He had three heads; one which drank Soma, one Surā and one which ate food. He promised openly the share to the gods, secretly to the asuras. Men promise openly the share to every one; if they promise anyone secretly, his share is indeed promised. Therefore Indra was afraid (thinking), 'Such a one is diverting the sovereignty (from me).' He took his bolt and smote off his heads. (tr. by Keith, p. 188)

This myth brings forth the reason of the rivalry between Viśvarūpa and Indra. Viśvarūpa is the priest of the gods. Still he is doing something against the gods, and is thereby supporting the demons, who are related to him through his mother. Naturally, therefore, Indra is afraid of the loss of his own powers and is worried that Viśvarūpa would, in this way, snatch away the kingdom from him. In the myth in the *KāṭhS* and the *MaiS* it is stated that Indra was afraid that Viśvarūpa would become **this**. If interpreted with the help of the myth in the *TaiS*, this **this** means 'the sovereign'. It becomes clear thus that it was a struggle for power; either a struggle between Viśvarūpa and Indra or that between gods and *asuras*, or perhaps between both of them.

There is one more myth about Indra and Viśvarūpa in *AitBrā*, XXXV.2, which should be taken into account for a fuller interpretation of the myths in connection with the *sautrāmaṇī*. In the previous chapter, i.e. the 4th chapter of the *AitBrā*, there is a discussion of how to enable a kṣatriya sacrificer to perform a sacrifice. As a solution to this problem, it is concluded that at the time of performing a sacrifice, the kṣatriya should put aside his qualities as a kṣatriya and become a brāhmaṇa. Then, after the performance, he should again become a kṣatriya. Thus he will be able to perform a sacrifice and again become a kṣatriya without losing the fruit of the sacrifice.

Thus, the priests have allowed a kṣatriya sacrificer to perform a sacrifice. However, to maintain the supremacy of the priestly class, they did not allow him to partake of *soma* in the sacrifice. It is considered as a privilege exclusively of the brāhmaṇas. While all the priests are partaking of *soma*, the kṣatriya sacrificer is given a drink prepared from the juice of the roots of a banyan tree and the juice of the fruits of *aśvattha*, *plakṣa* and *udumbara*.

With a view to justifying this act of the priests, there is cited a myth at the beginning of the 35th chapter of the *AitBrā*. It tells that even the gods — the supernatural beings — had done previously the same thing in the case of Indra. The myth reads:

> when the gods excluded Indra, (saying). 'He hath misused Viśvarūpa, son of Tvaṣṭṛ, he had laid low Vṛtra, he hath given the Yatis to the hyaenas, he hath killed the Arurmaghas, he has contended with Bṛhaspati, then Indra was deprived of the Soma drinking. Indra obtained later a share in the Soma drinking, having stolen the Soma of Tvaṣṭṛ, but to day even the lordly power is deprived of Soma drinking. (tr. by Keith, p. 314)

In his commentary on this passage, Sāyaṇa has mentioned that Viśvarūpa and Vṛtra were of brāhmaṇa caste. The Arurmaghas were *asuras*, but they were also at that time in the brāhmaṇa attire. Bṛhaspati of course was a brāhmaṇa and a teacher, and a priest of Indra.

It seems that Indra had offended brāhmaṇas and as a punishment of that act, he was not allowed to drink *soma* in the sacrifice. And from that time onwards, the kṣatriya caste also was deprived of *soma*-juice.

Indra most probably used his force and stole away the *soma* of Tvaṣṭṛ and drank it off. Therefore, perhaps to avoid such probabilities, the priests might have created a taboo that nobody should partake of *soma*, unless he was invited to do so. In other texts also, we notice the mention of this taboo, though, in the *AitBrā* it is not mentioned specifically.

What Kluckhohn has said about the myth and ritual suits perfectly well in this context. He has stated, "the function of both myths and rituals is the discharge of the emotion of individuals in socially accepted channels".[10]

The struggle between Indra and Viśvarūpa or the struggle for power and supremacy between the kṣatriya caste and brāhmaṇa caste in general was a historical fact. This historical event is, so to say, an explanatory cell or a mini-myth, which has the property and potentiality of expanding into a full-fledged myth. This explanatory cell is further accorded to many occasions and is then transformed, expanded and rearranged for specific purposes. The static and repetitive character of mythology in contradistinction with history, which is an open system, becomes clear from this example.[11]

These myths have not been paid much attention to, in connection with the ritual of the *sautrāmaṇī*. The myth, much discussed in this connection, is only that of Indra and Namuci, viz. the one described in *ŚatBrā*, XII.7.1.10-14 and XII.7.3.1-4.[12]

The myth described in *ŚatBrā*, XII.7.1-13 reads thus — "Now at that time he (Indra) had to do with Namuci, the

10. Clyde Kluckhohn, *op.cit.*, p. 64.
11. See Levi Strauss, *op.cit.*, pp. 39ff.
12. For various interpretations of the Indra Namuci myths, *see* M. Bloomfield, "Contributions to the Interpretation of the Veda", *JAOS*, Vol. 15, pp. 143ff.

    A.K. Coomarasvami, in *JAOS,* Vol. 55, 1935, pp. 373-7; K. Rönnow, "Zur Erklärung des Pravargya, des Agnicayana and der Sautrāmaṇī", *Le Monde Oriental*, Vol. 23, pp. 113-73; H. Oldenberg, *Kleine Schriften*, pp. 635ff.; Narayan Aiyangar, *op.cit.*, Part II, pp. 172ff.

> *asura*." Namuci bethought him, "He has been undone once for all: I will seize upon his energy, his vital power, his *soma* drink, his food." By (taking) that *surā*-liquor of his he seized upon his energy, or vital power, his *soma*-drink, his food. He lay there dissolved. The gods gathered around him and said, "Verily, he was the best of us; evil has befallen him: let us heal him".
>
> They said to the two Aśvins "You are *Brahman* physicians: heal you this one!" They replied, "Let there be a share for us!" They spoke, "That he-goat there shall be your share". They said, 'So be it!' and hence the smoke coloured (he-goat) is sacred to the two Aśvins.
>
> They (the gods) said to Sarasvatī, "Verily you are healing medicine 'heal thou this one!" she replied, "Let there be a share for me!" They spoke, "That ram there shall be your share!" She agreed to it!" and therefore the ram is sacred to Sarasvatī.
>
> They then spoke, "Verily, there is even now as much in him (Indra) as that bull: that one shall belong to himself". They said, 'So be it!' and therefore the bull is sacred to Indra.'

Thus, in this myth, the *Brāhmaṇa* text has tried to explain why certain animals are offered to certain deities in the primordial performance of the *sautrāmaṇī*.

At the end of the myth is explained the name *sautrāmaṇī* in the following way,

> The two Aśvins and Sarasvatī, having taken the energy, the vital power, from Namuci, restored them to him (Indra), and saved him from evil. 'Truly, we have saved him from evil so as to be well-saved (sutrāta)', they thought, and this became the Sautrāmaṇī; and this is the (saving) nature of the Sautrāmaṇī, it saves the self from death, and repels evil for whosoever thus knows that (saving) nature of the Sautrāmaṇī. (tr. by Eggeling, pt. V, pp. 216, 217)

Besides the explanation about the offerings in the primordial performance of the rite, there is one more important purpose behind creating this myth. It is about the use of *surā*.

It has been already discussed that the *surā*-ritual was first admitted into the Vedic hieratic religion, when the rites of the kṣatriyas were included in the Vedic *śrauta* ritual. Thus, in the *rājasūya* sacrifice described in the *AitBrā* the sacrificer is given the *surā*-drink in the *abhiṣeka* and the *punarabhiṣeka* ceremony.

Later the *surā*-ritual is elaborated; and to it are added the offerings of *surā* and those of animals to the Aśvins, Sarasvatī and Indra Sutrāman. It is but natural, therefore, that the verses which had a reference to these deities and also, though remotely, to *surā* were employed in this rite. The verses are:

yuvaṁ surāmam aśvinā namucāv āsure sacā | *vipipānā*
śubhaspatī indraṁ karmasv āvatam | —*ṚV*, X.131.4

and

putram iva pitarāv aśvinobhā indra āvathuḥ kāvyaiḥ
daṁsanābhiḥ |

yat surāmam vy apibaḥ śacībhiḥ sarasvatī tvāṁ maghavan
abhiṣṇak | —*ṚV*, X.131.5.

These verses are used as the *puronuvākyā*s (the invitatory verses) and the *yājyā*s (the offering verses) of the *surā*-offerings in the *sautrāmaṇī* sacrifice.

In the *ŚatBrā* an attempt has been made to establish a sort of inseparable connection of these verses with the primordial performance of the rite, and therefore, the story of Indra and Namuci is created. However, the superficialness of the connection between the verses and the myth and the deliberate attempt of the *brāhmaṇa* becomes clearly perceptible when one reads the myth told next to it in the *ŚatBrā*.

There is one more verse which has a reference to Indra and Namuci and which is employed in the *sautrāmaṇī* sacrifice for propitiating the ancestors. It reads:

> *apām phenena namuceḥ śira indrodavartayaḥ* I
> *viśvā yad ajayaḥ spr̥dhaḥ* I — *R̥V*, VIII.14.13.

The next myth in the *ŚatBrā* is based on this verse and on *R̥V* 10.131.5. It reads:

> By means of the Surā liquor Namuci, the Asura, carried off Indra's (source of) strength, the essence of food, the Soma-drink. He (Indra) hasted up to the Aśvins and Sarasvatī, crying, 'I have sworn to Namuci', saying, 'I will slay thee neither by day nor by night, neither with staff nor with bow, neither with the palm of my hand nor with the fist, neither with the dry nor with the moist' and yet has he taken these things from me: seek ye to bring me back these things!
> — (*ŚatBrā*, XII.7.3.1, tr. by Eggeling, pt.V, p.222)

It is to be noted here that the *ŚatBrā* contradicts its own version told in XII.7.1.1 by this myth. Previously it is stated there that it was the gods who went to the physicians with the request to cure Indra, while in this myth, it is told that Indra himself approaches them. This internal discrepancy is no doubt an indication of a later attempt of elaborating the myth.

Further on, the myth reads:

> They spoke, 'Let us have a share therein, and we will bring them back to thee'—'These things (shall be) common to us,' he said, 'bring them back, then!'

The Aśvins and Sarasvatī then poured out foam of water (to serve) as a thunderbolt, saying, 'It is neither dry nor moist'; and when the night was clearing up, and the sun had not yet risen, Indra, thinking 'It is neither by day nor by night', therewith struck off the head of Namuci, the *asura*. Wherefore it has been said by the *r̥ṣi*, "With foam of water, Indra, you severed the head of Namuci, when you were subduing all your enemies."

The myth goes on further,

> Now, Namuci is evil: having thus, indeed, slain that evil, his hateful enemy, Indra wrested from him his energy, or vital power. Let him who has an enemy perform the *sautrāmaṇī*: he thereby slays that evil, his hateful enemy, and wrests from him his vital power or energy.

In the next part of the myth, it is told,

> In his (Namuci's) severed head there was the *soma*-juice mixed with blood. They loathed it. They perceived the means of drinking separately the two liquids, 'King *soma*, the drink of immortality, is pressed'; and having thereby made that (*soma*) palatable, they took it in (as food).
>
> — *ŚatBrā*, XII.7.3.2-4.

Even though, these myths in the *ŚatBrā* appear in every probability to be the later ones and deliberately created to explain certain verses used in the sacrifice, they have received much attention of the scholars.

Thus, on the basis of these myths in the *ŚatBrā* and the verses *R̥V*, X.131.4 and 5, Bloomfield has asserted,

> I am for my part incapable of believing that even a single Vedic hymn was ever composed without reference to ritual application and without that environment of legendary report.[13]

Gonda also has posed a hypothesis, mainly on the basis of the *mantras* used in the *sautrāmaṇī*, that,

> There is, it would appear to me, hardly any room for doubting, with Geldner, whether the *Sūkta* X.131 was intended for a form of the Sautrāmaṇī ritual; for uncertainty as to whether it proves the existence of a probably comparatively simple Sautrāmaṇī in the period preceding the codification of that corpus.[14]

---

13. M. Bloomfield, *op.cit.*, p. 144.
14. J. Gonda, *The Mantras of the Agnyupasthāna and the Sautrāmaṇī*, Amsterdam, 1980, p. 71.

It is difficult, however, to agree with them. It is already seen in the previous chapter that the simple form of the *sautrāmaṇī* is present in the oldest part of the oldest *Brāhmaṇa*, i.e., *AitBrā*, XXXVII. The important feature of the rite, i.e., the partaking of *surā* by the sacrificer, is present there. There are certain other striking similarities also. The peculiar way of placing the stool for the sacrificer, the optional use of the *vyāhṛtis* in the *abhiṣeka* ceremony, the separate *nidhanas* 'final parts of the *sāman*' used for a *kṣatriya* sacrificer do have some connection with the *punarabhiṣeka* ceremony described in the *AitBrā*. Bloomfield also is of the same opinion that the *punarabhiṣeka* ceremony is itself a form of the *sautrāmaṇī*.[15]

It would not be incorrect then to expect that if the hymn *ṚV*, X.131 presupposes a form of the *sautrāmaṇī*, the *AitBrā* in which such an earlier form appears to be described would have given the employment of these verses in this context and further more surely when *ṚV*, X.131.4, 5 are used as the *yājyā* and the *puronuvākyā*.

There is one more point to be taken into account in this regard. The first verse of the hymn *ṚV*, X.131 is employed, according to the *AitBrā* in the *punarabhiṣeka* ceremony itself (*AitBrā*, XXXVII.7), that is to say, after the ritual performance of the rite of the victory over the enemies, the sacrificer comes home from the battlefield, reciting the verse, *apa prāca indra viśvān amitrān* . . . *ṚV*, X.131.1. The non-mention of the next two verses viz. *ṚV*, X.131.4 and 5 in this context further asserts that the latter were not used in the simpler form of the *sautrāmaṇī*.

From the discussion above, it should be clear that the quarrel between Indra and Viśvarūpa is the nucleus of many myths cited in connection with various rites. The myth regarding the *sautrāmaṇī* is also expanded around the same. Consequently, it has become difficult to understand the social importance of the *sautrāmaṇī* without taking into account these myths.

---

15. M. Bloomfield, *op.cit.* In a foot-note on p. 152, he has stated, "In addition to the Sāutrāmaṇī. only the Punarabhiṣeka-ceremony which is itself a form of Sautrāmaṇī prescribes the use of Surā."

The holistic study of all the myths regarding Indra and Viśvarūpa reveal the real picture of the relation between the brāhmaṇa and the kṣatriya castes. The quarrel between Indra and Viśvarūpa is representation of the quarrel between the gods and the *asura*s and also between the kṣatriyas and the brāhmaṇas.

It is only after studying these myths that one becomes aware that in order to safeguard their supremacy and power, the brāhmaṇas have denied to the kṣatriyas the right of drinking the *soma*-juice in the sacrifice and for validating this behaviour they have created, on the basis of the myth, a taboo that nobody, who is not invited to the sacrifice should partake of the *soma*-juice; if he did so, he would be deprived of his faculties.

However, schlolars have so far paid little attention to these myths and, as a result, the real significance of the rite has slipped out of their sight. It appears that they have unduly attached great importance to the later myths which occur in the *ŚatBrā* in connection with the *kaukilī*, and that their interpretation of the myths has, therefore, become lop-sided.

Part II

7

The Ritual of the Caraka Sautrāmaṇī

THE *sautrāmaṇī* sacrifice is of four days' duration, yet it is sometimes performed in two days also (*ŚatBrā*, V.5.4.20 and optionally according to *KātyŚS*, XV.10.1 and *VaikhāŚS*, XI.2). The animal-offerings and the *surā*-offerings are performed on the main day of the sacrifice. Three days before it, *surā* is prepared. The rites which are performed on this day are also considered here as the preparatory rites together with the preparatory rites performed on the main day of the sacrifice.

The Preparatory Rites to be Performed three days before the actual Performance of the Sacrifice

BaudhŚS, XVII.31 gives a long list of the necessary paraphernalia to be arranged on this day by one who is desirous of performing the *sautrāmaṇī* sacrifice. He keeps ready a bull's hide, lead, a eunuch (*klība*), sprouted barley *śaṣpa*, sprouted paddy *tokma*, powder of pulses *nagnahu*, paddy, flour of three different grains, three pots made from the wood of three different trees, hairs of three different animals, viz. a lion, a wolf and a tiger, a sacrificial post *yūpa*, an eagle-wing feather, a pregnant mare, a stool, supporting ring *iṇḍva*, a pitcher, a kind of plate used as a lid *kārotara*, two two-branched poles, a long bamboo, a loop of rope, a vessel with a hundred holes *śatātṛṇṇā*, a piece of hundred *mānas* of gold *śatamāna hiraṇya*, a pot called *sata*, a purifier made of hair and a brāhmaṇa for drinking the remnants of *surā*. If he is not able to get such a brāhmaṇa, he should arrange for the earth from an ant-hill.

After the Adhvaryu has offered the new-moon offerings, he begins the preparation of *surā* with buying the ingredients of it.[1]

According to the *ĀpaŚS*, the *HirŚS* and the *VaikhāŚS* the ingredients of *surā* are bought first, the paddy which is bought is tied in a cloth for germination and then the Adhvaryu adds fuel to the fires. He then prepares a sacrificial broom *veda*, strews sacrificial grass around the fires, goes through the rites beginning with the washing of the hands and places the necessary implements within the altar. Instead of the potsherds he places a vessel, since he has to cook rice for the preparation of *surā* (*ĀpaŚS*, XIX.1.3,4; *VaikhāŚS*, XI.1; *HirŚS*, XIII.8.3.)

After the *agnihotra* is performed, the Adhvaryu mixes the ingredients of *surā* and keeps the mixture for fermentation.

When the sacrificer is sure that *surā* will be ready on the next day, he observes fast for the animal-sacrifice (*MānŚS*, V.2.4.6).

The Preparatory Rites to be Performed on the day of the Offerings

After three nights have passed commences the performance of the *sautrāmaṇī* sacrifice. The procedure of the animal-sacrifice in it is similar to that of the *nirūḍhapaśubandha* (*VaikhāŚS*, XI.2; *VārāŚS*, III.2.7.7; *ĀpaŚS*, XIX.1.2).

The Adhvaryu cuts off a sacrificial post, (*ĀpaŚS*, XIX.1.11; *HirŚS*, XIII.8.9). According to *VaikhāŚS*, XI.2 the *yūpa* is already cut off on the previous day. He does not prepare a new *veda*. He uses that one which is prepared previously, i.e., three days before.

The altar is already measured and traced on the day before (*VaikhāŚS*, XI.2; *BaudhŚS*, XVII.32). When the Adhvaryu is preparing the northern altar, the Pratiprasthātṛ takes the earth from the *cātvāla* and prepares a mound to the south of that altar.

1. The ritual of the preparation of *surā* beginning with the buying of the ingredients up to its purification is dealt with in chapter 8: 'The Preparation of Surā'.

It is quadrangular in shape and is two *aṅgula*s high (*VaikhāŚS*, XI.2; *ĀpaŚS*, XIX.1.15). He prepares another mound to the east of the southern fire. The pots made of *palāśa*, *aśvattha*, *udumbara* and *nyagrodha* wood are put upon it. Sometimes, this mound is made of sand (*VārāŚS*, III.2.7.13,14). *MānŚS*, V.2.4.8 prescribes that the Adhvaryu should prepare one more mound to the north of the altar, for placing the cups of milk.

After he has prepared the altar, the Adhvaryu carries forth the fire from the *āhavanīya* fire. At that time the Pratiprasthātr̥ also takes some embers from the southern fire and places them on the mound which is prepared to the south of the altar (*ĀpaŚS*, XIX.1.16). According to *MānŚS*, V.2.4.11, he takes, at that time, some earth from the mound as a support for the fire and places that fire on the front half of that mound

However, in the *VārāŚS* it is prescribed that no separate mound should be prepared for the southern fire. After placing the fire on the northern altar, the Adhvaryu should again carry forth the fire, take it along the south of the fire and place it on the southern buttock of the altar. Or, after carrying the fire around the animals, he should put the fire-brand itself on that part of the altar. The same fire should be used for cooking the parts of the animals (*VārāŚS*, III.2.7.8, 9).

The reason why two fires should be carried forth is given in *ŚatBrā*, V.5.4.21. It is said,

> he should carry forth two fires, otherwise the oblations of *soma* and the oblations of *surā* would get mixed. Therefore, the Adhvaryu places the fire from the *āhavanīya* on the northern altar and the southern fire he places on the raised mound. There is no separate altar for it.
>
> (cf. also *KātyŚS*, XV.10.7, 8)

At that time, the Pratiprasthātr̥ does not wash his hands, (*VaikhāŚS*, XI.2, *HirŚS*, XIII.8.14). Then, at the time of placing the utensils, the Adhvaryu arranges three vessels for Indra, the Aśvins and Sarasvatī, a pot called *sata*, a purifier made of hair, an eagle-wing-feather and the things to be mixed in *surā*. He puts them on the second mound (*ĀpaŚS*, XIX.1.17; *VaikhāŚS*, XI.2). These vessels for the deities are made of *vikaṅkata*-wood according to *VaikhāŚS*, XI.2 and *HirŚS*, XIII.8.15; or they are made of *palāśa*, *udumbara* and *nyagrodha* wood according to *VārāŚS*, III.2.7.14. Together with these pots a golden plate (*rukma*) and a *śatātr̥ṇṇā* vessel are also placed on the mound (*HirŚS*, XIII.8.2; *VaikhāŚS*, XI.2).

The *MānŚS*, prescribes that the Adhvaryu should arrange the paraphernalia, which is necessary for the animal-sacrifice. The Pratiprasthātr̥ should place three earthen vessels, a wooden pot and three wooden vessels also, on the southern mound together with the *śatātr̥ṇṇā* and the hair-strainer. At that time, the Adhvaryu puts three wooden vessels and two strainers made of sprouts (*śaṣpapavitre*) on the northern mound, which is prepared by the Adhvaryu.

The Adhvaryu takes clarified butter and milk. He puts the clarified butter within the altar and the milk on the mound. He takes the clarified butter four times in the ladles and takes the *pr̥ṣadājya*[2] in the proper vessel and places these things within the altar (*MānŚS*, V.2.4.11-13).

Some more details regarding the preparatory rites are given in *BaudhŚS*, XVII.32, 33. After strewing the sacrificial grass around the altar, the Adhvaryu carries the *stambayajus*. The procedure of carrying it is described in the *Paurodāśika kāṇḍa*. Thrice he carries it with a *Yajus*-formula and at the fourth time, without reciting any formula. He performs the first tracing out of the altar. He mutters the *karaṇa* formula, i.e., *imāṁ naraḥ kr̥ṇuta*. . . . He digs the spot which is intended for the altar. The Āgnīdhra takes away thrice the earth which has been dug up. At that time, the Adhvaryu prepares the *cātvāla*. After preparing the northern altar, he prepares the navel on it, and digs a pit for the sacrificial post. The Adhvaryu and the Pratiprasthātr̥ then carry forth two fires in the normal procedure. The *sūtrakāra* has not mentioned about the second altar or the

---

2. *Pr̥ṣadājya* is the mixture of curds and ghee.

second mound. It is to be understood from the description in the *Varuṇapraghāsaparvan*. There, it is described that, of the two altars, the northern one should be prepared like that in the animal-sacrifice and the southern one like that in the new-moon or the full-moon sacrifice. The two altars should be in a line on the western side but not on the eastern side. There should be a span's length on the eastern side between the two (*BaudhŚS*, V.5).

The Adhvaryu performs the second tracing out of the altar, after the fire is already carried forth. Then he levels the altar with a wooden sword (*sphya*), holds that sword crosswise within the altar and gives out the call to the Āgnīdhra to put down the *prokṣaṇī* water, to bring the sacrificial faggot and grass and to cleanse the ladles, spoons and knife with the relevant formulas. He tells him to cleanse the ladle of *pṛṣadājya* without any formula. Then he tells him to fasten the girdle around the sacrificer's wife and to come with clarified butter and curds. After that he tells the Pratiprasthātṛ to see whether the *surā* is ready. (The procedure of the purification of *surā* is described in chapter 8 'The Preparation of Surā).'

The Offering of Animals

In this sacrifice, before the offerings of *surā* animals are immolated for certain deities. A grey-coloured goat is offered to the Aśvins, a ram to Sarasvatī and a bull to Indra. The reason why these animals are immolated for these deities is given in the *brāhmaṇa*s thus:

> The Aśvins are the doctors of the gods. With their help the priests cure the sacrificer. An animal is offered to Sarasvatī, as she is speech. Thus, with the help of speech, the priests cure the sacrificer. A bull is offered to Indra, to obtain strength. (*TaiBrā*, I.8.5.6; *ŚatBrā*, V.5.4.15-17.)

If the sacrificer is a *somavāmin* or a *somātipūta*, an additional animal is immolated for Bṛhaspati (*TaiBrā*, I.8.6.4; *ĀpaŚS*, XIX.2.1, 2; *HirŚS*, XIII.8.19; *VaikhāŚS*, XI.3; *BaudhŚS*, XVII.35; *VārāŚS*, III.2.7.26; *ĀśvaŚS*, III.9.2). The reason for making this offering is stated in *TaiBrā*, I.8.6.4 as, "Bṛhaspati is the *Brahman* of the gods.

When an animal is offered to Bṛhaspati, whatever is lacking in the sacrifice is made perfect."

The animal to Bṛhaspati is not prescribed in the *MaiS*, the *TaiS*, the *KāṭhS* and in the *MānŚS*, and the *KātyŚS*.

In *ŚatBrā*, V.5.4.1 and also in *KātyŚS*, XV.10.4 an option is given to the animals prescribed for these deities. It is stated there,

> These specific animals are difficult to be obtained. Therefore, if the sacrificer is not able to obtain them, he may offer goats to all the deities, as they are easy to be cooked. If he is going to offer goats, then a reddish white should be offered to the Aśvins.

Regarding the order of the animal-offerings and the filling up of the cups with *surā*, a difference of opinion is found in Vedic texts. According to some texts, viz. the *MānŚS*, the *BaudhŚS* and the *VārāŚS*, the cups are filled first and then the animals are offered; while according to the *ŚatBrā*, the *KātyŚS*, the *ĀpaŚS*, the *HirŚS* and the *VaikhāŚS*, the cups are filled with *surā* after the animal omenta are offered and all the persons concerned have sprinkled themselves with water near the *cātvāla*.[3]

The animals are formally dedicated by one single sacrificial post. In *KātyŚS*, XV.10.6 it is stated that optionally three sacrificial posts can be erected and the animals can be dedicated by separate posts, since this procedure of a separate post for a separate animal is found in *ekādaśinī*.[4] This option is mentioned is *VaikhāŚS*, XI.2 also.

---

3. The word in *KātyŚS*, XV.10.9 is *vapāmārjanānte*. The word *vapā* (omentum) is to be understood here as *vapāhoma*, i.e., the offering of the omentum. For a detailed discussion of this word, *see* G.U. Thite, 'Vapāmārjana in the Śrauta Sūtras', *Archive Orientałny*, Vol. 46, pp. 338-40.

4. In the *jyotiṣṭoma* sacrifice, a sacrificial animal is offered. It is called *stomāyanasañjñaka savanīya paśu*. Optionally, additional eleven animals are also offered with this animal. If these are offered, one sacrificial post is erected for the *savanīya paśu* and a separate post for those eleven animals. Sometimes, eleven separate posts are erected for these eleven animals.

According to *TaiBrā*, I.8.6.1, however, three posts should not be used. The reason is given as

> If the priest immolates the animals by three posts, he places the vital powers outside the sacrificer and creates an enemy for him. Therefore, he should not immolate them by three separate posts. He should erect only one post. He places thereby the vital powers together in the sacrificer and does not create an enemy for him.

After the omenta of these animals are offered, the priests, the sacrificer and the sacrificer's wife go near the *cātvāla* and besprinkle themselves with water as an act of purification (*ĀpaŚS*, XIX.2.1-3; *HirŚS*, XIII.8.19, 20; *VaikhāŚS*, XI.3; *VārāŚS*, III.2.7.25, 26; *MānŚS*, V.2.4.22-4).

The sacrificer gives away a gold coin *niṣka*, a bull and a *sātvarī* mare as sacrificial gifts *(dakṣiṇā)* (*ĀpaŚS*, XIX.2.3; *HirŚS*, XIII.8.20; *VaikhāŚS*, XI.3). According to *ĀpaŚS*, the adjective *sātvarī* means 'a mare, which is reunited with a lost horse', while according to the commentary on *HirŚS*, XIII.8.20, *sātvārī* means 'one who goes fast' (*śīghragāminī*). According to some teachers a mare with a colt and a piece of a hundred *māna*s of gold and silver are given as *dakṣiṇā* (*ĀpaŚS*, XIX.2.5 and 6).

Filling the Cups with Surā for the Deities

The cups are filled for the deities either after the preparatory rites, when the clarified butter is placed within the altar (*MānŚS*, V.2.4.17,19; *VārāŚS*, III.2.7.10; *BaudhŚS*, XVII.34, and also optionally *ĀpaŚS*, XIX.2.14) or after giving the offerings of the omenta of the animals (*KātyŚS*, XV.10.9-11; *ŚatBrā*, V.5.4.21, 22; *ĀpaŚS*, XIX.2.7; *VaikhāŚS*, XI.3; *HirŚS*, XIII.8.21).

According to *VaikhāŚS*, XI.2, *HirŚS*, XIII.8.15 and also according to the commentary of Vidyādhara on *KātyŚS*, XV.10.11, the cups used are made of *vikaṅkata* wood. The *BaudhŚS*, and the *VārāŚS*, on the other hand, prescribe pots of different wood for each deity. It is only according to the *MānŚS*, that the earthen cups are used for taking the *surā* for the deities.

The Adhvaryu takes *surā* in the cup with the *mantra, kuvidaṅga yavamanto yavañcit. . .* In *TaiBrā*, I.8.5.5,6 it is stated,

> The deity is not mentioned in this verse. Therefore, it belongs to Prajāpati. He obtains Prajāpati thereby. The Adhvaryu takes the *surā* with only one verse. He places the vital powers collectively in the sacrificer.'

In the *TaiBrā* it is not mentioned as to how many cups should be drawn.

According to *ŚatBrā*, V.5.4.23 and *KātyŚS*, XV.10.11, 12, either one or three cups should be drawn. However, after stating this option, the *ŚatBrā* further asserts that only one should be drawn as there is only one *puronuvākyā*, one *yājyā* and one *praiṣa*.

When three cups are taken, they are taken for the Aśvins, Sarasvatī and Indra Sutrāman.

The Adhvaryu first takes a cup of *palāśa* wood. He recites the verse *kuvidaṅga yavamanto . . .* and takes *surā* in it with the formula *upayāmagṛhito'si aśvibyāṁ tvā juṣṭaṁ gṛhṇāmi*. He mixes the powder of *kvala* and lion's hair in it, putting two *darbha*-blades over the cup. Then he removes the *darbha*-blades, wipes the cup with the eagle-wing-feather and places the cup within the altar with *eṣa te yonir aśvibhyāṁ tvā sādayāmi*.

He then takes a cup of *nyagrodha* wood, recites the verse *kuvidaṅga yavamanto. . .* and fills the cup with *surā* reciting the verse *upayāmagṛhīto'si sarasvatyai tvā juṣṭaṁ gṛhṇāmi*. He mixes the tiger's hair and the power of *badara* in it, keeping two *darbha*-blades over the cup. He then removes the *darbha*-blades, wipes the cup with the eagle-wing-feather and places it within the altar saying *eṣa te yonir sarasvatyai tvā. . . .* Then he takes the cup of *aśvattha* wood, recites the verse *kuvidaṅga yavamanto . . .* and takes *surā* in it with *upayāmagṛhīto'si indrāya tvā sutrāmne juṣṭaṁ gṛhṇāmi*. He then mixes the wolf's hair and the powder of *karkandhu* in it, keeping two *darbha*-blades over the cup. Then he removes the *darbha*-blades, wipes the cup with eagle-wing-feather and keeps the cup within the altar, saying *eṣa te yonir indrāya tvā sutrāmṇe. . .* (*BaudhŚS*, XVII.34).

The Adhvaryu puts those cups to the west of the ladles. He places them in such a way that their row ends towards the east. This is the way prescribed by Bodhāyana. Śālikī prescribes that he places them in such a way that the row ends towards the east (*BaudhŚS*, XXIII.16).

The procedure of filling the cups is almost similar in *MaiS*, II.3.9 and *KāṭhS*, XII.10 and in *ĀpaŚS*, XIX.2.8-12; *VaikhāŚS*, XI.3 and 4, and *HirŚS*, XIII.8.21,22 except a few variations.

According to *ĀpaŚS*, the *HirŚS* and the *VaikhāŚS* the cup for the Aśvins is drawn by the Adhvaryu, that for Sarasvatī, by the Pratiprasthātr̥ and the one for Indra Sutrāman by the Brahman priest or by the sacrificer himself. According to the *HirŚS* the one for Indra Sutrāman is drawn by the sacrificer. Brahman priest is not mentioned in it.

MānŚS, V.2.4.21 states that it is the Pratiprasthātr̥, who draws all the three cups.

According to the *MaiS*, the *KāṭhS*, the *MānŚS* and the *VārāŚS*, the hairs of different animals are not put in the cups. Instead, it is prescribed in *VārāŚS*, III.2.7.17, 20-3, and in *VaikhāŚS*, XI.4 that the Adhvaryu should meditate upon two lions, the Pratiprasthātr̥ upon two tigers and the sacrificer upon two wolves.

But, if the hairs of these particular animals are not available, then only the priests should meditate upon the respective animals, (*ĀpaŚS*, XIX.2.11 and *HirŚS*, XIII.8.23)..

The cups are then put at their proper places, after wiping them with eagle-wing-feathers (*ĀpaŚS*, XIX.2.12; *VaikhāŚS*, XI.4 and *VārāŚS*, III.2.7.24). According to *HirŚS*, XIII.8.24, they are put on the head of a brāhmaṇa. The *MaiS* also prescribes similarly. It is stated therein that the Adhyaryu puts it thus to make it sacrificial, as *surā* is food and food is sacrificial.

One important point should be noted here. According to *MānŚS*,

V.2.4.19, when the Pratiprasthātṛ is drawing the cups of *surā*, the Adhvaryu draws at the same time the cups of milk. In *VaikhāŚS*, XI.4 and *ĀpaŚS*, XIX.2.13, it is stated that optionally the cups of milk should be drawn instead of *surā*. In the *BaudhDvaiSū*, the opinion of Śālikī is mentioned; according to him, cups of milk also should be drawn.

The Preparation of the Cakes

After the offerings of the animal-omenta have been offered and the cups of *surā* are drawn for the deities, the Adhvaryu draws paddy for a cake to Bṛhaspati.

The *MaiS*, the *KāṭhS*, the *ŚatBrā* and the *KātyŚS* do not prescribe this fourth animal to Bṛhaspati and, therefore, they do not prescribe the Bārhaspatya cake also. In *VaikhāŚS*, XI.3 and *VārāŚS*, III.2.7.26 it is prescribed that a fourth animal should be immolated for Bṛhaspati, if the sacrificer is *somātipūta*, yet a cake in connection with that animal is not prescribed.

The Adhvaryu draws paddy for an eleven-potsherd cake for Indra, a twelve-potsherd cake for Savitṛ and a ten-potsherd cake for Varuṇa also (*ĀpaŚS*, XIX.2.15 and *HirŚS*, XIII.8.25).[5] According to *VaikhāŚS*, XI.4, the one which is offered to Varuṇa is prepared on twelve potsherds; *VārāŚS*, III.2.7.26 prescribes that for Savitṛ a cake should be prepared on eight potsherds; and for Varuṇa should be prepared barley-pap instead of a cake. The deities to whom the animals are offered and the deities to whom the cakes are offered are different. The texts do not make it clear as to which cake should be offered in connection with which animal. It is only the commentary on *ĀśvaŚS*, III.9.2 which states specifically that in connection with the animal dedicated to the Aśvins, a cake should be offered to Indra, with the animal dedicated to Sarasvatī, a cake should be offered to Savitṛ and in connection with that dedicated to Indra the barley-pap should be to Varuṇa.

---

5. In *Śrautakośa* it is stated that, according to *ĀpaŚS* a cake is to be offered to Sarasvatī.

It is only *TaiBrā*, I.8.6.1 which states that the cakes are not offered in connection with the animals; they are offered for the cups of *surā*. However, a cake is offered for the animal which is immolated for Bṛhaspati, since no cup is drawn for Bṛhaspati. Thus it is said *naiteṣām paśūnām purodāśā bhavanti grahapurodāśā hy'ete* "There are no cakes to be offered in connection with these animals. The cups offered serve, as it were, as the cakes for them." Bhaṭṭa Bhāskara has, however, explained the sentence differently thus: "the deities of the cups and of the animals are the same, and, therefore, the cups are considered to be the cakes for the animals." But, in the light of the explanation given by the *TaiBrā* in connection with the Bārhaspatya cake, the explanation of Bhaṭṭa Bhāskara does not seem to be satisfactory.

Perhaps keeping this explanation of the *TaiBrā* in mind, the commentator on *ĀśvaŚS*, III.9.6 mentions that, according to some, there are no cakes to be offered in connection with the animals since the cups themselves suffice as the cakes in connection with the animals.

After drawing paddy for the cakes for the respective deities, the Adhvaryu bakes the cakes properly and puts them within the altar. Then he begins the procedure of the offering of *surā*.

The Offering of Surā

The Adhvaryu takes the *surā* cup for the Aśvins, the Pratiprasthātṛ that for Sarasvatī and the Brahman priest or the sacrificer takes that for Indra (*VaikhāŚS*, XI.4; *HirŚS*, XIII.8.27). The *VārāŚS* does not offer this option between the Brahman and the sacrificer. According to it, the sacrificer himself takes the cup for Indra Sutrāman (*VārāŚS*, III.2.7.28). *BaudhŚS*, XVII.35 prescribes that the cups for the Aśvins and Sarasvatī should be taken by the Adhvaryu and that for Indra should be taken by the Pratiprasthātṛ.

While drawing the cups, they are drawn in earthen cups according to the *MānŚS*. At the time of the offering of *surā*, the Pratiprasthātṛ pours it from those earthen cups into the wooden ones (*MānŚS*, V.2.4.25). This might be due to the influence of *TaiS*,

II.5.4 wherein the use of the earthen pots is prohibited for offering. Thus it is said,

> *dārupātreṇa juhoti na hi mṛṇmayam āhutim ānaśa iti* |
>
> He offers with a wooden vessel, for an earthen pot does not hold the offering. (tr. by Keith)

Then the Adhvaryu, the Pratiprasthātṛ and the sacrificer stand between the two fires, each one having a cup of milk in his left hand and a cup of *surā* in the right hand. They stand in a row, first the Adhvaryu, then the Pratiprasthātṛ and then the sacrificer (*MānŚS*, V.2.4.25).

Even though, the cups are taken by more than one person, the calls are given only by the Adhvaryu, (*ĀpaŚS*, XIX.2.17). Thus, while getting up after taking the cups, the Adhvaryu says, "Do you recite the *puronuvākyā* relating to the Aśvins, Sarasvatī and Indra Sutrāman." The Maitrāvaruṇa recites the *puronuvākyā*, *yuvaṁ surāmam aśvinā*. . . .

The Adhvaryu then steps beyond the altar towards the south, causes the Āgnīdhra to announce and after he has responded, directs the Maitrāvaruṇa with the words, "Do you address the Hotṛ to recite the *yājyā* in connection with the offerings of *surā* taken for the Aśvins, Sarasvatī and Indra." The Maitrāvaruṇa gives a call to the Hotṛ saying, *hotā yakṣad aśvinā sarasvatī indraṁ sutrāmāṇam*. The Hotṛ recites the verse *putram iva pitarāv aśvinobhā* . . . as the *yājyā*. At the *vaṣaṭ* utterance by the Hotṛ, the Adhvaryu and the Pratiprasthātṛ offer an oblation with the verse *ahāvy agne havir āsye te*. . . . At the second *vaṣaṭ* utterance by the Hotṛ the Adhvaryu and the Pratiprasthātṛ offer the second oblation with the verse, *yasminn aśvāsa ṛṣabhāsa ukṣaṇā* . . . (*BaudhŚS*, XVII. 35, 36; *MānŚS*, V.2.4.25; *VārāŚS*, III.2.7.28, 29; *ŚatBrā*, V.5.4.24-26; *KātyŚS*, XV.10.13, 14).

The *puronuvākyā*s and the *yājyā*s to all the deities are the same. It is only *ŚāṅkhāŚS*, XV.15.10-11 which first states that, "according to some teachers, there should be different calls for the different deities and they should be modified suitably" and then it rejects it, stating that 'this is a practice of the *asuras*'.

After the *vaṣaṭ* utterance, the respective cups are offered. At the second *vaṣaṭ* utterance, the Hotṛ should utter the formula *somasyāgne vīhi* . . . at the second offering (*ĀpaŚS*, XIX.2.19, and XIX.3.1; also *VaikhāŚS*, XI.4) or he should optionally utter the formula *surāsutasyāgne vīhi* . . . (*ĀśvaŚS*, III.9.4).

The employment of the two verses, viz. *ahāvy agne havir āsye te* . . . and *yasminn aśvāsa ṛṣabhāsa ukṣaṇaḥ* . . . is different in the *ĀpaŚS*. It prescribes at XIX.3.2 that with the recitation of these two verses, the sacrificer should follow the *surā* which has been offered or which is being offered (cf. also *VaikhāŚS*, XI.4).

These *surā*-offerings are offered on the southern fire (*KātyŚS*, XV.10.16).

After these offerings are offered, the Adhvaryu should meditate upon the formula *siṁhayor imaṁ yaśaḥ āgacchatu*. The Pratiprasthātṛ should meditate upon the formula *vyāghrayor imaṁ yaśaḥ āgacchatu* and the sacrificer should meditate upon the formula *vṛkayor imaṁ yaśaḥ āgacchatu* (*MānŚS*, V.2.4.28).

The Disposal of the Remaining Surā

After the *surā* has been offered, the Adhvaryu pours the remnants of the Āśvina cup into the Sārasvata one and then pours the remnants of the Sārasvata cup into the cup which was taken for Indra (*BaudhŚS*, XVII.36). Or as *MānŚS*, V.2.4.29 prescribes, the Adhvaryu and the Pratiprasthātṛ pour the remnants of their cups into the cups of the sacrificer.

The Hotṛ and the Adhvaryu partake of the remnants of *surā*, (*KātyŚS*, XV.10.16). *VārāŚS*, III.2.7.31 prescribes that the sacrificer should give some money to these priests for drinking it. The priests eat the remnants with the verse *yad atra śiṣṭam*. . . . According to *ĀśvaŚS*, III.9.5 only the Hotṛ priest partakes of it, i.e., he just smells it. At the time of smelling the *surā* in each cup, he recites the *mantra* beginning with the words *yad atra riptam*. *ŚāṅkhāŚS*, XV.15.13 prescribes a different verse to be recited at the time of eating the remnants. According to it, the Hotṛ eats the remnants with the recitation of the verse *yam aśvinā namucāv āsure dadhi. . . .*

Or a brāhmaṇa should be hired to partake of the remnants. After the cups are filled with *surā*, the Adhvaryu prepares a mound of old ashes to the east of the sourthern fire and makes the brāhmaṇa sit upon it. If he doesn't get a brāhmaṇa, then he heaps there the ant-hill-earth, (*BaudhŚS*, XVII.35).

But, according to *VaikhāŚS*, XI.5, this alternative is not open to all. If the sacrificer is a brāhmaṇa, only then a brāhmaṇa is hired. *TaiBrā*, I.8.6.4 states the opinion that it is very natural that a brāhmaṇa is hired since it is the usual practice that the brāhmaṇa drinks whatever remains after the offerings. *MaiS*, II.3.9 and *KāṭhS*, XII.11 also mention that when he gives *surā* to the brāhmaṇa, he, as it were, offers an oblation thereby.

The brāhmaṇa should consume it with the recitation of the verses, *nāna hi vām* . . . and *yad atra śiṣṭam* . . . (*BaudhŚS*, XVII.36). Or the brāhmaṇa recites only one verse viz. *yad atra śiṣṭam* . . . and while he is drinking *surā*, the sacrificer consecrates him with the verse *nānā hi vām* . . . (*HirŚS*, XIII.8.29).

If the Adhvaryu and the Hotṛ are not ready to drink it, or if it is not possible to hire a brāhmaṇa, the Adhvaryu pours the remnants of *surā* on the ant-hill-earth (*TaiBrā*, I.8.0.2; *ĀpaŚS*, XIX.3.5; *BaudhŚS*, XVII.36; *VārāŚS*, III.2.7.32; *HirŚS*, XIII.8.30; *VaikhāŚS*, XI.5).

It is in a way an atonement for not getting a brāhmaṇa. What is lacking in the *sautrāmaṇī* is thus made perfect, when he pours that *surā* on the ant-hill-earth (*TaiBrā*, I.8.6.2).

While pouring it down on the ant-hill-earth, the Adhvaryu should recite the verses *nānā hi vām* . . . and *yad atra śiṣṭam* . . . (*BaudhŚS*, XVII.36).

A different verse is prescribed by *ĀpaŚS*, XIX.3.5 and *HirŚS*, XIII.8.30, to accompany this act. According to them, at this time the verse *dve sṛtī aśṛṇavam* . . . should be recited.

According to Baudhāyana, while pouring down, one should take it along the south and pour it down along the north; whereas, according to Śālikī, one should take it along the north and pour it down along the south.

Still more options are prescribed besides these ones. Optionally, the sacrificer himself should drink it (*ĀpaŚS*, XIX.3.3; *VārāŚS*, III.2.7.31; *HirŚS*, XIII.8.31; *VaikhāŚS*, XI.5). When he does so, he deposits vigour in himself, as it were (*MaiS*, II.3.9. and *KāṭhS*, XII.11).

While drinking it, he should recite the verses, *nānā hi vām* . . . and *yad atra śiṣṭam* . . . (*ĀpaŚS*, XIX.3.3 and *VaikhāŚS*, XI.5).

The *MānŚS* does not offer any option as such. According to it, the sacrificer takes both his cups,viz. that of *surā* and that of milk, in which the remnants are poured; and then goes along the east of the two fires, to the south and eats the remnants. While consuming the remnants of milk, he recites the verse *yad atra śiṣṭam* . . . and while consuming those of *surā*, he recites the verse *nānā hi vām*. . . . If he does not actually drink the remnants, he smells those cups.

Aupamanyava suggests an altogether different way. According to him, the remaining *surā* should again be poured into the pot from which the cups are filled; whereas, according to *VārāŚS*, III.2.7.32, *HirŚS*, XIII.8.31 and *VaikhāŚS*, XI.5, it should be offered on fire. The Adhvaryu should offer it on the southern fire, while reciting the verse *dve sṛtī aśṛṇavam* . . . (*VaikhāŚS*, XI.5). When he offers it on the fire in this way, he thereby achieves perfection (*MaiS*, II.3.9 and *KāṭhS*, XII.11).

If the Adhvaryu offers it on the *āhavanīya* fire, he heals the sacrificer thereby, but he does not make him free from evil. When he offers it on the southern fire, he heals the sacrificer and also makes him free from evil (*MaiS*, II.3.9; *KāṭhS*, XII.11).

The Trickling of the Surā on the Southern Fire

The *surā*, which remains in the pot after the cups are drawn for the deities, is poured in a perforated pitcher *śatātṛṇṇā* and is made to trickle on the southern fire. This is considered to be an offering to the fathers.

The preparation of this rite is made beforehand, when the cups are filled for the deities and are put towards the west of the ladles. The Adhvaryu then takes the remaining *surā* and goes to the southern fire. He gets two pits dug near it; one to the north of the fire and the other to its south. He keeps there two two-branched poles, a long pole, a loop of rope, the *śatātr̥ṇṇā* vessel, a hundred *māna*s of gold, the pot called *sata* and a filter made of hair.

After disposing of the *surā* which is remaining in the cups, the Adhvaryu fills those cups with the sediments of *surā* and hides the eagle-wing-feather in the cup of *palāśa* wood (*BaudhŚS*, XVII.35, 36).

The Adhvaryu then offers three offerings on the fire with the three verses beginning with *ye bhakṣayanta* ... (*VārāŚS*, III.2.7.33). Then he ties up the *śatātr̥ṇṇā* vessel and holds it suspended on the southern fire (*ĀpaŚS*, XIX.3.7; *HirŚS*, XVIII.8.22 and *VaikhāŚS*, XI.5).

The method for keeping the pot hanging on the fire is described only in the *BaudhŚS*. It is described there that the Adhvaryu raises the two two-branched poles in the two pits already dug. He places the long pole (of bamboo) on them. Then he hangs a sling on that bamboo and places in it the *śatātr̥ṇṇā* vessel (*BaudhŚS*, XVII.36).

ŚatBrā, V.5.4.27 gives the reason why the *śatātr̥ṇṇā* is used. It states, "Man has a hundred years of life, he has hundred-fold vigour and hundred-fold strength. Therefore, the *śatātr̥ṇṇā* is used." Optionally, the pitcher might have nine holes according to this *Brāhmaṇa* as 'nine are the vital airs in man'.

Following the *Brāhmaṇa*, the *KātyŚS* also suggests that the pitcher may optionally have nine holes. This is not explicitly mentioned. The *sūtra* XV.10.16 states that a pot having the holes like a *rukma* 'a golden plate' should be used. This golden plate is mentioned in connection with the *rājasūya* in *KātyŚS*, XV.5.27, and there it is mentioned that it has either a hundred or nine marks upon it.

It is only *ŚatBrā*, V.5.4.28 which states that the pitcher should be hung on the *āhavanīya* fire. (But Eggeling perhaps rightly adds a foot-note to translation of this passage that the southern fire is meant here by the word *āhavanīya*). The *KātyŚS* also supports this. Further, the commentator Karkācārya has mentioned, while commenting upon *sūtra* XV.10.15, that all the necessary sacred or consecratory acts, which are to be observed in connection with the *āhavanīya*, should be performed in connection with the southern fire.

After placing the *śatātṛṇṇā* in the loop of rope, the Adhvaryu spreads a filter made of hair in it with its fringes to the north, and places upon it a golden plate *rukma* (*BaudhŚS*, XVII.36; *ĀpaŚS*, XIX.3.7; *HirŚS*, XIX.8.31). According to *TaiBrā*, I.8.6.4, the Adhvaryu holds a golden plate between the fire and the pot. *VaikhāŚS*, XI.5 prescribes that a *rukma* or two or three *niṣka*s or a golden ear-ring or a hundred *māna*s of gold should be kept in the *śatātṛṇṇā* whereas neither the filter nor the *rukma*, etc., is mentioned in the *MānŚS*, V.2.4.31 and in *VārāŚS*, III.2.7.34. According to *MānŚS*, V.2.4.31, the rites regarding *surā* are performed by the Pratiprasthātṛ. In *ĀpaŚS*, XIX.3.7 verse *yan me manaḥ parāgatam*. . . is prescribed to be recited while placing the filter in the pitcher, and according to *VaikhāŚS*, XI.5, while placing the *niṣka*, etc.

Then the remaining *surā* is poured by the Adhvaryu (or by the Pratiprasthātṛ, according to the *MānŚS*) in the pitcher (*VārāŚS*, III.2.7.34). In the commentary on *HirŚS*, XIII.8.33 it is stated that, while pouring the *surā*, the Adhvaryu should have his sacred thread on the right shoulder. In *ĀpaŚS*, XIX.3.7 and *BaudhŚS* a verse is prescribed to be recited at the time of pouring *surā* and it is *somapratīkāḥ pitaras tṛpṇuta* . . . *ĀpaŚS*, XIX.3.7 prescribes that *somapratīkāḥ pitaro madantām* may also be sung at this time. According to *HirŚS*, XIII.8.33, the *surā* is poured with the recitation of the verses *somapratīkāḥ pitaro madantām* and *yan me manaḥ parāgatam*. . . . *LāṭyāŚS*, V.4.14 prescribes that, when the *surā* is being poured in the sieve, all persons including the Brahman priest should pray to it with *yat te pavitram arciṣy agne vitatam antaram* | *brahma tena punīhi mā*. The *surā* poured in this way begins to trickle down on the fire. The reason as to why *surā* is made to trickle down is stated in *MaiS*, II.3.9 and *KāṭhS*, XII.11:

> The *surā* is made to trickle this way, as the life of man also trickles away. The *surā* trickles in a hundred-fold way. In the same manner, the life of man also trickles away in a hundred-fold way and he obtains a hundred years of life and hundred-fold vigour thereby. (also *TaiBrā*, I.8.6.4)

The priests consecrate the *surā*, which is trickling down in the fire. When they pray to it, they thereby supply Indra, as it were, with that part of his, which had gone away from him, when *soma* flowed through him (*ŚatBrā*, V.5.4.28).

When anybody has lost, or is deprived of something, it has gone to his fathers. Therefore, the priests consecrate the down-trickling *surā* by the verses which have the word *pitr̥* in them. Thus they make him impelled by the fathers (*MaiS*, II.3.9; *KāṭhS*, XII.11; and *TaiBrā*, I.8.6.5).

The priests, viz. the Adhvaryu, the Hotr̥ and the Brahman, pray to the down-trickling *surā* with the *pāvamānī* verses which begin with *pavamānaḥ suvarjanaḥ* or if the sacrificer is a *somātipavita*, then they consecrate it with the verses which are used as *puronuvākyās* and *yājyās* for the offerings to the fathers, viz. *udīratām avara utparāsaḥ* (*BaudhŚS*, XVII.36).

At that time, the Adhvaryu should stand towards the east facing towards the west. The Brahman should stand to the south facing the north and the Hotr̥ to the west facing the east (*ĀpaŚS*, XIX.3.10; *HirŚS*, XIII.8.35, *VaikhāŚS*). *VārāŚS*, III.2.7.35 adds that the Āgnīdhra should stand towards the north.

According to *MānŚS*, V.2.4.31, the Brahman is to the south, the sacrificer to the west, the Adhvaryu to the north and the Pratiprasthātr̥ to the east.

They pray to the down-trickling *surā* with the twelve verses beginning with *tvaṁ soma pracikitaḥ*. . . . Each one recites three verses (*ĀpaŚS*, XIX.3.8; *HirŚS*, XIII.8.35). The Āgnīdhra prays with the *kāvyavāhanī* verses beginning with *yad agne kavyavāhana* . . . (*HirŚS*, XIII.8.35), or according to *ĀpaŚS*, XIX.3.11 these *kāvyavāhanī* verses are employed while the *śatātr̥ṇṇā* is put upon the southern fire and that also if the sacrificer is a brāhmaṇa.

When all the *surā* has trickled down, the Adhvaryu keeps the *śatātṛṇṇā*, as it is, for some time, and then puts it to the south of that fire. Then he puts on the mound of the old ashes the pots filled with sediments, with the formula,

> *pitṛbhyaḥ svadhāyibhyaḥ svadhā namaḥ* ।
> *pitāmahebhyaḥ svadhāyibhyaḥ svadhā namaḥ* ।
> and
> *prapitāmahebhyaḥ svadhāyibhyaḥ svadhā namaḥ* ।
> —*BaudhŚS*, XVII.36.

At this time, he gives a pregnant mare as a gift. According to *MāiS*, II.4.2 and *KāṭhS*, XII.11 a *sṛtvarī* mare is given as a gift. *ĀpaŚS*, XIX.4.1 and *HirŚS*, XIII.8.35 prescribe that, if the sacrificer is a *rājanya* or a vaiśya, the Adhvaryu should not carry forth the southern fire and the sacrificer himself should partake of the remnants of *surā*. But in such case, these *sūtra*s do not mention, in which fire the *surā*-offerings are to be offered. Therefore, the *VaikhāŚS* seems to be more right. According to it, even if the southern fire is carried forth, the sacrificer, who is a *rājanya* or a vaiśya himself should partake of the remnants of *surā* (*VaikhāŚS*, XI.5).

In this connection a myth is cited in *MaiS*, II.4.2 and *KāṭhS*, XII.12. The myth reads:

> One half of Prajāpati was courage and the other was foolishness. Courage was placed forward and foolishness was kept behind. Courage was *soma*. From it was born the brāhmaṇa. Therefore, the brāhmaṇa is courageous. Foolishness was *surā*. *Rājanya* or kṣatriya was born from that. Therefore, after drinking *surā*, the elder one and the younger one, the daughter-in-law and the father-in-law chatter foolishly. It is foolishness and foolishness is evil. Hence a brāhmaṇa should not drink *surā*, otherwise, he would connect himself with evil. This *Brāhmaṇa* (portion) should be told to a kṣatriya. Thus, *surā* does not harm one, who, knowing this, drinks it. This is the form of Prajāpati which has vigour in it. Prajāpati is vigour. The sacrificer thus places vigour in himself.

The Remaining Animal-sacrifice and the Offerings of Cakes

After the disposal of the remnants of *surā*, the Adhvaryu touches water and begins the rite of offering the cake to Bṛhaspati. The grains for all the cakes are already drawn and the cakes are already baked before performing the offerings of *surā*. Only the *MānŚS* is an exception to this. According to it, the grains for the cakes are also drawn at this time. For all the deities, the cakes are baked on eleven-potsherds (*MānŚS*, V.2.4.32). The Adhvaryu then performs the rites beginning with the offerings to the divinity up to the *iḍā* as regards the Bārhaspatya cake. It is only the *HirŚS* according to which the Bārhaspatya cake is offered immediately after the offerings of *surā*.

After the offerings of the Bārhaspatya cake, the Adhvaryu performs the ritual regarding the animal-sacrifice, beginning with the *manotā*-offerings up to the *iḍā*. After that he begins the ritual of the offering of the cakes.

The deities of the animals and the deities of the cakes are different. The animals are offered to the Aśvins, Sarasvatī and Indra Sutrāman, whereas the cakes are offered to Indra, Savitṛ and Varuṇa. *TaiBrā*, I.8.6.2 remarks that this is for the perfection (*samṛddhi*) of the sacrifice.

The animal and the omentum of the animal to Indra are offered the last and the cake for Indra is offered the first. When the Adhvaryu offers the same, he connects the sacrificer with vigour. But, the *VārāŚS* does not show the acceptance of this procedure. According to it, the offerings of the animal for Indra are offered the first and the offerings of the animal for the Aśvins are offered the last (*VārāŚS*, III.2.7.37).

The Adhvaryu offers a cake prepared on eleven potsherds to Indra. By this offering, the sacrificer gains the strength (*TaiBrā*, I.8.6.3). Indra is the deity of the sacrifice. The Adhvaryu thus heals him with the help of the deity of the sacrifice.

A twelve or eight-potsherd cake is offered to Savitṛ. Savitṛ is the impeller of the gods and impelled by him the priest heals the sacrificer (*TaiBrā*, I.8.6; *ŚatBrā*, V.5.4.30; *MaiS*, II.4.2 and *KāṭhS*, XII.12).

A ten-potsherd cake is offered to Varuṇa. This act is explained by *ŚatBrā*, V.5.4.31 as, "Varuṇa is the injurer. When the Adhvaryu offers a cake to Varuṇa, he heals the sacrificer with the injurer also." *MaiS*, II.4.2 and *KāṭhS*, XII.12 state that he offers the cake to be free from Varuṇa.

The ritual of the *sviṣṭakṛt* offerings and the partaking of *iḍā* in connection with the animals and the cakes is performed together. This is done for achieving wholeness (*saṁhiti*) of the sacrifice and to keep the *iḍā* unseparated. What is lacking in the *sautramaṇī* is thereby made perfect. Something is lacking in the *sautrāmaṇī*, because the deities of the animals are different from those of the cakes. This shortcoming of the *sautrāmaṇī* is thus overcome and the rite is made perfect. It is interesting to note here that, according to *TaiBrā*, I.8.6.2 this very speciality of the *sautrāmanī* achieves the perfection of the rite.

Then the after-offerings (*anūyājas*) of the sacrifices are performed. A different procedure is prescribed in the *ŚatBrā*, V.5.4.33 and the *KātyŚS*, XV.10. 20-2. If the sacrificer is a *somātipūta*, he should offer the cakes after the after-offerings, when the ladles are not yet separated. The *soma* passes excessively from behind. When he offers in this way, he covers him from behind with this sacrifice. In that case, he should draw the oblation-material for a cake which is to be prepared on two potsherds and to be offered to the Aśvins. This cake he offers, when he has performed the ritual regarding the offering of the omenta.

However, this alternative is rejected by the *ŚatBrā* itself at V.5.4.34. Thus it is said there,

> this should not be done. One, who goes away from the right path of the sacrifice, is, as it were, going astray from the right path of the sacrifice. One, who offers in this way, is as it were, going away from the right path of the sacrifice. Therefore, he should offer these oblations, only when he is performing the offerings of the omenta and, in that case, he

> should not offer the two-potsherd cake.

A mare is given away as a sacrificial gift of this sacrifice.

> The mare gives birth to a horse or to a mule. The *sautrāmaṇī* is either a *soma* (sacrifice) or a *surā* (sacrifice). Therefore, for the perfection of the sacrifice the mare is given as gift.
> — *TaiBrā*, I.8.6.4.

ŚatBrā, V.5.4.35 prescribes that a castrated bull is to be given as a sacrificial gift,[6] since such a bull is neither male nor a female. Or, a female horse which is yoked to a chariot should be given, as

> she is yoked to a chariot. She is not a female. If she is a female, then she is certainly not a male. Therefore, a mare which is yoked to a chariot is the sacrificial gift.[7]

VārāŚS, III.2.7.40 prescribes that a mare and also a bull should be offered as sacrificial gifts.

The Avabhṛtha Bath

After the description of the offerings of the animals and that of the cakes, the *avabhṛtha* bath is prescribed in the ritual of the *caraka sautrāmaṇī* (*VārāŚS*, III.2.7.4; *ĀpaŚS*,XIX.4.6; *HirŚS*. XIII.8.38). Generally, the *avabhṛtha* is performed only after a *soma*-sacrifice.[8]

---

6. Regarding the nature and function of *dakṣiṇās* in general *see*, G.U. Thite, "Non-attractive Dakṣiṇās in Śrauta Rituals", *Viśveśvarānanda Indological Journal*, Vol. 7, pp. 36-44, Hoshiarpur, 1969.
7. Von Henry Falk has referred to this sacrificial gift in his article 'Die Legende von Śunaḥśepa vor ihrem rituellen Hintergrund', in *ZDMG* Band 134, Heft 1, 1984, p. 127.

   While explaining why this particular gift is given, he has overlooked the explanation occurring in the same passage and has tried to connect it with the passage in *MaiS*, II.3.3 which describes some other rite.
8. The *avabhṛtha* is explained as, 'final purificatory bath in *agniṣṭoma*' in the General Index of *History of Dharma Śāstra*, P.V. Kane, Vol.II, Part II, p. 1287. The rite is described on p. 1198 of the same. While describing the ritual of *sautrāmaṇī* it is stated 'There is the final purificatory bath as in *somayāga*', p. 1228.

It is not performed in an *iṣṭi* or in an animal-sacrifice. It is evident from the singing of the *sāman* in it. As a part of the ritual of the *avabhṛtha* a *sāman* is sung by the Prastotṛ. This priest has no part either in an *iṣṭi* or in an animal-sacrifice. Naturally therefore, even if the *avabhṛtha* is introduced in the ritual of the *sautrāmaṇī*, there is no singing of the *sāman* due to the absence of the priest Prastotṛ (*BaudhŚS*, XVII.38; and comm. on *HirŚS*, XIII.40). Besides the *soma*-sacrifice, the *avabhṛtha* is found prescribed in the ritual of the *vanuṇapraghāsa* and that of the *sautrāmaṇī*. And in both these rites it is stated that the procedure of the *avabhṛtha* in a *soma*-sacrifice is followed here also. (cf. *HirŚS*, XIII.8.39; *VārāŚS*, III.2.7.41 and I.7.2.42).

Nothing can be said at present as to why the *avabhṛtha* is introduced in the *varuṇapraghāsa*; however, with regard to the *sautrāmaṇī*, it can be said that the rite of *avabhṛtha* is added to it later, and it is for achieving similarity of the *sautrāmaṇī* with the *soma*-sacrifice. It is worth to note in this regard that the Saṁhitās and the *Brāhmaṇa*s do not present any description of the *avabhṛtha*. The description of the *caraka sautrāmaṇī* in the *KātyŚS* also does not include the same. The *MānŚS* also does not prescribe it. It describes only the disposal of the pots. It is stated in that *ŚS* that the pots, etc., stained with *surā* or milk, are thrown into the water (*MānŚS*, V.2.4.38).

After the offerings of *surā*, the sediments of *surā* are poured in those cups and the eagle-wing-feather is also kept hidden in it. While going for the *avabhṛtha*, they take with them those pots, the *māsara*, the heart-pike and also whatever is stained with *surā*. The *māsara* is treated as *ṛjīṣa* 'the dregs of *soma*' (*ĀpaŚS*, XIX.4.6-8; *HirŚS*, XIII.8.38; *VaikhāŚS*, XI.6; *BaudhŚS*, XVII.36). *VārāŚS*, III.2.7.41 suggests that the *māsara* should be considered as a cake for Varuṇa.

While going for the *avabhṛtha*, the Adhvaryu recites the verse *dve sṛtī aśṛṇavam....* They go to the north between the *cātvāla* and the rubbish heap. First, they dispose of the heart-pike in the usual procedure (*BaudhŚS*, XVII.37, 38). The procedure is described in *BaudhŚS*, IV.10 in connection with the animal sacrifice. There it is described: the Adhvaryu, the sacrificer and the wife of the sacrificer go to the north between the *cātvāla* and the rubbish heap. The Adhvaryu digs up a little to the east of the sacrificial post by means of the wooden sword, sprinkles that spot with water by means of the hand with the palm turned downwards and stick up the heart-pike upon the joint of the dry patch of the ground and the wet patch of the ground with *śug asi tam abhi śoca*. . . . Then all of them sprinkle themselves with water, with the formula, *dhāmno dhāmno rājann itaḥ*. . . .

After they have disposed of the heart-pikes, they go to the water. At that time, no *sāman* is sung. *BaudhŚS*, XVII.38 prescribes that they do not recite even the formula *devīr apaḥ eṣa vo garbhaḥ* . . . *HirŚS*, XIII.8.40,41 also prescribe that they go without reciting anything.

After going near the water, they put the pots upon the border of the water. The Adhvaryu throws into the water the cup which was taken for the Aśvins. At that time, he recites the formula *yas te deva varuṇa gāyatracchandaḥ pāśaḥ* . . . (*ĀpaŚS*, XIX.4.9 and *HirŚS*, XIII.8.42).

The cup taken for Indra he throws into water with *yas te deva varuṇa jagatīcchandaḥ pāśaḥ* . . . and the cup for Sarasvatī he throws with the formula *yas te deva vanuṇa triṣṭupchandaḥ pāśaḥ*. . . .

According to *ĀpaŚS*, XIX.4.9, *HirŚS*, XIII.8.42 and *VaikhāŚS*, XI.6 the heart-pikes are not to be disposed of in the way prescribed in connection with the animal-sacrifice. According to these *sūtra*s, the Adhvaryu throws them into water at this time with the formula, *yas te deva varuṇa paṅkticchandaḥ pāśaḥ taṁ ta etena avayaje*. . . . The Hotṛ should follow the disposal of the heart-pikes with the relevant formula and go away (*ĀpaHauPari*, II.3). The pot *sata*, the *śatātṛṇṇā*, the eagle-wing-feathers, etc., are thrown into water with the recitation of the formula *yas te deva varuṇa anuṣṭupchandaḥ pāśaḥ taṁ ta etena avayaje*. According to the *BaudhŚS* these things should be thrown without reciting any formula. While coming back after the performance of this rite they do not recite any formula, (*ĀpaŚS*, XIX.3.10; *HirŚS*, XIII.8.43), and do not look behind, so that they should be concealed from Varuṇa (*BaudhŚS*, XVII.38).

According to *BaudhŚS*, XVII.38 the procedure of the *avabhṛtha* is established, viz. it is the same as that prescribed in connection with the *soma*-sacrifice. It means that all such rites, which are not described here, such as pushing back the border of waters, plunging into water, etc., are to be performed. This is not prescribed in the other *sūtras*.

While coming back, they should collect three fire-sticks each, with the formula, *edho'si edhiṣīmahi*. After coming back into the fire-hall, the Adhvaryu puts the fire-sticks upon the *āhavanīya* fire with the formula *samid asi, tejo'si, tejo mayi dhehi*. They all pray to the *āhavanīya* fire with *apo anv acāriṣam rasena samasṛkṣmahi* (*BaudhŚS*, XVII.38). After that, the Adhvaryu offers the flour of parched barley upon the fire, with the recitation of the *kusīda* verses, i.e., *yat kusīdam apratītam*. . . . Then the sacrificer prays to the sacrificial post. Here ends the *caraka sautrāmaṇī* (*BaudhŚS*, XVII.38).

8

Preparation of Surā

DRINKS are known to man right from the palaeolithic age. The hunters of Western Europe of that period prepared drinks from the trees like Maple or also from the bark of trees, etc.[1] The use of corn for the preparation of fermented liquor is as old as its use for food.[2] A beverage prepared by alcoholic fermentation of the cereals is called beer.[3] The use of malted grains is probably later than the simpler principle of infusion. The term beer is generally employed to include the products of both. In majority of early kinds of beer, however, only infusion is used.[4]

About the origin of liquor prepared from corn, it is conjectured that man came across it serendipitiously. In the neolithic period, there was, in the cereal-eating civilisation, a custom of eating soups made from cereals. After the soups were consumed, the remnants began to ferment. Perhaps, the peculiar acid-flavour might not have, at first, appealed to man, but gradually, it certainly became delicious for refined palates.[5] The originator of beer, in Greek opinion, was Egypt; although the Sumero-Akkadians, another

---

1. *Gastronomy, The Anthropology of Food and Food Habits,* ed. by Margaret L. Arnott; Mouton; *The Origin of Grape Wine: A Problem of Historical-Ecological Anthropology*" by Getano Forni, pp. 69ff.
2. *ERE*, 'Drinks and Drinking' by A.E. Crawley, pp. 72ff.
3. *Encyclopaedia Britannica*, Vol. 3, '*Beer*', p. 313.
4. *ERE*, *op.cit.*, p. 72.
5. *Gastronomy*, *op.cit.*, p. 74.

agricultural community, which prepared it since the dawn of history, may share the claim.[6] In Egypt, it was an important drink in daily life. There are so many references to beer, such as, it was donated as food, was used in divine offerings, evening offerings, mortuary offerings and in the offerings to obelisks. One becomes convinced, thereby, of the importance of that drink.

In Vedic literature also, we get many references to liquor, i.e., *surā* as it is called, and, therefore, can infer that the Vedic people might be drinking *surā* in their normal life. But it can be said with certainty that *surā* was used in Vedic ritual also. The word is sometimes translated as 'wine'. But, from the description of its preparation in the ritual texts, it is clear that it was prepared through fermentation of grains and therefore, 'beer' seems to be the appropriate translation of it. The use of *surā* is mentioned in the *vājapeya* sacrifice. It is used in some *gṛhya* rites also.[7] But, there is no offering of *surā* in these rites. The offerings of *surā* are found only in the *sautrāmaṇī* sacrifice. According to some texts, the sacrificer himself partakes of the remnants after the offerings are made.

Even though *surā* is used in various rites, the procedure of its preparation is described only in connection with the ritual of the *sautrāmaṇī* — the description is found in both of its varieties, viz. the *caraka* and the *kaukilī*. By and large, the description found in connection with the *caraka* is brief (only the *BaudhŚS* is an exception in this regard), and in the context of the *kaukilī*, it is given in details.

In the Saṁhitās the *mantra*s used in the preparation of *surā* are cited in the description of both the varieties, but the *Brāhmaṇa* portion is found only in the *MaiS* and the *KāṭhS* and that again referring to the *caraka sautrāmaṇī* alone. It will be convenient, therefore, to discuss the method of the preparation of *surā* in both the varieties, jointly.

---

6. *Food, the Gift of Orisis*, Vol. 2 by William J. Darby, Paul Ghalioungui, Louis Grivetti, pp. 530ff.
7. See J. Gonda, *Vedic Ritual — The Non-Solemn Rites*, p. 185.

The ritual description of the preparation of *surā*.[8]

In the Caraka

THE BUYING OF THE INGREDIENTS

Three days before the actual performance of the *sautrāmaṇī* sacrifice, is performed the rite of purchasing some of the ingredients of *surā* (cf. *ĀpaŚS*, XIX.11; *HirŚS*, XXIII.1.1; *VaikhāŚS*, XI.1). According to *ŚatBrā*, V.4.6.20 and *KātyŚS*, XV.10.1 (here, optionally) they are purchased only on the previous day of the sacrifice.

BaudhŚS, XVII.31 prescribes that the ingredients necessary for the preparation of *surā* should be kept ready at the time of placing the paraphernalia. At that time, the *surāsoma* (i.e., substance for the preparation of *surā*, here the *śaṣpa* 'sprouted barley') is kept on a red bull's hide to the east of the fire-hall. (It is outside the fire-hall).

After the new-moon offerings, (in this case, the main *iṣṭi* will be on the third day of the bright half of the month) or under any auspicious constellation, the Adhvaryu buys the *śaṣpa* near the altar (*MānŚS*, V.2.4.2). He buys it from a eunuch (*klība*) for lead (*BaudhŚS*, XVII.31; *TaiBrā*, I.8.5.17; *ĀpaŚS*, XIX.1.1; *VaikhāŚS*, XI.1). It is only *VārāŚS*, III.2.7 which prescribes that optionally it should be bought from a seller of *soma*. The reason as to why it is to be purchased for lead is given in the Saṁhitās, thus: "Untruth is lead, untruth the eunuch and untruth is *surā*. Thus, he buys untruth from untruth, with untruth" (*MaiS*, II.4.2;[9] *KāṭhS*, XII.11). The reason which is given for this in *TaiBrā*, I.8.5.17 is a little different. It states,

> Lead is neither iron nor gold. A eunuch is neither a man nor a woman. This *sautrāmaṇī* is neither a *soma* (sacrifice) for

---

8. For the 'Preparation of *surā*' *see also* A. Weber, *Indische Studien*, Vol. X, pp. 349ff.

9. The word in the text is *kāryā*. However, from the verb *krīṇāti* in the next sentence, it seems that is must be *kreyā*.

a *surā* (sacrifice). Therefore, it is for perfection that the Adhvaryu buys it with lead.

It is worth noting here that *KāṭhS*, I.12.11 prescribes the buying of *tokma* instead of the *śaṣpa* whereas *KātyŚS*, XV.9.23 prescribes that together with the sprouted paddy unsprouted paddy also should be purchased. According to *MānŚS*, V.2.4.2, besides *śaṣpa*, paddy, barley, wheat and *nagnahu* are also to be bought. *MaiS*, II.4.2 uses the word *surā* instead of *śaṣpa*. One cannot be certain, whether according to this tradition *surā* itself was bought or the word is to be taken to mean, here secondarily as an ingredient of *surā*. It is possible that prepared *surā* was bought, since such an option is noted in *BaudhDvaiSū*, XXIII.16, where it is stated that 'according to Aupamanyava, *surā* should be brought from where it is ready'.

At the time of buying, the Adhvaryu says to the eunuch (*klība*), "This lead is yours and this is mine; bought is the *surāsoma*" (*BaudhŚS*, XVII.31). According to *MānŚS*, V.2.4.3 he says, "O seller of *surāsoma*, I buy this *surāsoma* with this lead."

After buying it, the Adhvaryu enters into the fire-hall through the eastern door and places it behind the *gārhapatya* fire.

THE MIXING OF THE INGREDIENTS

It may be noted here that in the Saṁhitās and in the *TaiBrā* the actual mixing of the ingredients is not described. Only the explanation of the employment of the verses is given in Brāhamanical style. Thus it is stated in *KāṭhS*, XII.9 that "as the Adhvaryu recited the verse *svādvīṁ tvā svādunā* . . . he mixes *surā* with the *Brahman*". According to *TaiBrā*, I.8.5.17, the Adhvaryu makes the *surā* a form of *soma* thereby; and as he recites the formula *somo'si aśvibhyām pacyasva* . . . *surā* becomes ready for the deities.

In *MānŚS*, V.2.4.4, it is stated that the Adhvaryu mixes the ingredients of *surā* with the verse *svādvīṁ tvā svādunā* and touches that mixture with the recitation of *somo'si aśvibhyāṁ pacyasva*. . . . According to *ŚatBrā*, V.5.4.20 however, the ingredients are mixed with the recitation of the verse *somo'si aśvibhyām pacyasva*. The verse *svādvīṁ tvā svādunā* . . . is not cited in it. Following it, the *KātyŚS* also does not employ it. The procedure given there is as follows: The Adhvaryu first cooks the rice of the unsprouted paddy and pulverises the sprouted paddy. Then he mixes that flour in the cooked rice with the recitation of the verse *somo'si aśvibhyām pacyasva* . . . (*KātyŚS*, XV.9.24).

A few more details are added in the *VārāŚS*. The Adhvaryu cooks the rice on the *gārhapatya* fire and mixes the *tokma*, the *nagnahu* (not explained here) and the *lājā* 'parched grains' in that rice. This mixture is called the *māsara*. He mixes the *śaṣpa* in it with the recitation of the verse *svādvīṁ tvā svādunā*, and saying *somo'si aśvibhyām pacyasva* . . . he puts it near the mounds (*VārāŚS*, III.2.7.4, 5)

According to *ĀpaŚS*, XIX.1.5, the Adhvaryu draws paddy for the three deities, namely the Aśvins, Sarasvatī and Indra Sutrāman. He cooks rice of that paddy (*ĀpaŚS*, XIX.1.6). According to *VaikhāŚS*, XI.1, only one half of the paddy is cooked and the remaining half is parched on the *gārhapatya* fire. Then the Adhvaryu digs a ditch to the east of the *gārhapatya* fire and mixes *surā* in it in the usual procedure. Now the mixture is called the *parisrut* (*ĀpaŚS*, XIX.1.7, 8). He mixes the *śaṣpa* in that mixture with the recitation of the verse *svādvīṁ tvā svādunā* . . . (*ĀpaŚS*, XIX.1.9). The procedure described in *HirŚS*, XIII.8.4-6 and *VaikhāŚS*, XI.1 is similar up to this point. Further, it is added in *VaikhāŚS*, XI.2 that the Adhvaryu should touch the mixture while saying, *somo'si aśvibhyām pacyasva*. . . . According to *HirŚS*, XIII.8.7, the sacrificer consecrates the *surā*, with the recitation of *somo'si aśvibhyām pacyasva* . . ., while it is being mixed with *śaṣpa*.

According to *BaudhŚS*, XVII.31, paddy is already drawn at the time of placing the paraphernalia. The Adhvaryu pounds a half of it and putting a new pot on the *gārhapatya* fire, cooks it pouring much water in it. The other half he parches on a potsherd. Thus are produced the *lājās*. Those, which do not burst open after parching are called *tarī*. He pours the cooked rice in a perforated container called *pājaka* or *kaṭhina*, hangs that pot and collects the scum of the rice in a pot. He pulverises the *tarī* and mixes its powder in the scum. This mixture is called the *māsara*. Then he takes one measure of sprouted barley *śaṣpa*, two measures of sprouted paddy *tokma*, three of parched grains and four of pulses *nagnahu* (cf. *BaudhŚS*, XXVI.22). After pulverising these substances, he pours that powder and the *māsara* in the rice while reciting *svādvīṁ tvā svādunā*.

Then he takes a stool through the eastern door of the *āhavanīya* fire and puts it outside the fire-hall in the southern direction. He puts the supporting ring *iṇḍva* on that stool. Then he puts the pitcher on that ring and puts the lid *kārotara* upon that pitcher. The *kārotara*, as described in *BaudhŚS*, XXVI.22 is "made of wood or bamboo or clay. It is covered with hide on all sides. It is called *sutāsutī*, for, the *surā*, which flows out, conduces to the attainment of heaven, while that which does not flow out indeed causes one remain on earth." After putting the lid on that pitcher he plasters the cooked rice around the rim of the *kārotara* and thus covers the pitcher. Then he touches the pitcher with the recitation of *somo'si aśvibhyām pacyasva*. . . .

Thus mixed, the mixture remains for three nights (*BaudhŚS*, XVII. 32; *ĀpaŚS*, XIX.1.10; *KāṭhS*, XII.9; *VaikhāŚS*, XI.2; *HirŚS*, XIII.8.8). It is kept for three nights, since *soma*, after it is bought, also remains for three nights[10] (*KāṭhS*, XII.9. and *TaiBrā*, I.8.5.17).

It is clear thus, that the period of the fermentation is decided with a view to achieving similarity with *soma*. In some texts, however, the time prescribed is different. According to *ŚatBrā*, V.5.4.22 and *KātyŚS*, XV.10.1, the mixture is kept only for one day. *KātyŚS*, XV.10.1 prescribes that it may optionally be kept for a period which is necessary for the proper fermentation. Similar is

---

10. The reason why the *soma*, which is bought, is kept for three nights is told in a myth in *TaiS*, VI.1.5. It reads, *taṁ somaṁ āhriyamāṇaṁ gandharvo viśvāvasuḥ paryamuṣṇāt sa tisro rātrīḥ parimuṣito avasat* | *tasmāt tisro rātrīḥ somo vasati* "Gandharva Viśvāvasu stole the *soma*, which was being brought. Thus stolen it remained for three nights."

the prescription in *MānŚS*, V.2.4.6 which states that the sacrificer observes fast for animal-sacrifice, only when he is sure that the *surā* will be ready the next day.

THE PURIFICATION OF *SURĀ*

On the fourth day, i.e., on the day of the actual performance of the *sautrāmaṇī*, *surā* is purified after the ritual regarding the animal-sacrifice is performed up to the offering of the omenta and the formal sprinkling (*ŚatBrā*, V.5.4.21; *BaudhŚS*, XVII.33,34 and *KātyŚS*, XV.10.9). According to *ĀpaŚS*, XIX.1.13 and *HirŚS*, XIII.8.17, it is purified when the ritual regarding the animal-sacrifice is performed up to the formal dedication of the animals, whereas *MānŚS*, V.2.4.17 and *VārāŚS*, III.2.7.10 prescribe that the purification takes place after the clarified butter is kept at its proper place, in the preparatory rites.

The Adhvaryu digs out *surā* and puts it on the head of a brāhmaṇa (*VārāŚS*, III.2.7.11; *ĀpaŚS*, XIX.1.18) or on a mound (*ĀpaŚS*, XIX.1.18). According to *VaikhāŚS*, XI.2 and *HirŚS*, XIII.8.17, *surā*, after it is dug out, is poured into the pot *sata*.

According to *BaudhŚS*, XVII.33, it is the Pratiprasthātṛ, who purifies *surā*. After the animal-offerings are made, he is told by the Adhvaryu to see if *surā* is ready. Then the Pratiprasthātṛ goes out of the fire-hall, filters the *surā*, and with the implements necessary for the purification, he brings it in by the eastern door and puts it within the altar. While the Adhvaryu is doing his own work, the Pratiprasthātṛ, purifies the *surā* in the *sata*. He purifies it with a strainer made of hair, putting the ends of the strainer towards the north (*BaudhŚS*, XVII.34).

According to *MānŚS*, V.2.4.14 also, the Pratiprasthātṛ purifies the *surā*. After the clarified butter is put within the altar, in the preparatory rites, the Pratiprasthātṛ puts the pitcher of *surā* on the head of the Āgnīdhra, who is standing near the rubbish-heap. Then he goes along the west of the fire-hall to the south of it and puts that pitcher on his own mound, i.e., the mound, which is prepared to the south of the altar. Since the Pratiprasthātṛ performs the ritual regarding the *surā* on this mound, it is called his own mound.[11]

Then the Adhvaryu (or the Pratiprasthātṛ, according to *BaudhŚS*, XVII.34 and *MānŚS*, V.2.4.18), purifies *surā* reciting the verse *punātu te parisrutaṁ somaṁ sūryasya duhitā | vāreṇa śaśvatā tanā |* (cf. *TaiBrā*, I.8.5.17; *ĀpaŚS*, XIX.1.18; *VaikhāŚS*, XI.2; *VārāŚS*, III.2.7.11 and *HirŚS*, XIII.8.17).

In *KāṭhS*, XII.9 and *MaiS*, II.3.8 only the *mantra* is cited. Its employment is not prescribed.

According to *TaiBrā*, I.8.5.17, he purifies it thus for making it distinct (*vyāvṛttyai*). Bhaṭṭa Bhāskara, while commenting upon this text, explains the idea that the Adhvaryu makes it distinct from the *surā* used in day-to-day life (*laukikī surā*) and makes it fit for ritual purpose.

Surā is purified with a strainer, as *soma* also is purified with a strainer. The Adhvaryu recites *vāreṇa śaśvatā tanā*, as with *vāra* or *vāla*, i.e., with hair only, *soma* is purified (*TaiBrā*, I.8.5.17).

According to *ŚatBrā*, V.5.4.22 and *KātyŚS*, XV.10.9, *surā* is purified with the *darbha* blades and not with the strainer made of hair. The verse to be recited at the time of the purification is also, according to them, different. The verse prescribed by these texts is,

vāyuḥ pūtaḥ pavitreṇa pratyaṅ somo'tidrutaḥ |
indrasya yujyaḥ sakhā |

But *TaiBrā*, I.8.5.17 protests that *surā* should not be purified with *vāyuḥ pūtaḥ pavitreṇa*, as this verse is imperfect (*vyṛddha*). Only for one, who is excessively purged by *soma*, *surā* should be purified by this verse. This prescription is found in *BaudhŚS*, XVII.34;

---

11. In the *Śrautakośa*, this portion is translated as, "The Pratiprasthātṛ should place the pitcher of wine upon the head of the Āgnīdhra who is standing near the rubbish-heap, and cause him to carry it along the rear of the sanctuary of the sacred fires towards the south and to put it down upon the (southern) mound." *ŚK*, Vol.1 English Section, Part II, p. 914.

HirŚS, XIII.8.18; *VārāŚS*, III.2.7.12; *VaikhāŚS*, XI.3 and *KāṭhS*, XII.9 also. In *KāṭhS*, XII.9, it is prescribed also for one who is deprived of something.

The same verse, but with a little modification is prescribed to be employed while purifying *surā* for one, who has vomited *soma*. Thus it is prescribed in *ĀpaŚS*, XIX.1.19; *HirŚS*, XIII.8.18; *VaikhāŚS*, XI.3; *VārāŚS*, III.2.7.12 that for a *somavāmin*, the verse should be *vāyuḥ pūtaḥ pavitreṇa, prān somo'tidrutaḥ. . . .*

It is only the *ŚatBrā* and the *KātyŚS*, which prescribe that the Adhvaryu should pour, at this time, the powder of *kuvala*, *karkandhu* and *badara* in *surā*; for, when Indra spat out thrice, these were the three things produced therefrom. The Adhvaryu now supplies the sacrificer with these things and makes him whole (*ŚatBrā*, V.5.4.22 and *KātyŚS*, XV.10.10).

The Procedure in Connection with the Kaukilī

THE BUYING OF THE INGREDIENTS

The ingredients of *surā* are enumerated in *ŚatBrā*, XII.7.2.9. They are paddy, wheat, millet (*śyāmāka*), *indra*-grains (*upavāka*), barley, sprouted paddy *śaṣpa*, sprouted barley *tokma* and three kinds of berries called *badara*, *karkandhu* and *kuval*, "Thus the sacrificer acquires food which is cultivated and which is not cultivated. Verily, by means of both these kinds of food the sacrificer duly places energy and vital power in himself."

ŚatBrā, XII.7.2.12 strongly protests against the view expressed in the *TaiBrā*, the *KāṭhS* and the *MaiS* that the ingredients should be bought from a eunuch (*klība*). Thus it states,

> The other priests buy the *śaṣpa* from a eunuch saying, a eunuch is neither a man nor a woman and the *sautrāmaṇī* is neither an *iṣṭi* nor an animal-offering. But this should not be done. The *sautrāmaṇī* is both an *iṣṭi* as well as an animal-offering. The eunuch is someone imperfect among men. Therefore, those who buy with lead place imperfection

> in the very mouth (i.e., the beginning)[12] of the sacrifice. Hence, it should be bought from a seller of *soma*. He thus puts a form of *soma* at the very mouth of the sacrifice, for the perfection of the sacrifice.

The reason why *śaṣpa* is to be bought with lead is also given differently in *ŚatBrā*, XII.7.2.10. Thus it is stated,

> The Adhvaryu buys *śaṣpa* with lead, as the lead is the form of both — gold and iron, and both is the *sautrāmaṇī* — an *iṣṭi* and an animal-offering. Therefore, to secure both of these, he buys it with lead.

It is not only the *śaṣpa* that is bought. According to *ŚatBrā*, XII.7.2.10, the Adhvaryu buys *śaṣpa*, *tokma* and paddy. *KātyŚS*, XIX.1.18 states that instead of paddy the Adhvaryu buys parched grains. According to *ĀpaŚS*, XIX.5.7, the Adhvaryu has already bought paddy, barley and millet. It does not prescribe *śaṣpa*; however, it is stated that after buying these things, the Adhvaryu ties the paddy in linen cloth and keeps it for germination.

The additional ingredients are bought in exchange of some other additional things. The paddy, barley and millet are bought with black iron, black thread and black garment (*ĀpaŚS*, XIX.5.7). The *tokma* is bought with wool and parched grains or the paddy is bought with thread (*KātyŚS*, XIX.1.18; *ŚatBrā*, XII.7.2.11).

After buying them, the Adhvaryu enters into the fire-hall through the southern door and places the same behind the *gārhapatya* fire.

MIXING OF THE INGREDIENTS

At the time of preparing *surā*, the Adhvaryu parches the barley a little and pulverises it (*ĀpaŚS*, XIX.5.7). The fine powder he mixes with curds or buttermilk and stirs it with *darbha* blades. This mixture is called *māsara* (*ĀpaŚS*, XIX.5.8-9).

12. For the meaning of *yajñamukha* see also J. Gonda, "Vedic Gods and the Sacrifice", in *Numen*, Vol. XXX, Fasc. 1, July 1983, p. 5.

It is only in the *ĀpaŚS* and the *HirŚS* that curds or buttermilk is prescribed in the procedure of *surā*.

The barley, which is crushed, but has not become fine powder, he mixes into the remnants of the oblation material (*saṁsrāva*). In this context, he mixes it into the milk that is remaining after making the *agnihotra* offerings. This mixture is called *nagnahu*.

The Adhvaryu pulverises millet. At the time of preparing *surā*, he mixes together *tokma*, *māsara* and *nagnahu*. Then he scatters one-third of the millet-flour in that mixture and, reciting the verse *parito ṣiñcatā sutam* . . ., he pours milk of one cow in it. On the second day, he pours for a second time one more third part of the millet-flour and the milk of two cows in it. On the third day, he pours the remaining flour and milk of three cows in it (*ĀpaŚS*, XIX.5.11).

In connection with the *caraka sautrāmaṇī*, it is said in *ĀpaŚS*, XIX.1.7 and *HirŚS*, XIII.8.5 that the pitcher containing this mixture is put into a pit. In connection with that, it is further stated in *ĀpaŚS*, XIX.6.1 and *HirŚS*, XXIII.1.10 that some teachers prescribe a *kārotara* instead of a pit. The pitcher should be put in a *kārotara* and then put into a pit or the pitcher should be put in a *kārotara* instead of in a pit. The *kārotara* is made of bamboo and is covered with hide. A spout is attached to that *kārotara*. Its opening is covered with hide. When *surā* flows into it, it is called *parisrut* (*ĀpaŚS*, XIX.6.2 to 5 and *HirŚS*, XXIII.1.11-14). Though clear in meaning, the *sūtra*s do not give a clear picture of the exact procedure.

It is to be noted here that the employment of the verses *svādvīṁ tvā svādunā*. . . and *somo'si aśvibhyām pacyasva* . . . is not stated by the *sūtrakāra*s. According to the commentary on *HirŚS*, XXIII.1.11, the verse *svādvīṁ tvā svādunā* . . . is employed at the time of mixing together *tokma*, *māsara* and *nagnahu*.

According to *MānŚS*, V.2.11.3 and *VārāSS*, III.2.8.1, the procedure in connection with the *kaukilī sautrāmaṇī* is similar to that which is described in connection with the *caraka sautrāmaṇī* up to the mixing of the ingredients. Then, at the dawn of the second day, the Adhvaryu pours in it fresh milk of a cow. At the dawn of the third day, he pours fresh milk of two cows in it. Both the times, he pours it, saying *parīto ṣiñcatā sutam*. . . .

According to these two *sūtra*s, milk is not poured for a third time.

The procedure in the *KātyŚS* is as follows:

> After the Adhvaryu has bought the ingredients, he first pulverises the *nagnahu*. The word *nagnahu* is explained variously in different texts. In *BaudhŚS*, XXVI.22, it is the pulses; in *ĀpaŚS*, XIX.5.10, the mixture of *surā* is called the *nagnahu*, whereas the commentator Karkācārya explains it at *KātyŚS*, XIX.1.20 as a kind of root, used as catalytic agent, which accelerates the process of fermentation. Vidyādhara on *KātyŚS*, XIX.1.20 and Mahīdhara, in his commentary on *VājaS*, X.31, have stated that *nagnahu* means some medicinal herbs.[13]

After pulverising the *nagnahu*, he cooks paddy and millet separately, putting much extra water in them. After cooking, he separates the scum from the rice and mixes the flour of *nagnahu* in the scum. This mixture is called *māsara* (*KātyŚS*, XIX.1.20). Then he mixes the rice of paddy and millet with the *māsara*, reciting *svādvīṁ tvā svādunā* . . . *ŚatBrā*, XII.7.3.5 explains that as he recites this verse he makes *surā* sweet and makes it a form of *soma*.

According to *ŚatBrā*, XII.7.3.6, he recites the verse *somo'si aśvibhyām pacyasva*. . . . It then explains the reason for this as, 'the Aśvins, Sarasvatī and Sutrāman Indra were the deities', who first performed this sacrifice. As he recites this verse, he performs the sacrifice with this verse. He thereby gives them their own share and makes the *surā* a form of *soma*-pressing.

---

13. To add herbs, while making beer is an old practice as is stated in *Encyclopeadia Britannica*, article mentioned above, p. 314. Thus it is said there, As from ancient times, it was the custom to add spices and herbs to beer. P. Gogoi and S. Boissya give a long list of various herbs used by the people of Mongolian origin residing in the State of Assam. These people use these herbs, it is stated, for yeast formation in the procedure of the preparation of country-liqour. See, "A Method of Preparation of Beer from Rice. . .", *Anthropos*, 1979-84, 1-3, pp. 248-50.

The *KātyŚS*, does not prescribe the employment of this verse. Instead, it prescribes the verse *aṁśunā te aṁśuḥ. . .* (*KātyŚS*, XIX.1.21).

On the first night, he milks a cow after having touched her, saying *aśvibhyāṁ tvā apākaromi* 'I take you away for the Aśvins', and pours the milk in the mixture. On the second morning, he touches two cows saying, *sarasvatyai tvā apākaromi* 'I take you away for Sarasvatī', milks them and pours the milk in the mixture. On the third day, he milks three cows after touching them, saying, *indrāya sutrāmṇe apākaromi* 'I take you away for Indra Sutrāman', and pours their milk in the mixture. "As he so pours he thereby provides the sacrificer with suitable forms and suitable deities." (*ŚatBrā*, XII.8.2.11).

While pouring the milk, he recites the verse, *parīto ṣiñcatā sutam. . .* to make the *surā* a form of *soma* (*ŚatBrā*, XII.8.2.12).

On the first day together with the milk for the Aśvins, he spreads the powder of sprouted paddy also in that mixture (*KātyŚS*, XIX.1.23). The reason is given in *ŚatBrā*, XII.8.2.8 as

> The sprouted paddy is indeed the form of the morning-pressing. The morning-pressing is this world and it relates to the Aśvins. When on the first night the Adhvaryu pours the milk for the Aśvins in it, he thus provides the sacrificer with the morning-pressing with its own world, with its own deity and with its own form.

On the second day, together with the milk for Sarasvatī, he pours the powder of sprouted barley also in the mixture (*KātyŚS*, XIX.1.25). The reason given in *ŚatBrā*, XII.8.2.9 is,

> The sprouted barley is the form of the midday-pressing. The midday-pressing is, as it were, the air and it relates to Sarasvatī; when the Adhvaryu pours in that mixture the milk taken for Sarasvatī, he thus provides the sacrificer with the midday-pressing with its own world, own deity and own form.

On the third night, together with the milk for Indra Sutrāman, he pours the powder of parched grains (*KātyŚS*, XIX.1.27). The reason stated in *ŚatBrā*, XII.8.2.10 is,

> The parched paddy is, as it were, the form of the evening-pressing, the evening-pressing is the sky and it relates to Indra. When the Adhvaryu pours in that mixture the milk taken for Indra, he thus provides the sacrificer with the evening-pressing, with its own world, own deity and own form.

Mahīdhara, in his commentary upon *VājaS*, XIX.1, explains the division of these powders. According to him, the powders of *śaṣpa, tokma,* and *lājā*s are divided into three parts. The first one-third he further divides into two and pours separately into the scums of paddy and millet. The other one-third also he divides into two and pours into the rice of paddy and rice of millet; and the remaining one-third of the powders of the *śaṣpa*, *tokma* and the *lājā*s he pours into the mixture on the first, the second and the third day.

Thus mixed, the mixture remains for three nights. The period of the fermentation is decided so as 'to make the mixture a form of *soma*' (*ŚatBrā*, XII.7.3.6).

THE PURIFICATION OF *SURĀ*

According to *KātyŚS*, XIX.2.6, *surā* is first filtered and then purified. The Adhvaryu digs a pit to the west of the right buttock of the altar. He places a hide in that pit. He then pours *surā* on that hide and places the *kārotara* 'sieve' upon it so that the liquid portion of *surā* oozes out into the *kārotara* and the thick residue remains at the bottom. Alternatively the Adhvaryu pours *surā* into the *kārotara* and takes the purified *surā* from the *kārotara* on the hide. In this case, the residue remains in the *kārotara*.

The latter option is indicated by the line *kārotareṇa dadhato gavāṁ tvaci* (*VājaS*, XIX.8). "They take it with the *kārotara* on the hide of the bull (or cow)."

The filtered *surā* is collected with the recitation of the verse, *siñcanti pariṣiñcanti*. . .

According to *ŚatBrā*, XII.7.3.11,

> the Adhvaryu purifies *surā* with *punātu te parisrutam* . . . for one who is desirous of prosperity, to get the prosperity. When he recites *somaṁ sūryasya duhitā*, *surā* becomes *soma* by faith. By faith only he makes it *soma* (also *KātyŚS*, XIX. *MānŚS*, V.2.4.18).

If the sacrificer is one, who is excessively purged by *soma*, the Adhvaryu purifies *surā* with *vāyoḥ pūtaḥ pavitreṇa pratyaṅ somo-'tidrutaḥ indrasya yujyaḥ sakhā*, and, if the sacrificer is one who has vomited *soma* then he purifies it with the modification, *vāyoḥ pūtaḥ pavitreṇa prāṅ somo'tidrutaḥ* . . . (*ŚatBrā*, XII.7.3.9.10; *KātyŚS*). The *mantra* is modified differently in the *MānŚS*. Thus according to *MānŚS*, V.2.11.13, the *surā* is purified with the *mantra*, *vāyuḥ pūtaḥ pavitreṇa* . . . if the sacrificer is a *somavāmin* and if he is a *somātipūta*, it should be purified with the verse *vāyoḥ pūtaḥ pavitreṇa*. . . .

It is stated in the *ŚatBrā* that

> when the Adhvaryu purifies *surā* in this manner, he thereby purifies the sacrificer in the right manner, and deposits in him the strength and power which had gone away from him.

VārāŚS, III.2.8.8 prescribes that the Adhvaryu purifies *surā*, following the prescription for its purification in the *caraka*.

The *ĀpaŚS* and *HirŚS* prescribe for the purification of *surā* a different verse. Thus, *ĀpaŚS*, XIX.6.13 and *HirŚS*, XXIII.1.23 prescribe that the Pratiprasthātṛ purifies *surā* through a strainer made of hair of a cow and a horse. He purifies it with the verse *brahma kṣatram pavate teja indriyam*. . . .

VaitāSū, XXX.7 prescribes that the verse *vāyoḥ pūtaḥ pavitreṇa* . . . should be used for the consecration of *surā*,with the necessary modifications in it.

When the Adhvaryu is purifying *surā*, the Brahman priest

recites the verse,

adhvaryo adribhiḥ sutaṁ somam pavitra ānaya ǀ
punāhīndrāya pātave ǀ— *VaitāSū*, XXX.9 and *KātyŚS*.

In *LāṭyāŚS*, V.4.11, it is prescribed that, whenever the Adhvaryu is going through any rites connected with the preparation of *surā*, the Brahman priest should sit down by his side.

It is evident from the discussion above that the procedure of the preparation of *surā* is almost the same in all theVedic texts. The difference lies only in the measures of the ingredients, and in respect of what they mean by the words *nagnahu*, *māsara*, etc. The only difference is between the procedure described in the *Taittirīya* tradition and that in the other texts in connection with the *kaukilī*. It is only according to the *sūtra* texts of the *Taittirīya*s (i.e., *ĀpaŚS* and the *HirŚS*) that the curds, buttermilk and the *saṁsrāva*s of the *agnihotra* offerings are used in the preparation of *surā* — such is not the case elsewhere. Similarly, there is not much difference between the procedures described in connection with the *caraka* and the *kaukilī*. The only and main difference is the **addition** of milk in the preparation of *surā* in the *kaukilī*. There is no reference to the pouring of the milk in the description of the preparation of *surā* in the *caraka sautrāmaṇī*. Even in the *kaukilī* ritual, it is clear, milk was not an important ingredient of *surā*. It is added for an altogether different purpose. In *ŚatBrā*, XII.8.2.11 it is stated that when he pours in that mixture the milk taken for the Aśvins, the Adhvaryu provides the sacrificer with the morning-pressing. On the second night, when he pours in that mixture the milk taken for Sarasvatī, he provides the sacrificer with the midday-pressing and when, on the third night, he pours the milk taken for Indra, he thereby provides the sacrificer with the evening-pressing.[14] Thus the main purpose behind the addition of the milk is to achieve similarity with

---

14. The original passage in *ŚatBrā*, XII.8.2.5-10 reads: *āśvinena payasā prathamām rātriṁ abhiṣiñcati svenaivainametallokena svayā devatayā svena rūpeṇa prātassavanena samarddhayati* ǀ*sārasvatena payasā . . . mādhyandinena savanena . . .* ǀ *aindreṇa payasā. . . tṛtīyasavanena. . .* ǀ

the *soma*-ritual, and to elevate the drink *surā* by comparing it with *soma*.

Similar tendency of elevating the *surā*-drink by comparing it with *soma* or *soma*-ritual is found when the time of the fermentation is decided. Nothing can be said with certainty about the necessary period of fermentation of *surā* in the Vedic texts. It is observed that, in these texts, the time varies from one day up to whatever period is necessary for fermentation. Thus it is said in *KātyŚS*, XV.10.1, 2

> *tripaśuḥ paśubandhaḥ śvaḥ* |
> *caturthyām pakvāyāṁ vā* |

> The animal-sacrifice consisting of three animals is performed on the next day or on the fourth day or when *surā* is ready.

In *MānŚS*, V.2.4.6 also, it is said,

> *śvaḥ surā janiteti paśubandhāyo'pavasati* |

> When he is sure that the *surā* will be ready 'tomorrow', he observes fast for the animal-sacrifice.

In other texts the period is of three days, and this period is fixed mainly for achieving similarity of that procedure with the procedure of the preparation of *soma*.

The knowledge of the Vedic ritualists about the preparation of *surā* seems to be quite advanced, since the use of sprouted grains is a later development in the process of preparing liquor. Previously it was prepared only through infusion. About the importance of the sprouted grains in the process of fermentation it is stated,

> The basis of all beer production is the fermentation of starch in amylaceous cereals. Grain always contains a small quantity of directly fermentable sugar, but this is inadequate in amount for producing an alcoholic drink. As starch itself cannot ferment unless split into fermentable sugars, it is usually first subjected to malting, i.e., letting grain germinate, a process during which starch is converted

into maltose and considerable amounts of diastose are developed. . . .[15]

One more point should be discussed in connection with the preparation of *surā*. It is stated by Rajendralal Mitra that *surā* was used in important rites like the *vājapeya* and the *sautrāmaṇī*. It was first fermented and then distilled. However, (he adds further), he could not find any description of a still in which the distillation was effected.[16] Allchin also has similarly argued that distillation was known in ancient India. He held that the existence of a still of Vedic times, could be proved. This argument is based mainly on the pots found by Prof. Marshall in his excavations and some words occurring in the *Śrauta Sūtra*s in connection with the preparation of *surā*. The words he has quoted are *śuṇḍa*, *kārotara* and *iṇḍva*. He has stated that if these pots are arranged suitably, they would represent a still. It should be noted here, however, that these words are from the different *sūtra*s. No single *sūtra* uses all these words together. According to *BaudhŚS*, XVII.32 *iṇḍva* is used, *kārotara* is also used but the *śuṇḍa* (the sprout) is not used. It states further that a *kārotara* is used just as a lid. There is no reference in any *sūtra* to the placing of the mixture on burning fire, which is essential for distillation. From the detailed description of the preparation of *surā*, it is evident that the beverage was prepared only through fermentation and it did not at all undergo the process of distillation.[17]

While learning about the Vedic religion, it is useful to take into consideration the Avestan religion as both are connected to each

---

15. *Food, the Gift of Orisis*, *op.cit.*, p. 534 and also *Gastronomy*, *op.cit.*, pp. 74ff.

    For a detailed description and analysis of the procedure of malting and making a fermented drink, see also D.E. Briggo *Barley*, pp. 526 ff. and also pp. 573-7.

16. Rajendralal Mitra, *Indo-Aryans*, Vol. 1, p. 390.

17. See F.R. Allchin, "India: The Ancient Home of Distillation" in '*Man*' *The Journal of the Royal Anthropological Institute*, New Series, Vol. 14, 1979, pp. 55-63.

other. In the Avesta, also, one comes across the word *hurā*, which means *surā*. In a dictionary[18] it is translated as Milchwein, Kumys, *der Wein der (aus) Pferdemilch*. It seems to be a wine prepared from milk, especially the horse's milk. In Vedic *surā* also, as we have seen, milk is used, but only superficially. It is not an important invariable ingredient. Vedic *surā* is basically a beer prepared from cereals. One cannot be sure, therefore, about whether both these words denote the same drink. Further, there is no reference in the Avesta to the offering or any ritual use of *surā*.

In the Vedic texts, the description of the preparation of *surā* is very brief, compared to the description of *soma*. It is possible that since *soma* was the drink of the brāhmaṇas, it has got more attention in the ritual texts. And if it is so, there is no wonder in it. In the literature of the other countries, also, similar tendency is found. Regarding Egypt also, it is observed, that less is known about beer than about wine, as beer was the usual drink of the commoners, while wine was the beverage of the rich.[19]

---

18 *Altiranisches Wörterbuch*, von Christian Bartholomae, Berlin, 1961 (Reprint), p. 1837.

19. *Food, the Gift of Orisis, op.cit.*, pp. 531ff.

9

The Ritual of the Kaukilī Sautrāmaṇī

THE ritual of the *kaukilī sautrāmaṇī* is similar to the ritual of the *caraka sautrāmaṇī*. The duration also is the same; just like the *caraka*, the *kaukilī* also lasts for four days (*ĀpaŚS*, XIX.5.2; *HirŚS*, XXIII.1.2; *MānŚS*, V.2.11.1). Similarly, there are animal-offerings and also the offerings of milk and *surā* in this sacrifice. These animal-offerings and the *iṣṭi*s are performed separately (*KātyŚS*, XIX.6.1).

On these days, the sacrificer offers the regular *agnihotra* offerings.[1] He eats only that whatever has remained after these offerings are made and he observes the vow of speaking truth (*KātyŚS*, XIX.1.12-15).

There is some discussion in the *ŚatBrā* in this regard. Suplā, the son of Sṛñjaya asked Pratīdarśa, the son of Ibhāvata,

> In this sacrifice, neither the sacrificer is initiated, nor are pressed the *soma*-stalks, then how can it be considered to be a *soma* sacrifice?

On this answered Pratīdarśa,

---

1. It is only the *KātyŚS* which directly mentions that the daily *agnihotra* offerings are offered (*KātyŚS*, XIX.1.15). But an indirect reference to it is found in the *ĀpaŚS* also. In connection with the preparation of *surā*, it is stated in *ĀpaŚS*, XIX.5.10 that "coarse flour of paddy, barley and millet is mixed with the *saṁsrāvas*", i.e., the remnants of milk of the *agnihotra* offerings.

> The observance of a vow is the head of the sacrifice, and the initiation (*dīkṣā*) is its soul. The truth is a kind of a vow. And the faith is a kind of initiation. Mind is the form of the sacrificer and the speech represents, the sacrificer. When the sacrificer observes the vow through speech, he places the head of the sacrifice in himself; he places the truth in faith and places himself in the sacrifice. And therefore, the observance of the vow in connection with speech is considered as the initiation in this sacrifice. — *ŚatBrā*, XII.8.2.3-6

The Rites to be Performed three days before the Actual Performance of the Sacrifice

The main rite on this day is that of the preparation of *surā*. At the time when the Adhvaryu draws grains for *surā*, he immolates an animal for Indra. The sacrificer gives away a bull as the sacrificial gift of that offering. Then the Adhvaryu offers *caru* to Aditi and the sacrificer gives away a calf as sacrificial gift (*ŚatBrā*, XII.9.2.11; *ĀpaŚS*, XIX.5.3-6; *HirŚS*, XXIII.1.3-5). *VārāŚS*, III.2.8.4 prescribes that this *caru* should be prepared in ghee.

According to some teachers, the order of these rites can be changed. One may first offer the animal to Indra and then the *caru* to Aditi (*KātyŚS*, XIX.1.7). The *VaitāSū* also follows this order (*VaitāŚū*, XXX.45).

There is a difference of opinion among the Vedic texts as regards the order of these offerings and the preparation of *surā* also. The order in the *VārāŚS* and the *MānŚS* is that, *surā* should be prepared first, following the procedure of the *caraka* and these offerings should be offered afterwards, whereas, according to the *ĀpaŚS*; the *HirŚS* and the *KātyŚS* these offerings should be offered first and *surā* should be prepared afterwards. The *MānŚS* does not prescribe the offering of the *caru*. According to it, only a bull to Indra is to be offered. The procedure of some other rites is also given in it differently. Thus it is stated in it:

When the sacrificer is sure that the *surā* will be ready on

> the third day, he observes fast in connection with the animal offering to Indra. Then, on the next, i.e., on the second day, are given the animal-offerings to Indra and on the same day, the sacrificer observes fast in connection with the animal-sacrifice to be preformed on the next day. On the third day, when the *surā* is ready, the priests move towards the north and perform the ritual of the *surā*-offerings and the animal-offerings (*MānŚS*, V.2.11.5-11).[2]

The *hautra* in connection with this animal-offering to Indra is similar to that in an animal-sacrifice (*ĀpaHauPari*, II.3). There are seventeen *sāmidhenī* verses in connection with that offering and also in connection with the *iṣṭi* (*KātyŚS*, XIX.6.2). When the Adhvaryu gives out the call *samidbhyaḥ preṣya*, the Maitrāvaruṇa gives out the call to the Hotr̥, with *hotā yakṣad samiddhendraṁ iḍaspade....* The Hotr̥ then recites the offering verse (*yājyā*). In this manner the Maitrāvaruṇa gives out the calls to the Hotr̥ regarding the *prayāja*s and the Hotr̥ recites the respective *yājyā*s of those *prayāja*s, (*ĀpaHauPari*, II.3). The first *anuvāka* (*MaiS*, III.2.1), which begins with the verse *samiddha indra uṣasām aṇīke* . . . is used as the *prayāja-yājyā*s (*MānŚS*, V.2.11.7 and *KātyŚS*, XIX.6.12). If the sacrificer belongs to the Vasiṣṭha or the Śaunaka *gotra*, the second divinity in the *prayāja* offerings should be *narāśaṁsa* instead of *tanūnapāt*. According to some teachers, this modification should be followed also in the case of the sacrificer who belongs to the Atri-*gotra* (*KātyŚS*, XIX.6.8,9). The calls relating to the *prayāja*s and the *anūyāja*s of this animal offering are the normal ones, viz. those listed in the *praiṣādhyāya* of the *R̥gveda-Khilas*, V.7.1.

---

2. The *ŚrautaKośa* (Vol. 1, English Section, Part II, p. 926) interprets these *sūtra*s differently. According to it, "After three days, on the very day on which he expects the wine to be ready, he should go through the Upavasatha rites in connection with the animal-offerings to Indra, as prescribed (in the animal-sacrifice). On the following day, he should offer a bull to Indra. On the same day, he should move towards the north and treat that day as the Upavasatha-day (in connection with the offering of the three animals)."

The *mantras* relating to the carrying round of the fire and the offering of the *ājyabhāgas* are the same as those prescribed in connection with the animal sacrifice, (*ĀpaHauPari*, II.3). Thus, the *ājyabhāgas* should have the word *vṛtraghna* in them. Or, since the animal-offering is a modification of *sānnāyya*, they should have the word *vṛdhanvat* in them (*KātyŚS*, XIX.6.3,4).

In connection with the offering of the omentum, the verse *ā carṣaṇiprā*... is used as the *puronuvākyā* and the verse *viveśa yan mā* ... is used as the *yājyā*. The Maitrāvaruṇa recites the verse *taṁ sadhrīcīr ūtayaḥ* ... as the *puronuvākyā* and the Hotṛ recites the verse *satyam it tan nā*... as the *yājyā*. The verses *pra sasāhiṣe*... and *sa sevṛdham adhi dhā* ... are used respectively as the *puronuvākyā* and the *yājyā* relating to the offering of the organs (*ĀpaHauPari*, II.3 and *MānŚS*, V.2.11.9).

The verses to be used as the *puronuvākyās* and the *yājyās* in connection with the offering of the omentum, the animal-cake and in connection with the organs of the animals are different according to *KātyŚS*, XIX.6.13. The six verses beginning with *āyātv indro-'vasā* (*VājaS*, XX.47-52) are used for this purpose.

The *mantras* relating to the principal offering are to be recited in low tone. Since there is no specific injunction regarding the *puronuvākyās* and the *yājyās* relating to the *sviṣṭakṛt* offerings, they are in *virāj* metre (*KātyŚS*, XIX.6.7).

While performing the *anūyājas*, etc., the Adhvaryu gives out the call, *devebhyaḥ preṣya.* At that time, the Maitrāvaruṇa gives out the call to the Hotṛ with *devam barhir indram*.... The Hotṛ then recites *devam barhiḥ* ... as the *yājyā* regarding the *anūyāja* of the animal-sacrifice. When the Adhvaryu gives out the call for the *sūktavāka*, the Maitrāvaruṇa gives out the call to the Hotṛ with *agnim adya* .... The Hotṛ then recites the *nigadas* beginning with *idaṁ dyāvāpṛthivī* .... While reciting the *nigadas*, he includes into them the names of the relevant divinities in the sacrifice. The *śaṁyuvāka* and the verses relating to the *patnīsaṁyājas* are the usual ones.

After the offering of the *caru* to Aditi, the Adhvaryu adds three fire-sticks to the *āhavanīya* fire, with the three verses beginning with *abhyādadhāmi*. . . (*KātyŚS*, XIX.1.11).

The Preparation of the Altar

One day before the actual performance of the sacrifice, the priests prepare two altars, like those in the *varuṇapraghāsa*. The northern one is prepared by the Adhvaryu and the southern one is prepared by the Pratiprasthātṛ. The northern one is prepared like that of the *soma*-sacrifice. The difference is only in the size. It is one third of the altar prepared in the *soma*-sacrifice. To the west of these two altars are prepared two mounds. The northern mound is prepared to place the milk cups and the southern one to place the *surā*-cups (*KātyŚS*, XIX.2.1-3).

There is no reference to the preparation of the altar in any other *sūtras*. The procedure seems to be similar to that in the *caraka sautrāmaṇī*. It should be noted here that in the *caraka* an altar is not prepared for the southern fire, only a mound is sufficient for it, even according to *KātyŚS*, XV.10.8. Since the procedure in connection with the *kaukilī* is different, according to the *KātyŚS*, and a separate altar is to be prepared, the *sūtra* describes the procedure of it.

Placing the Necessary Paraphernalia

On the fourth day, he arranges the utensils necessary for the *surā* offerings and the animal-offerings. The Adhvaryu places three vessels for the Aśvins, Sarasvatī and Indra Sutrāman. Then he arranges the powder of three berries viz. *kuvala, karkandhu* and *badara*; the flour of barley, paddy and millet, two eagle-wing-feathers and two strainers of hairs.[3] The strainer which is to be used

3. In the *ŚrautaKośa*, the words *śyenapatre vāle droṇe* are taken as the forms in locative singular and the *sūtra* is translated as, "He should take up, upon the feather of a *śyena* or upon the filter of hair of tail or in a wooden vessel, the flour of parched *kuvala*, *badara* and *karkandhu* . . .", *ŚrautaKośa*, Vol. 1, English Section, Part II p. 923.

by the Adhvaryu is prepared from the hairs of a goat and a ram, while that which is to be used by the Pratiprasthātr̥ is prepared from the hairs of an ox and a horse (*ĀpaŚS*, XIX.5.6-8; *HirŚS*, XXIII.1.15.18). *ŚatBrā*, XII.7.3.13 mentions some more things to be arranged. According to it, the Adhvaryu arranges also the *śatātr̥ṇṇā*, the pot *sata*, the vessel *cappa*, a hundred *māna*s of gold, vessels made of *aśvattha*, *udumbara* and *nyagrodha* wood, some earthen plates and also some additional vessels of *palāśa* wood.

According to *KātyŚS*, XIX.2.4,5 the Adhvaryu performs the rites up to the placing of the clarified butter regarding the northern altar. Regarding the southern one, he performs the rites beginning with taking the wooden sword, etc., following the procedure of the *varuṇapraghāsa*. All the rites regarding *surā* are performed on this altar.

After he has drawn the clarified butter, the Adhvaryu draws much milk. According to Āśmarathya, it is drawn with *mantra*s, while Ālekhana prescribes that it should be drawn without reciting anything (*ĀpaŚS*, XIX.6.9, 10; *HirŚS*, XXIII.1.19-21).

MānŚS does not describe the procedure regarding the placing of the paraphernalia. It only mentions that the ritual up to the purification of milk and *surā* is similar to that in the *caraka sautrāmaṇī* (*MānŚS*, V.2.11.12).

The Purification of Milk and Surā

After he has purified the clarified butter, the Adhvaryu purifies the milk, with the *mantra*, *vāyoḥ pūtaḥ pavitreṇa*. . . . If the sacrificer is a *somavāmin*, he purifies it with the modification *prāṅ somaḥ*. . . and if he is a *somātipūta*, he modifies it as *pratyaṅ somaḥ*. . . (*ĀpaŚS* XIX.6.11-3; *HirŚS*, XXIII.1.22, 23). "When he thus purifies it with this verse, he thereby restores to the sacrificer whatever strength and vigour have gone away from him" (*ŚatBrā*, XII.7.4.9, 10).

It should be noted here, that in connection with the *caraka sautrāmaṇī* the *surā* is purified by this verse, which is used here for the purification of the milk. However, it is not surprising, since the milk is compared to the *soma* by the *ŚatBrā*. Thus it is stated in

XII.7.3.8,

> the milk is like *soma* and the *surā* is food. Since he has taken the milk as the oblation material, he obtains the *soma* thereby and by *surā*, he obtains food.

The *surā* is purified by Pratiprasthātṛ and it is purified with the *mantra*, *brahma kṣatram pavate*. . . . It does not become clear from these *sūtras* whether the *surā* is purified first and the milk afterwards, or the Adhvaryu and the Pratiprasthātṛ purify them simultaneously. The *ŚatBrā* however, specifically mentions at XII.7.3.8 that the *surā* should be purified first and afterwards the milk. It states further,

> Milk is the *kṣatra* and *surā* is the *viś* (i.e., the vaiśya class). When he purifies the milk after the purification of *surā* he produces the *kṣatra* from the *viś*, as it were, since the *kṣatra* is born from the *viś*.

Similar is the procedure in the *KātyŚS* also. The Adhvaryu first purifies the *surā* with *punātu te parisrutam*. . . . A modification is suggested in the *ŚatBrā*. According to it,

> If the sacrificer is one, who is performing this sacrifice with the desire of prosperity, the Adhvaryu purifies the *surā* with this verse. This he does for perfection and prosperity. And by means of faith, he makes that *surā* a form of *soma*.

KātyŚS, XIX.2.10 prescribes that if the sacrificer is *somātipūta*, the Adhvaryu purifies the *surā* with *vāyoḥ pūtaḥ pavitreṇa pratyaṅ somo'tidrutaḥ* . . . and if the sacrificer is a *somavāmin*, he purifies it with the modification *prāṅ somaḥ*. . . .

After he has purified the *surā*, he purifies the milk in a pot made of bamboo. He pours it in that pot through a strainer made of the hair of a goat and a ram. While purifying it, he recites the verse *brahma kṣatram pavate*. . . . While the Adhvaryu is thus purifying the milk, the Brahman consecrates it with the verse *adhvaryo adribhiḥ*. . . . Instead of the hair-strainer, *VārāŚS*, III.2.8.7 prescribes woollen threads to be used as strainer.

MānŚS does not prescribe the procedure of the purification of milk, either in the *caraka sautrāmaṇī* or in the *kaukilī sautrāmaṇī*. According to it, while the *surā* is being purified for a *somavāmin*, the verse should begin with *vāyuḥ pūtaḥ pavitreṇa* . . . and if it is to be purified for a *somātipūta*, the verse should begin with *vāyoḥ pūtaḥ pavitreṇa*. . . . This modification is different from all the other texts. They prescribe the modification in the second *pāda* of the stanza.

After the Pratiprasthātr̥ has thus purified it with this verse, he recites the verse, *brahma kṣatrám pavate*. . . (*MānŚS*, V.2.11.13,14).

It is clear from the description above, that only the *ĀpaŚS*, and the *HirŚS*, prescribe different *mantra*s for the purification of *surā*.

Drawing the Cups

After the purification of *surā* and milk, the cups are drawn for the deities. *ĀpaŚS*, XIX.6.14 prescribes that the Adhvaryu first pours the clarified butter for the animal-sacrifice, and then draws the cups of milk and *surā* (also *HirŚS*, XXIII.1.24).

First he draws the cups of milk and then the cups of *surā*. 'He thereby makes the *viś* follow the *kṣatra*' (*ŚatBrā*, XII.7.3.12).

While taking the cups of milk, he recites the verse *kuvid aṅga yavamanto* . . . as the Puroruk. For all the cups, the same verse is used as the Puroruk. "Thus, the Adhvaryu thereby places the prosperity wholly in the sacrificer." The *ŚatBrā* further explains why the above-mentioned verse is used. Thus it is stated, "The barley is, as if, the stalks of *soma*, and the milk also is *soma*. With the help of *soma*, he thus gives the milk the form of *soma*" (*ŚatBrā*, XII.7.3.13).

A cup made of *aśvattha* wood is used for the Aśvins, of *udumbara* wood for Sarasvatī and a cup of *nyagrodha* wood for Indra, (*KātyŚS*, XIX.2.18-20).

With *upayāmagr̥hīto'si aśvibhyāṁ tvā juṣṭaṁ gr̥hṇāmi*, he fills the cup for the Aśvins, mixes barley flour in it and after wiping it with the purifier puts it on its proper place, reciting the formula, *eṣa te yonir tejase tvā*. . .; with *upayāma* ° . . . *sarasvatyai tvā*. . . he fills the cup for Sarasvatī, mixes wheat-flour in it and after wiping it with the purifier puts it on its proper place, reciting the formula, *eṣa te yonir vīryāya tvā*. . .; with *upayāma*° . . . *indrāya tvā sutrāmṇe* he fills the cup for Indra Sutrāman, mixes the flour of Indra-grains (*upavāka*) in it and after wiping it with the purifier places it on its proper place with *eṣa te yonir balāya tvā*. . . (*ĀpaŚS*, XIX.7.1; *HirŚS*, XXIII.1.26).

According to *VārāŚS*, III.2.8.11, the Adhvaryu mixes paddy-flour in the Āśvina cup, barley-flour in the Sārasvata cup and wheat-flour in the Aindra cup. He wipes these cups with the eagle-wing-feather instead of the purifier and then puts them on their proper places.

KātyŚS, XIX.2.22 prescribes that together with the flour of wheat, *upavāka* and barley; he adds also the powder of *kuvala* in the cup for the Aśvins, powder of *badara* in the cup for Sarasvatī and powder of *karkandhu* in the cup for Indra.

While adding the powder of wheat and *kuvala* to the cup for the Aśvins, he recites the formula *tejo'si*. . ., while pouring the powders into the cup for Sarasvatī, he recites the formula *vīryam asi*. . . and while mixing it in the cup for Indra, he recites *balam asi*. . . . According to *ĀpaŚS*, XIX.7.1 with these formulas the Adhvaryu prays to the cups after he has put them on their proper places. *VaitāSū*, XXX.10 prescribes that, when the Adhvaryu is thus taking the cups of milk, the Brahman priest consecrates his act with the verse *kuvid aṅga yavamanto*. . . .

After the Adhvaryu has drawn the cups of milk, and put them on their proper places, the Pratiprasthātṛ draws the cups of *surā*. According to *KātyŚS*, XIX.2.14, 23 these are also drawn by the Adhvaryu himself. *ĀpaŚS*, XIX.7.2 prescribes that the Pratiprasthātṛ draws the cups of *surā* when it is being poured into the pot, keeping the purifier inbetween.

For all the cups, the verse *nānā hi vām* . . . is used as the Puroruk. *ŚatBrā*, XII.7.3.14 states, "as he uses only one and the same verse for all the cups, he places thereby the fame wholly in the sacrificer." The *MānŚS* does not mention the Puroṛuk. It is possible that for the cups of milk, as well as for the cups of *surā*, the verse *kuvid aṅga yavamanto* . . . is used as the Puroruk, since in *MānŚS*, V.2.11.15 the dual form of the verb *grah* is used. The *sūtra* reads —

kuvid aṅga yavamanto iti gṛhṇīto'dhvaryuḥ payograhān

With the verse: What then? etc. the Adhvaryu scoops the milk draughts, (the Pratiprasthātṛ the *surā* draughts). (tr. by Gelder, p. 177)

According to *KātyŚS*, XIX.2.23 *surā* is drawn in earthen vessels.

After the cups are filled with *surā*, the hairs of wolves, tigers and lions are put into them without making any distinction. Or, the hair of wolves are put into the cup for the Aśvins, those of tigers in the cup for Sarasvatī and those of lions in the cup for Indra (also *MānŚS*, V.2.11.16). The order is different in the *ĀpaŚS* and the *HirŚS*. The act of mixing is not described in connection with the *kaukilī sautrāmaṇī*. It is only stated that the usual procedure of mixing the things in *surā* is to be followed (*ĀpaŚS*, XIX.7.7; *HirŚS*, XXIII.1.26). In connection with the *caraka*, it is mentioned in *ĀpaŚS*, XIX.2.10 and *HirŚS*, XIII.8.23 that the hair of lion are to be put in the cup for the Aśvins, those of tiger in the cup for Sarasvatī and those of wolf in the cup for Indra. If the Adhvaryu does not get the hairs of respective animals, then he should meditate upon those animals. Together with these hairs, the powder of *kuvala, badara* and *karkandhu* is to be poured into the cups respectively for the Aśvins, Sarasvatī and Indra.

According to *MānŚS*, V.2.11.16 the powder of *badara* is poured in the cup for Indra and that of *karkandhu* in the cup for Sarasvatī. Together with these powders, he pours the flour of wheat, *upavāka* and *tokma* also in the cups respectively for the Aśvins, Sarasvatī and Indra. *VārāŚS*, III.2.8.11 prescribes that the flour of *tokma*, *śyāmāka* and *upavāka* should be poured into the cups respectively for the Aśvins, Sarasvatī and Indra.

Regarding the mixing of the hairs of the animals in the cups, it is stated in the *ŚatBrā*,

> In that there are those wild beasts, this is a form of that cruel deity; and if he were to mix the cups of milk with hairs of those beasts, he would thrust the cattle into the mouth of Rudra, and the sacrificer would be without cattle. Let him not mix them, or cattle would not be secured by him, for Rudra is the ruler of the animals. The cups of Surā alone, he mixes with hairs of those beasts. He thus puts into the Surā what belongs to Rudra, hence by drinking Surā one becomes of violent (*raudra*) mind and on the wild beasts alone he thus directs Rudra's shaft to ensure safety to the domestic animals: and cattle are secured by him and he does not thrust the cattle into the mouth of Rudra.
>
> — *ŚatBrā*, XII.7.3.20, tr. by Eggeling, pt. V, pp. 229-30

After filling the cups with *surā* and mixing them with certain things, they are wiped with eagle-wing-feathers[4] and then are kept on their proper places.

In this procedure, first, all the cups of milk are taken and then all the cups of *surā* are taken. An objection is raised by the *ŚatBrā* regarding this procedure. Thus it is stated,

> The cups of milk are the *kṣatra* and the cups of *surā* are the *viś*. When he draws them without interlinking them, he makes the *viś* detached from the *kṣatra* and the *kṣatra* detached from the *viś* and causes confusion between the higher and the lower, and also a failure of the sacrifice. Hence, he draws them, so as to be interlinked and thereby combines the *viś* with the *kṣatra* and the *kṣatra* with the *viś*, so that there would be no confusion between the higher

4. In *ĀpaŚS*, XIX.7.4, 5, 6 and also in *HirŚS*, XXIII.1.26, the reading is *pavitreṇa parimṛjya* 'after wiping them with the purifier'; however, in the commentary on *HirŚS*, XXIII.1.26, it is stated that the priest wipes those cups with an eagle-wing-feather. Caland is also of the same opinion. That the cups are purified with an eagle-wing-feather seems to be more acceptable, since the other texts prescribe the use of an eagle-wing-feather and similar is the prescription in *ĀpaŚS*, XIX.2.12 and in the commentary on *HirŚS*, XIII.8.24, in connection with the *caraka sautrāmaṇī*.

> and the lower, and there would be perfection in the performance of the sacrifice. — *ŚatBrā*, XII.7.3.15

Further, these cups are compared to some other things and it is insisted that the interlinking is necessary. Thus it is stated in *ŚatBrā*, XII.7.3.16,

> The cups of milk are the vital airs and the cups of *surā* are the body. When he draws the cups without interlinking them, the body becomes devoid of vital airs and the sacrificer is liable to destruction. Therefore, he takes the cups thus interlinking them and connects the body thereby with the vital airs. Thus he establishes life in the sacrificer.

The Adhvaryu, following this procedure, first takes the cup of milk for the Asvins and then the cup of *surā* for them, so as to interlink the cups of milk and *surā*. In the same way, he takes the cups of milk and *surā* for Sarasvatī and then for Indra. The *KātyŚS*, prescribes this procedure as an option (cf. *KātyŚS*, XIX.2.23, 24).

After the Adhvaryu has taken all the cups and put them on their proper places, he prays to them with the six verses of the *anuvāka* beginning with *somo rājā* . . . or with the first four verses, he prays to the cups of milk and with the rest of them he prays to the cups of *surā* (*KātyŚS*, XIX.2.27, 28: *VārāŚS*, III.2.8.16).

According to *ĀpaŚS*, XIX.7.8, the Adhvaryu and the sacrificer first pray with *ojo' si ojo mayi dhehi*. . . and then with the *anuvāka* beginning with *somo rājā*. . . .

The Purification of the Sacrificer

After the ritual of drawing the cups is thus completed, the Adhvaryu and the Pratiprasthātr̥ purify the sacrificer, who is sitting behind the altar facing towards the east. They purify him with the eagle-wing-feathers, following the procedure of the initiation ceremony in a *soma*-sacrifice. The only difference is that here the feathers are used instead of the *kuśa* grass. Twice they move the feathers above the navel and twice below it (*KātyŚS*, XIX.2.29; *MānŚS*, V.2.11.20). "They as if secure for him the upper and the lower breaths. The breath moves upwards and downwards in one's body" (*ŚatBrā*, XII.7.3.22).

At that time, the Adhvaryu recites the verse *yā vyāghraṁ viṣūcikā*. . . . According to *ŚatBrā*, XII.7.3.21 one more verse viz. — *yad āpipeṣa* . . . is recited at this time. *KātyŚS*, XIX.2.30 employs this verse for a different purpose. According to it, with the recitation of this verse, the sacrificer looks at the fire, while he is thus being purified.

Then the sacrificer touches the cups of milk with *saṁ pṛca stha saṁ mā bhadreṇa pṛṅkta*. According to *ŚatBrā*, "he makes himself rich thereby with wealth and glory". He touches the cups of *surā* with *vipṛca stha vi mā pāpmanā pṛṅkta*. The *ŚatBrā*, states that he thereby keeps himself away from evil (*ŚatBrā*, XII.7.3.22; *KātyŚS*, XIX.2.31, 32).

The Offering of the Omenta of the Three Animals

The procedure of the animal-offering in the *kaukilī* is similar to the procedure in the *caraka*. The animals offered are also the same. Following the usual procedure the Adhvaryu digs a pit and erects a sacrificial post (*MānŚS*, V.2.11.17). Even though the animals are more than one, only one sacrificial post is erected. This post is erected in the middle; to the south of it is erected the post for the animal to Indra and to its north is erected the post for the animal to Vayodhas Indra (*KātyŚS*, XIX.3.1-6).

Devayājñika describes the procedure of tying the three animals to one post. First, the priest ties the goat to the post; then the ram, which is taken for Sarasvatī, to the neck of the goat, and then the bull which is taken for Indra, to the neck of the ram.

The Adhvaryu formally dedicates the animals to the respective deities, as is mentioned previously in connection with the *caraka*. The ritual is similar up to the carrying round the fire. When he is carrying round the fire for the second time, he puts a portion of the fire brand on the mound and adds fuel to it. With the rest of the fire-brand he performs the carrying round and then takes that fire-brand to cook the animals (*ĀpaŚS*, XIX.8.1.4; *HirŚS*, XXIII.1.23-

31). The ritual is usual up to the offering of the omenta and the formal sprinkling of the water (*MānŚS*, V.2.11.19).

When the Adhvaryu has offered the omenta, the sacrificer gives away forty cows and a mare with a colt as the sacrificial gifts, (*ĀpaŚS*, XIX.8.5; *HirŚS*, XXIII.1.32).

After the Adhvaryu has given out the call relating to the animal-offerings, with *samidbhyaḥ preṣya*, the Maitrāvaruṇa addresses a call to the Hotṛ with *hotā yakṣat samidhā' gnim iḍaspade*. ... The Hotṛ then recites the verse *samiddho agnir aśvinā* ... as the *yājyā*. Thus, the Maitrāvaruṇa addresses the calls to the Hotṛ and the Hotṛ recites the relevent *yājyā*s of the *prayāja*s. The ritual of carrying round the fire and of the offering of the *ājyabhāga*s is similar to the animal-sacrifice. Three different verses are prescribed regarding the offering of the omenta of the three animals. Those are used as the *puronuvākyā*s as well as the *yājyā*s of the offering of the omenta, *aśvinā havir indriyaṁ* ..., *yam aśvinā sarasvatī*... and *tam indram paśavaḥ* ... are the three verses. The first and the second are recited respectively as the *puronuvākyā* and the *yājyā* relating to the offering of the omentum of the animal immolated for the Aśvins. The second and the third are recited respectively as the *puronuvākyā* and the *yājyā* relating to the offering of the omentum of the animal immolated for Sarasvatī; and the third and the first are recited respectively as the *puronuvākyā* and the *yājyā* relating to the offering of the omentum of the animal immolated for Indra. The *hautra* regarding the *barhihoma*, *sūktavāka*, *śaṁyavāka*, etc., is similar to that mentioned in connection with the animal which is immolated for Indra, three days before.

The Offerings of Milk and Surā

Optionally, the cups of milk and *surā* may be drawn at this time, i.e., after the offering of the omenta (*ĀpaŚS*, XIX.8.6; *HirŚS*, XXIII.1.33).

According to *KātyŚS*, XIX.2.33 the *surā*-cups are drawn in the earthen vessels. But as it is said in the *Brāhmaṇa*, *dāru-pātreṇa juhoti na hi mṛṇmayam āhutim ānaśa iti*. "He offers with a wooden vessel, for an earthenware does not hold the offering", the *surā* is poured from those earthen vessels into wooden ones, and then it is offered.

The Adhvaryu takes the milk-cups and the Pratiprasthātṛ the *surā*-cups. Or, according to *VārāŚS*, III.2.8.20 and also according to *MānŚS*, (following the procedure mentioned at V.2.4.25, in connection with the *caraka*) the sacrificer also takes the cups. Thus, the Adhvaryu, the Pratiprasthātṛ and the sacrificer take the cups of milk in the left hand and the cups of *surā* in the right hand.

The Adhvaryu gives out a call for the *puronuvākyā* as *aśvibhyāṁ sarasvatyā indrāya sutrāmṇe surāsomebhyo'nubrūhi*. The verse *yuvaṁ surāmaṁ aśvinā* . . . is recited as the *puronuvākyā*. In the call given out for the *yājyā*, he adds the word *prasthitān preṣya*. Thus he gives out the call, *aśvibhyāṁ sarasvatyā indrāya sutrāmṇe surāsomān prasthitān preṣya*. The verse *putramiva pitarāv aśvino-bha* . . . is recited as the *yājyā* of these offerings. When the Hotṛ utters the *vaṣaṭ*, the Adhvaryu, or the Adhvaryu, the Pratiprasthātṛ and the sacrificer offer the cups of milk reciting the verse *surāvantam barhiṣadam suvīram*. . . .

At the second *vaṣaṭ* utterance the cups are offered without uttering anything (*ĀpaŚS*, XIX.8.9; *HirŚS*, XXIII.1.37).

The milk-cups are offered on the northern fire. "The Adhvaryu thereby makes the sacrificer prosperous with pure *soma* drink" (*ŚatBrā*, XII.8.1.1). The *surā*-cups are offered on the southern fire. "The priest thereby keeps the sacrificer away from evil" (*ŚatBrā*, XII.8.1.3). It is only Āśmarathya, who is of the opinion that the *surā*-cups also should be offered on the *āhavanīya* fire. Regarding this a story is cited in *ŚatBrā*, XII.9.3.1-15. Thus reads the story:

> Duṣṭarītu Pauṁsāyana was expelled from the kingdom and so also was expelled Revottara Pāṭava Cākra Sthapati by the Sṛñjayas. He said to Duṣṭarītu, "I will perform the *sautrāmaṇī* sacrifice for you and will confer upon you that dominion over the Sṛñjayas." Duṣṭarītu allowed him to do so.

When Bāhlika Prātipīya, the Kauravya king heard this, he came to Revottara Sthapati, at the time of drawing the cups of milk and *surā*. He said to him:

> O Sthapati Cākra, it is said that *surā* should not be offered in the *āhavanīya*-fire, nor anywhere else than in the *āhavanīya*. If you will offer it in the *āhavanīya*, you will cause social confusion and a repetition in the sacrifice, since the milk-cups are already offered in it; and if you will offer it anywhere else than in the *āhavanīya*, you will exclude the king from the dominion.

Sthapati Cākra assured him that he would not offer the *surā*-cups in the *āhavanīya* nor anywhere else than in the *āhavanīya*, and would not cause social confusion or repetition in the sacrifice and would not exclude the king from the dominion.

> On the northern fire are offered the cups of milk. The sacrificial animals are also cooked on the northern fire. Thus the priest places the mortal animals into immortal womb and causes them to be born again. Thus he, for whom this sacrificial rite is performed, wards off the recurring death of his cattle and the sacrifice is not cut off from him.
>
> The cups of *surā* are offered on the southern fire, near the southern fire, they purify the *surā*.
>
> These two fires, the northern and the southern one, are taken from the *āhavanīya*, therefore, they are *āhavanīya*s; and as they do not again reach the *āhavanīya*, they are not *āhavanīya*s; he thereby obtains both kinds of oblations, that which is offered on the *āhavanīya* and that which is offered on what is not an *āhavanīya*.

With this explanation Bāhlika Prātipīya was satisfied and went home saying, now that kingdom belongs to Duṣṭarītu.

While offering the *surā*-cups is recited the verse *yas te rasaḥ sambhṛtaḥ oṣadhīsu* ... *VaitāSū*, XXX.11 prescribes that while the cups of milk and *surā* are being offered the Brahman priest recites the four verses beginning with *yuvaṁ surāmam aśvinā*... (*AV(Ś)*, XX.125. 4-7).

By offering thus the cups of milk and *surā* the priests

> restore to the sacrificer the strength and the vigour. Previously, when the strength and vigour had gone away from Indra, the gods had restored them to him with the help of this sacrifice. — *ŚatBrā*, XII.8.1.1,2

Before consuming the remnants of the cups of milk, a little milk is poured from each cup into the remaining two cups. Then the Adhvaryu, the Pratiprasthātṛ and the Āgnīdhra consume the remnants of the cup taken for the Aśvins. The Brahman, the Maitrāvaruṇa and the Hotṛ consume the remains from the cup taken for Sarasvatī and the sacrificer alone consumes that which is remaining in the cup taken for Indra. While partaking of those remnants, they recite the verse *yam aśvinā namuceḥ*. . . (*VārāŚS*, III.2.8.24, 25).

According to *ĀpaŚS*, XIX.8.10-2 and *HirŚS*, XXIII.1.37-9, the remnants of the milk-cup for the Aśvins are consumed only by the Adhvaryu while reciting the verse *yam aśvinā namuceḥ* . . .; the remnants of the milk-cup for Sarasvatī are partaken by the Pratiprasthātṛ and the Āgnīdhra while reciting the verse *yad atra riptam* . . . and the remnants of the milk-cup for Indra are consumed by the Brahman priest and the sacrificer with the recitation of the *mantra*, *idaṁ haviḥ*. . . .

The procedure described in *MānŚS*, V.2.12.23 is similar to that described in connection with the *caraka*. Before consuming the remnants of the cups of milk, the Adhvaryu meditates upon the formula *siṁhayor imaṁ yaśaḥ āgacchatu*; the Pratiprasthātṛ upon *vyāghrayor* . . . and the sacrificer upon *vṛkayor*. . . . Then they consume the remnants of the cups with the recitation of the *mantra* *yam aśvinā namuceḥ*. . . .

According to *KātyŚS*, XIX.3.13, 14, the priests partake of the cups in two turns. First, the Adhvaryu consumes the remnants from the cup for the Aśvins, then the Pratiprasthātṛ and then the Āgnīdhra. In the same way, they consume for the second time. Similarly, the Hotṛ, the Brahman and the Maitrāvaruṇa consume the remnants of the cup for Sarasvatī and the sacrificer consumes those of the cup taken for Indra.

Regarding the ritual of the remnants of *surā*, it is prescribed by *ĀpaŚS*, XIX.8.13 and *HirŚS*, XXIII.1.40 that it is similar to that of the *caraka*. According to *MānŚS*, V.2.11.23 it is similar to the ritual regarding milk. Only the verse is different. While partaking of the remnants of *surā*, they recite the verse *nānā hi vām*. . . .

According to *KātyŚS* also, the procedure is similar to that related to the ritual of the remnants of milk. However, while partaking the remnants of *surā* all the persons sit to the south of the fire-hall and put the sacrificial cord on the right shoulder. They may actually partake of *surā* or, according to some, they may just smell it. The *mantra* to be recited at this time is different from that prescribed in the *MānŚS*. They partake of it with the recitation of the verse *yad atra riptam*. . . . *VaitāSū*, XXX.11 prescribes that the Brahman priest may partake optionally of the remnants of *surā* from the cup for the Aśvins. At that time, he should recite the verse *yam aśvinā*. . . .

The *ŚatBrā* is of the opinion that the remnants should be consumed by all the persons to make the *sautrāmaṇī* a *soma*-sacrifice. It is in a *soma*-sacrifice that all consume the remnants of the oblation. If the sacrificer alone would consume it, the *sautrāmaṇī* would be only an *iṣṭi* or an animal-sacrifice. It would not achieve similarity with the *soma*-sacrifice. Therefore, the remnants are consumed by all the persons and the verse *yad atra riptam* . . . is recited at that time (*ŚatBrā*, XII.8.1.5).

There are certain other procedures also, prescribed to be followed regarding the remnants of *surā*.

According to some priests, optionally a rajanya or a vaiśya may be hired to drink the remnants (*ŚatBrā*, XII.8.1.6; *KātyŚS*, XIX.3.19).

Or, three embers are taken out from the southern fire and are placed to the south of it outside the enclosing sticks. The *surā* is offered on them while reciting the formulas *pitṛbhyaḥ svadhāyibhyaḥ svadhā namaḥ pitāmahebhyaḥ svadhāyibhyaḥ* . . . and *prapitāmahebhyaḥ svadhāyibhyaḥ* . . . (*ŚatBrā*, XII.8.1.7; *VārāŚS*, III.2.8.26). *KātyŚS*, XIX.3.20 suggests some further modifications. According to it, the remnants of the cup taken for the Aśvins are poured on the northern ember, those from the cup taken for Sarasvatī are poured on the middle one and those of the cup taken for Indra on the southern one, reciting the formulas separately for each cup.

Then the priest brings water and pours it on those embers. At that time, he recites some formulas. He says *akṣan pitaraḥ*, he gives food thereby to the fathers. After that he says *amīmadanta pitaraḥ*, he as if makes them rejoice thereby; *atītṛpanta pitaraḥ*, he says, he makes them satisfied thereby. When he says *pitaraḥ śundhadhvam* he purifies them (*ŚatBrā*, XII.8.1.8; *KātyŚS*, XIX.3.21, 22).

According to *ĀpaŚS*, XIX.8.14,15 it is milk instead of *surā* which is offered for the fathers. The sacrificer pours the remaining milk to the south of the *āhavanīya* fire, for the fathers, grandfathers, and the great-grandfathers. He pours it with *pitṛbhyaḥ svadhāyibhyaḥ svadhā namaḥ*. He then prays to the fathers with *punantu mā pitaraḥ somyāsaḥ*. . . (*see* also *HirŚS*, XXIII.1.41, 42).

Trickling of Surā on the Southern Fire

In connection with the *kaukilī*, this rite is described in very few texts. Only the *MānŚS* and the *KātyŚS* describe it. It is interesting that the *ŚatBrā* also does not describe it. The *sūtras* refer to the procedure in the *caraka* (*ĀpaŚS*, XIX.8.13 and *HirŚS*, XXIII.1.40). *VārāŚS*, III.2.8. reads: 'as all the priests consecrate the dripping *surā*'. This *sūtra* thus indicates that the *surā* is made to trickle following the procedure of the *caraka*.

Between the two texts, which describe this rite, there is a difference of opinion. According to the *KātyŚS*, it is performed before the *abhiṣeka*, whereas in the *MānŚS*, it is prescribed to be performed after the *abhiṣeka*.

After the Adhvaryu has sprinkled the sacrificer with the remnants of the fresh milk remaining after the *vājaprasavya* offerings, and has offered sixteen oblations with the hoofs and horns, the Adhvaryu pours the *surā* in the *śatātṛṇṇā* vessel and makes it trickle on the southern fire. While it is trickling down, he makes the sacrificer recite the verses beginning with *punantu mā pitaraḥ somyāsaḥ. . .* (*MānŚS*, V.2.11.27, 28).

According to *KātyŚS*, XIX.3.23-25 the Adhvaryu, following the procedure of the *caraka*, hangs the *śatātṛṇṇā* vessel on the southern fire, keeps the gold and the hair-strainer in it before pouring the *surā*. While the *surā* is trickling down, on the fire, he makes the sacrificer recite the verses beginning with *punantu mā pitaraḥ* . . . (*VājaS*, XIX.37-44). If the sacrificer is a *somātipūta*, the Adhvaryu makes him recite the verses beginning with *tvaṁ soma pracikitaḥ* . . . (*VājaS*, XIX.52-60). With these verses the sacrificer prays to the trickling *surā*. *VaitāSū*, XXX.14 states that when all the *surā* has trickled down the Brahman recites five verses, viz. *AV*, XVIII.1.44, 45; XVIII.1.51 and XVIII.3.45, 44.

After disposing the remaining *surā* in this manner, the Adhvaryu offers an oblation with *ye samānā samanasaḥ* . . . and the Pratiprasthātṛ with *ye sajātā samanasaḥ*... (also *MānŚS*, V.2.11.30). Then the Adhvaryu offers one more oblation with *dve sṛtī* . . . and the Pratiprasthātṛ with *idaṁ haviḥ* . . . .

The *ŚatBrā*, XII.8.1.18 gives the reason of these oblations.

> Those, who perform the ritual on the southern fire go as if, to the world of the fathers. Therefore, he (i.e., the sacrificer) offers an oblation of clarified butter. The clarified butter is, as if, the sacrifice. Thereby they become established in the sacrifice.

The sacrificer offers this oblation with *ye samānā samanasaḥ pitaro yamarājye. . . .* He wins over the world of fathers thereby. Then all of them go to the northern fire, putting their sacrificial cords on the left shoulder. "The northern fire is this world. They become established thereby in this world." The sacrificer then offers an oblation of clarified butter in the northern fire. "They become thus established in the sacrifice" (*ŚatBrā*, XII.8.1.19).

He offers that oblations with *ye samānā samanasaḥ jīvā jīveṣu māmakāḥ. . . .* He offers an oblation of milk, with the verse, *dve sṛtī aśṛṇavaṁ. . . .* At that time all the priests touch him. The milk remaining after the offering he consumes with the verse *idaṁ haviḥ prajananam*.... He alone consumes it. He thereby establishes prosperity in him, since milk is prosperity. Then the sacrificer, his wife and the priests go near the *cātvāla* and sprinkle themselves keeping gold in between (*ŚatBrā*, XII.8.1.20-22; *KātyŚS*, XIX.3.30)

The *VārāŚS* prescribes an altogether different employment of these verses. According to it, after the trickling of the *surā*, the priests stand between the shoulders and the buttocks of the altar and recite the four verses beginning with *ye samānā samanasaḥ* ... but each one recites the verse in a reverse order (*VārāŚS*, III.2.8.29).

The Offerings of the Animal's Organs and of the Cakes

After they have sprinkled themselves near the *cātvāla*, the Adhvaryu draws paddy for the cakes, to be offered for Indra, Savitṛ and Varuṇa. The cake for Indra is to be prepared on eleven potsherds, that for Savitṛ on twelve and the one for Varuṇa on ten potsherds. He draws paddy for one more cake which is to be offered at the time of the *avabhṛtha*. It is to be prepared on one potsherd (*KātyŚS*, XIX.4.2). *VārāŚS*, III.2.8.19 prescribes that the cakes should be like those prescribed in connection with the *caraka*, i.e., one to be prepared on eleven potsherds for Indra, one eight-potsherd cake for Savitṛ and a barley pap for Varuṇa (*see VārāŚS*, III.2.7.27).

The deities of the animals to be offered and the deities of the cakes to be offered for those animals are different. Regarding this an objection is raised as follows: "this is an improper performance (*viloma*). Then how to make it right and proper?" The answer is given thus:

> The animal which is to be immolated at the end belongs to Indra and the first cake belongs to Indra. Thus, through Indra's energy, the priest secures energy and vital power for the sacrificer, since Indra indeed is the energy or the vital power. —*ŚatBrā*, XII.7.2.16

A cake is offered to Savitṛ, "so that the sacrificer might be impelled by that deity", the cake for Varuṇa is offered the last, "he thus delivers him from Varuṇa's power and Varuṇa's noose, for, one who is seized by evil is as if seized by Varuṇa himself." (*ŚatBrā*, XII.7.2.17).

After he has baked those cakes and put them at their proper places, he offers the *ājyabhāga*s and performs the ritual regarding the animals up to the *sviṣṭakṛt* and the *vanaspati-homa*. From the description in the *ŚatBrā* it seems that according to it, first the animals' organs are offered, and then are offered the cakes, the one to Indra being the first among them. But the procedure in the *VārāŚS* is different. *VārāŚS*, III.2.8.30, 31 prescribe that the Adhvaryu should first offer the cakes and then the animals. Among the animals also, he should first offer the one immolated for Indra and the one immolated for the Aśvins he should offer the last. Since the animals to be offered are more than one, he should follow the procedure of eleven-animal-sacrifice. He gives away thirty-three cows and a mare with a colt as sacrificial gifts.

The *ĀpaŚS* gives the ritual of the animal-sacrifice very briefly at XIX.9.2,3. According to it, the Adhvaryu performs the ritual regarding the animal sacrifice up to the *manotā*-offerings and then offers the oblations of fat of the animals and then sprinkles the sacrificer with the remnants of that fat.

The procedure is different in the *MānŚS*. It prescribes at V.2.12 24-33 that, after eating the remnants, the Adhvaryu offers the *vājaprasavya* oblations with fresh milk, and the sacrificer is sprinkled with the remnants of that milk. The ritual regarding the animals' organs and the cakes is performed, according to it, after the *abhiṣeka* ceremony. The cakes for Indra, Savitṛ and Varuṇa are prepared, all on eleven potsherds. The procedure of the offering is the usual one. Thirty-three cows and a mare with a colt are given away as the sacrificial gifts.

The procedure of reciting the *yājyā*s and the *puronuvākyā*s is similar to that of those recited in connection with the offering of the omenta. The three verses, *aśvinā gobhir indriyam . . . tā nāsatyā supeśasā . . .* and *tā bhiṣajā sukarmaṇā . . .* are recited both as *puronuvākyā*s and the *yājyā*s relating to the offering of the organs of the animals and the three verses, *ya indra indriyaṁ dadhuḥ. . .*, *savitā varuṇa dadhat* . . . and *varuṇaḥ kṣatram indriyam* . . . are to be recited both as *puronuvākyā*s and *yājyā*s in connection with the offering of the three cakes. He should address to the Hotṛ with the three calls namely *hotā yakṣad aśvinau chāgasya haviṣā* . . ., *hotā yakṣad sarasvatīm meṣasya haviṣā* . . . and *hotā yakṣad indram ṛṣabhasya haviṣā* . . ., in connection with the offerings of the animals' organs. In connection with the *vanaspati-homa* and the *sviṣṭakṛt* offering the Hotṛ is addressed with the calls, *hotā yakṣad vanaspatim* . . . and *hotā yakṣad agniṁ sviṣṭakṛtam*. . . .

After these offerings, the sacrificer is given a sacred bath with the remnants of the oblations of the fat. This rite is important since it has some striking similarities with the ritual of the *punarabhiṣeka* which is described in *AitBrā*, XXXVII. Hence, it is dealt with in details in a separate chapter, viz. ch. 10.

The Avabhṛtha Ceremony

After the *abhiṣeka*, the ritual is the usual one from the *sviṣṭakṛt* up to the *barhihoma*, i.e., the offering of the sacrificial grass. Then the Adhvaryu offers an oblation with the three verses beginning with *yad devā devaheḍanam* . . . and then all go for *avabhṛtha* (*VārāŚS*, III.2.8.49). According to *MānŚS*, V.2.11.35, with these three verses, three oblations of clarified butter are offered before the *samiṣṭayajus* offering.

In connection with the *avabhṛtha* in the *caraka sautrāmaṇī*, it is observed that, it seems to be an addition in the ritual in order to achieve similarity with the *soma*-sacrifice. But, since the rite is not prescribed in the Saṁhitās or the *Brāhmaṇa*s, no explanation regarding this addition is found in the texts themselves. However, while prescribing the *avabhṛtha* in the *kaukilī sautrāmaṇī*, it is clearly mentioned in the *ŚatBrā* that, after the offerings are made, all go for the *avabhṛtha*; since after they have offered in the *soma*-sacrifice, they go for the *avabhṛtha* and the *sautrāmaṇī* is a *soma*-sacrifice (*ŚatBrā*, XII.9.2.1). Similarly, in *ŚāṅkhāBrā*, XVI.10 also, it is said, *avabhṛtham avaiti yathā some*. "He goes for the *avabhṛtha* as in a *soma*-sacrifice."

While going for the *avabhṛtha*, they take with them all the pots stained with milk and *surā* (*KātyŚS*, XIX.5.11).

According to Āśmarathya, the Adhvaryu offers five oblations in the *avabhṛtha* with the five verses beginning with *yad devā devaheḍanam*. . . Ālekhana is of the opinion that these offerings should be offered on the *āhavanīya* fire (*ĀpaŚS*, XIX.10.4). "When he recites these verses *yad devā* . . . etc., the men and the fathers make the sacrificer free from the sins of men and the fathers" (*ŚatBrā*, XII.9.2.2).

Then are performed the rites up to the consecration of the heart-pikes and from reaching the water up to the *avabhṛtheṣṭi* (*KātyŚS*, XIX.5.12). The Adhvaryu then puts the pitcher of sediments in the water with *yad devā* . . . (*KātyŚS*, XIX.5.13; and also *VaitāSū*, XXX.22). He drowns it in the water following the procedure mentioned previously in *KātyŚS*, X.10.3, with the verse *avabhṛtha nicumpuṇa*. . . (*KātyŚS*, XIX.5.14). *ĀpaŚS*, XIX.10.5 prescribes a different employment of this verse. According to it, with *avabhṛtha nicaṅkuna* . . . the sacrificer consecrates the place of the *avabhṛtha*.

The Adhvaryu offers an oblation in the waters with *dhāmno dhāmnaḥ* . . . the second oblation he offers while reciting the verse *yad grāme yad araṇye* . . , "Thus he makes the sacrificer free from all kinds of sins" (*ŚatBrā*, XII.9.2.3). According to *VārāŚS*, III.2.8.50 with the recitation of these two verses, the sacrificer sprinkles himself with water.

He takes water in his hands with *sumitriyā na āpaḥ* . . . and then taking two steps to the north, he throws it in the direction of his enemy with *durmitriyā na*. . . . He then takes a bath following the usual procedure of the *avabhṛtha*. At that time, he recites the verse, *pavitram asi* . . . (*VārāŚS*, III.2.8.51). According to *MānŚS*, V.2.12.27 both, the sacrificer and his wife take a bath and wash each others back. According to *KātyŚS*, XIX.5.16, with the recitation of *drupadād ivenmumucānaḥ* . . . the sacrificer throws away the wet garments into water.

With *ud vayam tamasas pari* . . . the sacrificer prays to the Āditya (*VārāŚS*, III.2.8.51). *ĀpaŚS*, XIX.10.5 prescribes that, before that he offers oblations with *sumitrā na āpaḥ* . . . and *drupadād ivenmumucānaḥ* . . ., and after praying in this way, he pushes back the border of waters with *pratiyuto varuṇasya pāśaḥ*. . . .

Following the procedure of the *soma*-sacrifice, the sacrificer comes out of the water and to the fire-hall (*KātyŚS*, XIX.5.17). On their way back, they collect the fire-sticks following the procedure of the animal-sacrifice (*ĀpaŚS*, XIX.10.6). The sacrificer prays to the fire with *apo adyānvacāriṣam*. . . . With *edho'si* . . . he takes the fire-sticks and adds them to the fire with *samid asi* . . . (*KātyŚS*, XIX.5.18,19; *VārāŚS*, III.2.8.52, *ĀpaŚS*, XIX.10.6; *ŚatBrā*, XII.9.2.10).

Then he prays to the *āhavaṇīya* fire with *samāvavarti* . . ., and offers an oblation with *bhūḥ svāhā*. According to *KātyŚS* he offers the oblation with *samāvavarti* . . . . *VārāŚS*, III.2.8.53 prescribes that with the recitation of *samāvṛtat pṛthivī* . . . . he offers a *pūrṇāhuti*; whereas, according to *MānŚS*, V.2.11.38, with the recitation of this verse, he offers on oblation in the *gārhapatya* fire with the help of *sruva* ladle.

The Ritual After the Avabhṛtha

After the *avabhṛtha*, the *piṇḍapitṛyajña* is performed, as is prescribed before[5] (*ĀpaŚS*, XIX.10.8).

After the Adhvaryu has performed the *udavasānīyā iṣṭi*, he offers the offering of whey (*payasyā*) to Mitra and Varuṇa (*KātyŚS*, XIX.5.21; *VaitāSū*, XXX.24 and *ŚāṅkhāBrā*, XVI.10).

The verses *śaṅ no bhavatu* . . . and *vāje vāje vata vājino*. . . are

5. According to *ŚrautaKośa* (Vol.1, English Section, Part II, p. 926) "the Piṇḍapitṛyajña is to be performed as is prescribed (in connection with the Sākamedhaparvan of the Cāturmāsya sacrifice)." But the basis on which these two are connected does not become clear.

According to Caland (pt. III, p. 182) the *piṇḍapitṛyajña* is to be performed following the procedure mentioned in connection with the new-moon offerings. Similar is the suggestion in the commentary on *HirŚS*, XXIII.1.57. This explanation seems to be more acceptable.

recited as the *puronuvākyā* and the *yājyā* of this offering. While reciting the *yājyā*, the Hotṛ should not breathe in. He should recite it in only one breath. For the *sviṣṭakṛt* offering of that whey are used the verses *ā no mitrāvaruṇa* . . . and *pra bāhavā sisṛtatam* . . . as the *puronuvākyā* and the *yājyā*.

Then an animal is offered to Indra Vayodhas. A bull is given away as a sacrificial gift of that offering. He offers rice pap to Aditi, after the animal-offering to Indra Vayodhas. As a sacrificial gift of this pap to Aditi, he gives away a milch-cow. This is the same milch-cow, of which the calf is given as the sacrificial gift in the previous offering to Aditi (*ĀpaŚS*, XIX.10.8-12; *VaitāŚū*, XXX.25,26). Similar is the procedure according to the *KātyŚS* also. It is suggested by *KātyŚS*, XIX.1.6 which reads *ante ca*. Or, the rice-pap should be offered to Aditi, before the offerings of the animal to Indra Vayodhas and of the whey to the Mitrāvaruṇau, as is prescribed in *KātyŚS*, XIX.17 which reads *āmikṣayā vā pūrvaḥ*.

The verses *sutrāmāṇam pṛthivīm* . . . and *mahīm u ṣu mātaram*. . . are used as the *puronuvākyā* and the *yājyā* of the *sviṣṭakṛt* offering of the rice-pap to Aditi.

VārāŚS, III.2.8.56 also prescribes that the animal to Indra Vayodhas should be offered after the *iṣṭi* of the rice-pap to Aditi is completed.

It is only the *MānŚS* which prescribes that, on this day, the sacrificer observes fast relating to the animal-offering to be performed for Indra Vayodhas on the next day. The actual offerings are made on the next day (*MānŚS*, V.2.11.43). The offerings of the rice-pap to Aditi, at the beginning and at the end of the sacrifice are not prescribed in this *sūtra*.

The Brahman priest should consecrate these offerings. It is told in the commentary on *VaitāSū*, XXX.25, 26.

The calls regarding the offerings of the animal to Vayodhas Indra are given as are given in a usual animal-sacrifice. The Hotṛ should recite the *prayāja-yājyā*s beginning with *samiddho agniḥ samidhā*. . . . The verses *vasantena ṛtunā* . . . and *grīṣmeṇa devā* *ṛtunā* . . . are used as the *puronuvākyā* and the *yājyā* relating to the offering of the omentum of that animal. The verses *varṣābhiḥ ṛtunā* . . . and *śāradena ṛtunā*. . . are the *puronuvākyā* and the *yājyā* relating to the cake offered for that animal and the verses *hemantena ṛtunā*. . . and *śisireṇa ṛtunā*. . . are those of the organs of that animal (*MānŚS*, V.2.11.43-45; *KātyŚS*, XIX.7.20, 21).

Similar is the hautra in the *Taittirīya* tradition. But it is not cited in the *ĀpaHauPari*. It is to be understood from *TaiS*, II.6.17 to II.6.20.

After these offerings ends the *kaukilī sautrāmaṇī*.

The expiation rites relating to the performance of the *sautrāmaṇī* sacrifice are prescribed only in the *VaikhāŚS*. In *VaikhāŚS*, XX.22, it is stated that if the sacrificer has expired before the conclusion of the *sautrāmaṇī* sacrifice, a portion is taken from all the oblations, the names of all the divinities are uttered and then those portions are offered with the utterance of *svāhā*.

And if, for some reason or other, the ritual of the *sautrāmaṇī* is interrupted many times, an *anvārambhaṇīyeṣṭi* is performed after the performance of the *sautrāmaṇī* and the fires are reorganized. According to some teachers, the sacred fires are either renewed or are set up again (*VaikhāŚS*, XX.31).

10

The Abhiṣeka of the Sacrificer

As it is already stated before, the *kaukilī sautrāmaṇī* developed as a separate rite, by elaboration of the ritual of the *caraka sautrāmaṇī*. While this happened, certain rites seem to have been added to the *caraka* ritual. *Abhiṣeka* 'the sacred bath'[1] is one of such rites. It is based on the ritual of the *punarabhiṣeka* described in *AitBrā*, XXXVII, which we have noticed earlier.

Among the Saṁhitās and the *Brāhmaṇa*s, it is only the *ŚatBrā* which describes this rite elaborately (*ŚatBrā*, XII.8.3.1-31). In the *MaiS*, *KāṭhS* and the *TaiBrā* only the *mantra*-portion is cited; the ritual is not described. In what follows, the order of the rites described in the *ŚatBrā* is kept in view.

The purpose of the rite is to restore to the sacrificer the strength and vital power, etc., which have gone away from him. This is made clear in a myth in *ŚatBrā*, XII.8.3.1, 2. The myth reads:

---

1. The word *abhiṣeka* is translated variously by scholars. Heesterman has translated it as 'unction' in *Ancient Indian Royal Consecration*. Keith has translated it as 'anointment' in *The Ṛgveda Brāhmaṇas*. Eggeling translates it as 'consecration'. But all these meanings seem to be unsatisfactory. In the *ŚrautaKośa* the word is translated as 'sanctificatory bath'. When one looks into the description of the actual procedure of the rite, it is clear that the fat is actually poured on the head of the sacrificer and therefore the translation of the *ŚrautaKośa* is more acceptable. Instead of sanctificatory the word sacred is used here for the sake of brevity.

> Tvaṣṭṛ, when his son was killed, performed a *soma*-sacrifice as a means of exorcism and did not invite Indra to that sacrifice. Indra caused nuisance to it and drank that *soma* per force. The *soma* came out of his body from every direction, i.e., from each of his limbs.[2]

From his mouth and breath passed out his fame and excellence. They entered into the cattle. Therefore, the cattle is the fame. He, who, knowing this, is given a sacred bath in the *sautrāmaṇī*, becomes fame.

At that time, the Aśvins and Sarasvatī performed this sacrifice to cure him. They gave him a sacred bath by this rite. Then he became the highest among the gods. One, who is given a sacred bath by this rite, becomes the highest among his own people.

The Ritual Sequence of the Abhiṣeka in the Kaukilī

This ritual of the sacred bath takes place between the *vanaspati-homa*[3] and the *sviṣṭakṛt*-offerings which form part of the animal sacrifice. The Adhvaryu performs the ritual beginning with the giving out a call (*praiṣa*) to Śamitṛ up to the performance of *vanaspati-homa* and then begins the rite of the *abhiṣeka* (cf. *KātyŚS*, XIX.4.7).

In this connection the *ŚatBrā*, remarks at XII.8.3.19, *sviṣṭakṛt* is the *kṣatra*, the Adhvaryu anoints the sacrificer with the help of the *kṣatra*. *Vanaspati* is the Soma and *sviṣtrakṛt* the Agni. As the Adhvaryu gives a sacred bath to the sacrificer after the *vanaspati-homa* and before the *sviṣṭakṛt*, he thus performs the *abhiṣeka* after encompassing the sacrificer by Agni and Soma. Therefore it is said, 'It is the kṣatriya, who gives the sacred bath to the kṣatriya.'

It has been stated previously that the *sautrāmaṇī* is basically one of the redressing rites which were performed for restoring to the

---

2. Eggeling has translated this sentence as "He (i.e., Indra) went asunder in every direction."
3. For *vanaspati-homa*, *see ŚatBrā*, III.8.3.33 and IV.5.2.11. In both the cases it is followed by the offerings to Agni Sviṣṭakṛt.

sacrificer the *kṣatriyatva* which had been rendered inoperative at the time of the sacrifice. It is set into action again by the performance of the *sautrāmaṇī*.[4] It is no wonder that the *ŚatBrā* has tried to establish some connection between the ritual procedure of the *abhiṣeka* and the *kṣatra*.

According to *VārāŚS*, III.2.8.32 and *ĀpaŚS*, XIX.9.3 also, the sacrificer is given the sacred bath before the *sviṣṭakṛt* offerings. However, the order of the rites is a little different from that of the rite described, in the *Śukla YV*. The *ŚatBrā*, and the *KātyŚS*, prescribe that the sacrificer is first seated on the stool (*āsandī*), then the offerings of fat are offered and afterwards the sacred bath takes place; whereas according to the *ĀpaŚS*; the *HirŚS* and the *VārāŚS*, the oblations of fat are offered first, then the sacrificer is seated on the stool for the *abhiṣeka*. The ritual described in *MānŚS*, V.2.12.24 is much different from both these traditions. According to it, first the *vājaprasavya* offerings[5] are offered as a part of the *sautrāmaṇī*. After these offerings, the sacrificer is anointed with the remaining milk and then are offered the oblations of fat.

Placing the Stool

The Adhvaryu spreads a black-antelope skin between the two altars. The hairy side is put upwards. The antelope-skin is connected by *ŚatBrā*, XII.8.3.3 with the sacrifice.

Then a stool (*āsandī*) is placed on that skin. It is made of *udumbara* wood and is woven with sacrificial *muñja*-grass. It is an *aratni* in length and its legs are knee-high, (cf. *KātyŚS*, XIX.4.7). According to *ĀpaŚS*, XIX.9.10 and *HirŚS*, XXIII.1.48, the legs of the stool are navel-high. According to the *ŚatBrā* the legs of the stool are knee-high. The reason for this is given, thus:

---

4. See chapter 3, "The Punarabhiṣeka and the Sautrāmaṇī".
5. For the description of the *vājaprasavya* offerings, *see MānŚS*, V.2.7.21 and VI.2.5.28-31. In *MānŚS*, VI.2.5.28-31, it is performed as a part of the *agnicayana*. The *vājaprasavya* oblations are offered with clarified butter mixed with some medicinal herbs. With the remnants of those offerings, the sacrificer is given the sacred bath afterwards.

> This world is knee-high. The kṣatriya is given the sacred bath for this world, i.e., to rule this world. One who is given the sacred bath in the *sautrāmaṇī* is the *kṣatra*. Therefore, the seat is knee-high if measured diagonally.
>
> — *ŚatBrā*, XII.8.3.5

It is remarkable that, though the *sautrāmaṇī* is prescribed for all the castes, the Brāhmaṇistic explanations connect it mainly with the kṣatriya and the *kṣatriyatva*.

Similarly *ŚatBrā*, XII.8.4.4 gives the explanation as to why a stool is placed for the sacrificer. It is stated,

> The sovereignty is seated on a stool. When the Adhvaryu places a stool for the sacrificer, he thereby leads the sacrificer to sovereignty by means of sovereignty.'

The Adhvaryu places the stool on the skin with the recitation of the *mantra*, *kṣatrasya yonir asi kṣatrasya nābhir asi*. He places it in such a way that the two legs of it are on the northern altar and the other two are on the southern one (cf. *KātyŚS*, XIX.4.7). In *ŚatBrā*, XII.8.3.6, the northern altar is said to be this world and the southern one, the world of the fathers. Also, it is said further that by placing the stool in this way, the Adhvaryu performs *abhiṣeka* for the sacrificer in both the worlds.

This peculiar way of placing the stool seems to have its origin in the rite of *abhiṣeka* in the *punarabhiṣeka* described in *AitBrā*, XXXVII.1. While placing the stool for the sacrificer it is put in such a way that two of its legs are within the altar and two are outside it. While giving the justification of it, it is said,

> Prosperity is the (earth). What is within the altar is its limited form; what is without the altar is the unlimited space. In that its two feet are within the altar, two outside of the altar, (it serves) to obtain both desires, that which is within the altar and that without the altar.
>
> (tr. by Keith, p. 322)

The procedure of this rite as described in the other *sūtra*s is different. Thus *ĀpaŚS*, XIX.9.11 and *HirŚS*, XXIII.1.48 prescribe that the stool should be put at the place of the sacrificer, and with a different verse, namely — *mitro'si varuṇo'si saṁ ahaṁ viśvair devair bhūyāsam. VārāŚS*, III.2.8.36 prescribes that the stool should be placed to the south of the *āhavanīya*, whereas according to *MānŚS*, V.2.11.24, it is placed to the north of the northern altar.

The Adhvaryu then spreads a black antelope skin upon the stool saying, *mā tvā hiṁsīt mā mā hiṁsīḥ*. He says this, lest there be any harm to him or to the sacrifice, as the skin is said to be the sacrifice (cf. *ŚatBrā*, XII.8.3.9; *KātyŚS*, XIX.4.8).

There is no reference to the spreading of the skin in the *ĀpaŚS*, *MānŚS* or *HirŚS*; however, according to the commentary on *TaiBrā*, II.6.5.1, the formula *kṣatrasya yonir asi kṣatrasya nābhir asi* is used for this purpose.

A somewhat different procedure is described in the *VārāŚS*. The verses prescribed in it are also different. According to it, the Adhvaryu first spreads the black-antelope-skin on the stool, saying *kṣatrasya yonir asi*. . . and then with *syonāsi suṣadāsi* places it to the south of the *āhavanīya* (*VārāŚS*, III.2.8.36).

The Sacrificer Sits upon that Stool

The sacrificer sits upon that stool with the verse, *niṣasāda dhr̥tavratah̤ varuṇaḥ pastyāsv ā sāmrājyāya sukratuḥ* (*KātyŚS*, XIX.4.9).

ŚatBrā, XII.8.3.10 gives the explanation of the employment of this verse; this also is in connection with a kṣatriya king. Thus it is stated, "The sacrificer mounts the seat with the verse referring to Varuṇa, as Varuṇa is the king of the gods." Thereby the Adhvaryu performs the *abhiṣeka* for the sacrificer with his own verse.

According to *ĀpaŚS*, XIX.9.12, the verses used in the *rājasūya* in similar rites should be employed here also. Thus, the sacrificer reaches the seat with *syonā mā sīda*. . . and when he has sat upon it, the Adhvaryu consecrates him with the verse *ni ṣasāda dhr̥tavrataḥ* . . . .

VārāŚS, III.2.8.37, 38 prescribe that the Adhvaryu should consecrate the sacrificer with *suṣadām āsīda* while he is mounting the stool, and with the *mantra*, *niṣasāda dhr̥tavrataḥ* . . . when he has sat upon it.[6]

The Adhvaryu then puts a golden and a silver plate under the feet of the sacrificer, with the recitation of the verse, *mr̥tyoḥ pāhi vidyot pāhi* (*KātyŚS*, XIX.4.10).

The explanation of this act is given in the *Brāhmaṇa* thus:

> The golden plate is the form of lightening and the silver, of hail. The Adhvaryu thus, bestows protection upon the sacrificer with the help of these two. Therefore, one who is performing the *sautrāmaṇī* has no fear from these deities.
>
> —*ŚatBrā*, XII.8.3.11

According to some teachers, the golden plate is put upon the head of the sacrificer with *vidyot pāhi* (*KātyŚS*, XIX.4.11). Vidyādhara in his commentary upon this *sūtra*, and Devayājñika, in his *Paddhati*, have prescribed that the plates are put on the feet of the sacrificer. Devayājñika has further quoted that, according to the information of Harisvāmin, some teachers prescribe that the plates should be thrown on the floor near the feet of the sacrificer.

The Offerings of the Fat

The Adhvaryu then offers thirty-two oblations of fat using the hoofs as the cups. He offers two oblations together, with each of the sixteen verses beginning with *sīsena tantram manasā manīṣiṇaḥ* . . . . The remnants of these oblations, he collects in a pot called, *sata* (*KātyŚS*, XIX.4.13).

For these oblations, the hoofs of the animals offered are used as cups. The *Brāhmaṇa* gives the reason why the hoofs are used:

6. It is further said in the 38th *sūtra*, *vyāghrāviṣṭadiveti ca*. The *ŚrautaKośa* has stated in a note that this *sūtra* is corrupt. In the translation, it is translated as, "he (the Adhvarya) should put a tiger's skin upon the sacrificer's body."

> With the help of the hoofs the cattle can stand erect. The Adhvaryu, by offering with the hoofs, leads the sacrificer to establishment. He offers these oblations with the verses in the *jagatī* metre, as the animals are of *jāgata* (moving) nature. He gains thereby the cattle for the sacrificer. He offers the oblations with sixteen verses, as the animals are of sixteen parts. He thus places excellence in him part by part. —*ŚatBrā*, XII.8.3.13

The oblations to be offered with the help of the hoofs are thirty-two, but it does not mean that those many hoofs are necessary. It is explained by Devayājñika in his *paddhati*, that the Adhvaryu takes two hoofs, makes them hot on the fire, and carves away all the flesh remaining in them. Then he takes the fat in them, offers it on the fire, takes the remnants in the *sata* and fills these hoofs again.

Though the number of the hoofs is not important in the tradition of the *Śukla YV*, in that of the other Vedas it is connected with the oblations. A separate hoof (and, if necessary, a dew-claw) also is taken each time for each oblation. Thus *VārāŚS*, III.2.8.32 prescribes that the Adhvaryu should offer sixteen oblations of fat by means of thirty-two hoofs and horns, reciting the verses beginning with *sīsena tantram*. . . . He should offer two offerings with a verse or a separate offering each time. After making the offerings, he collects the remnants in a pot, for the *abhiṣeka* of the sacrificer.

According to these texts, the fat of all the animals is taken in one and the same pot. But the procedure in the *ĀpaŚS* is different. At the time of the offerings to *manotā*[7], the Adhvaryu takes the fat of the animals in separate pots (*ĀpaŚS*, XIX.9.2). Before the *sviṣṭakṛt* offerings, he offers the subsidiary offerings (*upahomas*) by means of horns and hoofs. Every animal has eight hoofs and dew-claws. The Adhvaryu offers eight oblations of the fat immolated for the Aśvins; each of them is taken into a dew-claw and a hoof respectively. He offers them with eight verses beginning with *sīsena tantram*. . . . For the last oblation he takes two horns also together with a dew-claw

7. For the *manotā*-offerings, *see* *ĀpaŚS*, VII.2.4.1 and also the fn. given by Eggeling while translating *ŚatBrā*, II.8.3.14.

and a hoof. After the offerings are made, he pours the remnants of the offerings in the pot for that deity, and throws the dew-claws and the hoofs in the *āhavanīya* fire (*ĀpaŚS*, XIX.9.3-7).

In the same way, he offers the oblations of the fat of the animal immolated for Sarasvatī, with the remaining eight verses. The eight oblations of the fat of the animal, immolated for Indra, he offers with all the above-mentioned sixteen verses, each of these oblations being offered with two successive verses (*ĀpaŚS*, XIX.9.8-9).

The Abhiṣeka

After these oblations, the sacrificer is anointed with the fat. He is sitting on the stool with his face towards the east (*ĀpaŚS*, XIX.9.13). He is already anointed with some fragrant substances. According to some teachers, the fragrant substances are added to the fat (*KātyŚS*, XIX.4.14). Then the sacrificer is given the sacred bath with the fat. In the *ŚatBrā*, it is stated that the fat of the animals is wealth. It is further added there that the Adhvaryu thus pours the wealth on the sacrificer. Also, it is stated, the fat is the best of the food. The Adhvaryu thus bestows the best of the food upon the sacrificer.

The Adhvaryu stands near the sacrificer with his face towards the north and pours the fat on the sacrificer from east to west. He pours it on his head, and lets it flow towards his face. In this way, he anoints him in every direction.

While standing towards the east, the Adhvaryu pours the fat with *devasya tvā aśvinor bhaiṣajyena brahmavarcasāya abhiṣiñcāmi*; while standing towards the south with . . . *sarasvatyai bhaiṣajyena vīryāya annādyāya* . . . ; while standing towards the west with . . . *indrasya indriyeṇa balāya śriyai yaśase* . . . (*ŚatBrā*, XII.8.3.18; *KātyŚS*, XIX.9.14.15).

While standing towards the north of the sacrificer, the Adhvaryu pours the fat on the sacrificer for the fourth time with the verse addressed to all the three deities. The fourth pouring is an addition prescribed only in *KātyŚS*, XIX.9.15. It is not found in the *ŚatBrā*. It is further mentioned in the *KātyŚS*, XIX.9.15 that some teachers prescribe that the fourth pouring should be done with the *mahā-*

vyāhṛtis, i.e., with *bhūr bhuvaḥ* and *svaḥ*. While commenting upon this *sūtra*, Vidyādhara has stated that it should be poured first with the verse addressed to all the deities and then with the *mahāvyāhṛtis*.

In *ŚatBrā*, XII.8.3.18, it is stated, that, according to some teachers, the sacrificer is given the bath with both, viz. with the *yajus*-formula addressed to these deities and with the *vyāhṛtis*, saying that these *vyahṛtis* are all this (i.e., the universe) and with all this the sacrificer is given the sacred bath.

This seems to be a reference to the *abhiṣekas* performed in the *rājasūya* and in the *punarabhiṣeka* in the *AitBrā*. In these ceremonies the *abhiṣeka* is performed for the sacrificer with the *yajuṣ*-formula *devasya tvā* ... and also with the *mahāvyāhṛtis*, i.e., *bhūr*, *bhuvaḥ* and *svaḥ* (cf. *AitBrā*, XXXVII.3 and XXXIX.4).

However, this view is rejected by the *ŚatBrā* and it is prescribed in it that the sacrificer should be given the sacred bath only with the *yajus*-formula to deities, since the deities themselves are all this, i.e., the universe.

According to *VārāŚS*, III.2.8.42-3, the Adhvaryu takes the fat with *devasya tvā* . . . and while looking at the sacrificer offers an oblation reciting the verse *trayā devā ekādaśa* . . . and then pours the fat upon the sacrificer with the verse *prathamās tvā dvitīyaiḥ*. . . .

According to the *ĀpaŚS*, the Adhvaryu pours the fat on the head of the sacrificer from only one direction, not from all directions. He pours the remnants of the fat of the animal for the Aśvins with *devasya tvā . . . aśvinor bhaiṣajyena* . . . the fat of the animal for Sarasvatī, he pours with *devasya tvā . . . sarasvatyai bhaiṣajyena* . . ., and with *devasya tvā . . . indrasya indriyeṇa balāya śriyai yaśase*, he pours the fat of the animal immolated for Indra. The *vyāhṛtis* are not mentioned in this context (*ĀpaŚS*, XIX.9.13-5).

With the formula *ko'si katamo'si* the Adhvaryu touches the sacrificer and then offers an oblation of clarified butter reciting the *vyāhrtis* (*ĀpaŚS*, XIX.10.1). According to *KātyŚS*, XIX.4.19, he touches only the hands of the sacrificer and offers the oblations.

It is prescribed in *VaitāSū*, XXX.15 that, while the sacrificer is thus given the sacred bath, the Brahman should make him recite *om bhūr bhuvaḥ svaḥ*. . . .

The Rite of Lifting the Sacrificer

At the time, when the Adhvaryu is offering the oblations, the sacrificer should call out the auspicious names in the manner prescribed in the *rājasūya* (*ĀpaŚS*, XIX.9.2; *KātyŚS*, XIX.4.20).

With the verse *śiro me śrīḥ* . . . the sacrificer touches his relevant limbs (*ĀpaŚS*, XIX.10.2).

After this, the rite of lifting the sacrificer is described. He is lifted by the attendants, whose auspicious names he has called out. Though, the sacrificer is thus asked to call out the names of the attendants, the rite of lifting the sacrificer is not prescribed in the *ĀpaŚS*. It is prescribed only in the *ŚatBrā*, and the *KātyŚS*.

The attendants, called by the sacrificer, lift him up following the manner prescribed in the *śatarudriya* rite.[8] They lift him up first knee-high, then navel-high and then up to the level of the mouth (*KātyŚS*, XIX.4.22). According to *ŚatBrā*, XII.8.3.20, it is the priests who lift him up. The *ŚatBrā* glorifies the lifting as —

> The Adhvaryu places the sacrificer thereby in these worlds. Or, the *vājapeya* is doubtlessly an *abhiṣeka*, and the *sautrāmaṇī* also is an *abhiṣeka*. Therefore, as in the *vājapeya* rite, in the *sautrāmaṇī* also, the sacrificer climbs the pole. This is a form of that climbing.

The Sacrificer Gets down from the Stool

Then, the sacrificer descends upon the black antelope skin[9] (*KātyŚS*, XIX.5.23). Regarding this, it is stated in *ŚatBrā*, XII.8.3.21,

8. The *śatarudriya* rite is performed as a part of the *cayana*. These measures are observed in it. First, the oblation-material is taken up to the knees and is offered. At the time of the second offering, it is taken up to the navel and at the time of the third offering, it is taken up to the mouth and then offered (cf. *KātyŚS*, XVIII.1.1-4).
9. *KātyŚS* does not mention that a skin should be spread before →

> It is said that one, for whom *abhiṣeka* is performed in the *sautrāmaṇī*, falls down from this world. One descends on the black antelope skin. The skin is the sacrifice. Thus, one finally becomes established in this world.

The same idea, that the sacrificer becomes established in some thing when he descends from the stool is used by the *ŚatBrā* again while explaining the verse used in that connection. Thus it is stated in *ŚatBrā*, XII.8.3.22,

> The sacrificer descends with the verse, *prati kṣatre prati tiṣṭhāmi rāṣṭre*. He becomes thereby established in the *kṣatra* and in the kingly empires so as not to be driven away from them, (He says) *prati aśveṣu prati tiṣṭhāmi goṣu*, the sacrificer becomes established thereby in cows and horses, so that he should not go away from them. (He says) *prati aṅgeṣu prati tiṣṭhāmi ātman* the sacrificer becomes established thereby in limbs and soul, so that he should not go away from them. (He says) *prati prāṇeṣu prati tiṣṭhāmi puṣṭe*. The sacrificer becomes established thereby in the middle of heaven and earth, within which is established everything.

In other texts, different verses are prescribed for getting down from the stool. Thus, *VārāŚS*, III.2.8.47 and *ĀpaŚS*, XIX.10.2, prescribe that the sacrificer descends from the stool with the recitation of the verse, *jaṅghābhyām padhyāṁ dharmo'si viśi rājā pratiṣṭhitaḥ*; and after getting down, he murmurs the verse *prati kṣatre prati tiṣṭhāmi rāṣṭre*. . . .

The Singing of the Sāman

Then the Adhvaryu takes the thirty-third oblation in a hoof of a bull, reciting the verse *yo bhūtānām adhipatiḥ*. . . According to some, he takes the oblation of clarified butter in a cup made of *aśvattha* wood (*KātyŚS*, XIX.4.24, 25).

← placing the stool. It is to be understood from *ŚatBrā*, XII.8.3.3. Devayājñika has mentioned in this context that a black antelope skin is to be spread on the ground before placing the stool.

At this time, a *sāman* is sung as a part of the rite of anointment. According to *VārāŚS*, III.2.8.39, the *sāman* is sung when the sacrificer is being given the sacred bath.

When the procedure of the *abhiṣeka* begins, the brāhmaṇa priest stands up and goes beyond the two fires. When the Adhvaryu gives out to him the call to sing a *sāman*, he chants the *sāman* (*KātyŚS*, XIX.5.1; *VaitāSū*, XXX.16; *LāṭyāŚS*, V.4.16). At that time, thus informs Devayājñika, the sacrificer also sits near the Brahman priest.

In *ŚatBrā*, XII.8.3.23, the *sāman* is said to be the *kṣatra* and sovereignty. It is further stated,

> As the Brahman priest sings the *sāman*, he performs the *abhiṣeka* for the sacrificer with the *kṣatra* and leads him to sovereignty. The *sāman* is the essence of the Vedas. He gives the sacrificer the sacred bath thus with the essence of all the Vedas.

The *sāman* is sung on a verse in *br̥hatī* metre, which is related to Indra. And this is very appropriate as

> the *sautrāmaṇī* belongs to Indra, the sacrificer has Indra as his abode. The Adhvaryu thus performs his abhiṣeka in his own abode. —*ŚatBrā*, XII.8.3.25.

The *sāman* is called the *saṁśāna sāman*. The name also is connected with Indra. It is stated in *ŚatBrā*, XII.8.3.26 that

> By this very *sāman*, the gods made Indra sharp, and prepared him for strength and vigour. The priests now make this sacrificer prepared for strength and vigour.

The *R̥k* on which the *sāman* is based reads —

> *br̥had indrāya gāyata maruto vr̥trahantamam* I
> *yena jyotir ajanayan r̥tāvr̥dham devaṁ devāya jāgr̥vi* II
> — *R̥V*, VIII.89.1.

The procedure of singing the *sāman* is given in the *LāṭyāŚS*, the

DrāhyāŚS and the *VaitāSū*. Thus, it is prescribed in *LāṭyāŚS* V.4.16,18 and *DrāhyāŚS*, V.4.10, while chanting the *sāman*, the Brahman priest should chant the *stobha*, i.e., the initial part of the *sāman*, at each foot of the *Ṛk*.

The words *saṁśravase*, *viśravase*, *satyaśravase* and *śravase* are the *nidhanas*, i.e., the last parts of the *sāman*.

In the commentary *Ākṣepānuvidhi* on *VaitāSū*, XXX.18, an illustration is given of the manner of singing this *sāman*. It is thus,

> *saṁ tvā hinvanti dhāitāibhī3: bṛhad indrāya gāyata saṁśravase* । *saṁ tvā riṇanti dhāitāibhī3: maruto vṛtrahantamaṁ viśravase* । *saṁ tvā śiśanti dhāitāibhī3: yena jyotir ajanayann ṛtāvṛdhah satyaśravase* । *saṁ tvā tatakṣuḥ dhāitāibhī3: devaṁ devāya jāgṛvi śravase* ।

The *nidhanas* are sung by all the priests (*ŚatBrā*, XII.8.3.26; *KātyŚS*, XIX.5.3; *VaitāSū*, XXX.20). *LāṭyāŚS*, V.4.17 prescribes that when they are chanting the *nidhanas*, they should touch the head of the sacrificer.

These *nidhanas* are common to all the sacrificers, may they be of any caste (*KātyŚS*, XIX.5.6). They may differ according to the caste, optionally. In that case, these, viz. *saṁśravase*, etc., are used for a brāhmaṇa sacrificer. If the sacrificer is a kṣatriya, then the *nidhanas* should be *sañjityai*, *vijityai*, *satyajityai* and *jityai*, and if the sacrificer is a vaiśya, the *nidhanas* should be *sampuṣṭyai*, *vipuṣṭyai*, *satyapuṣṭyai* and *puṣṭyai* (*KātyŚS*, XIX.5.4, 5; *VaitāSū*, XXX.19; *LātyāŚS*, V.4.19).

The *nidhanas* chosen for a kṣatriya seem to have been accepted from a rite in *AitBrā*, XXXVII.5. In the *punarabhiṣeka* ceremony, after the *abhiṣeka*, the sacrificer gets down from the seat and bows before the priest saying, *namo brahmaṇe*, thrice. Then he releases his speech saying *atha yad varaṁ dadāmi jityai abhijityai sañjityai*. Because of the close relation between the *punarabhiṣeka* and the *sautrāmaṇī* it is not surprising that these terms are accepted in the latter, with a little variation (i.e., *satyajityai* instead of *abijityai*) and that also especially in connection with the kṣatriya sacrificer.

After the chanting of the *sāman*, the Hotṛ priest recites the relevant *śastra* of that *sāman*. At that time, the Adhvaryu sits down in front of him and gives the response (*pratigara*) as *om* (*KātyŚS*, XIX.5.7).

After the recitation of the *śastra* the Adhvaryu offers the thirty-third offering with the verse *trayā devā ekādaśa*. . . . It is obvious that the verse is connected with the offering because of the reference to the number thirty-three in it (*ŚatBrā*, XII.8.3.29). At that time, he recites also the verse *prathamās tvā dvitīyaiḥ*. . . . (*ŚatBrā*, XII.8.3.30).

According to the tradition of the black *YV* there is no lifting of the sacrificer and no singing of *sāman*. Only an offering is offered after the anointment. The Adhvaryu offers an oblation of clarified butter with the recitation of the verse *trayā devā ekādaśa*. . . . After the offering is made, the sacrificer touches his own relevant limbs, while reciting the verse *lomāni prayatir mama*. . . . (*ĀpaŚS*, XIX.10.2).

The *VārāŚS* prescribes a little different procedure of the ritual. After the *abhiṣeka*, the Adhvaryu offers an oblation in the *āhavanīya* fire saying, *bhūḥ svāhā*, following the manner of the *rājasūya* (*VāraŚS*, III.2.8.44). Then, while reciting the verse *śiro me śrīḥ*. . ., the sacrificer touches his own relevant limbs. At that time, the Adhvaryu offers an oblation (*pūrṇāhuti*) with the recitation of the verse, *lomāni prayatir mama*. After that, the sacrificer gets down from the seat, reciting the verse *jaṅghābhyām padbhyāṁ*. . . (*VārāŚS*, III.2.8.46,47).

According to *MānŚS*, V.2.12.24, the sacrificer is anointed with milk. After the anointment, the Pratiprasthātṛ offers the remaining milk on the southern fire saying *bhūḥ svāhā*.

After the offerings, the priests partake of the remnants of that oblation, smelling it, with the recitation of the verse *prāṇapā me* . . . (*KātyŚS*, XIX.5.9). The sacrificer actually partakes of it with the recitation of the verse, *lomāni prayatir mama*. . . (*ŚatBrā*, XII.8.3.31). Thus ends the ritual of the *abhiṣeka*.

At the beginning of the description of this rite, it is stated in *ŚatBrā*, XII.8.3.1, 2 that Indra had lost his strength and vigour. At that time, he was cured by the Aśvins and Sarasvatī. They restored to him his faculties by the performance of this rite *abhiṣeka*.

The same purpose is achieved for the sacrificer, when the *abhiṣeka* is performed for him. After the *abhiṣeka*, he becomes whole and perfect in all his limbs (*ŚatBrā*, XII.8.3.31).

Regarding the ritual procedure of the *abhiṣeka*, there is considerable difference between that of the white *YV* and the black *YV*. Some rites such as lifting the sacrificer, singing a *sāman* and partaking of the oblation material are not at all included in the ritual tradition of the black *YV*. Even among the ritual *sūtra*s of the black *YV*, almost each *Śrauta Sūtra* prescribes a different procedure. The employment of the verses also is different. The *MānŚS* prescribes quite a different material with which the sacrificer is anointed. Unlike all the other *sūtra*s, it prescribes that the *abhiṣeka* should be performed with milk.

11

The Difference between the Caraka Sautrāmaṇī and the Kaukilī Sautrāmaṇī

THE comparison of the descriptions of the rituals of these two forms of the *sautrāmaṇī*, viz. the *caraka* and the *kaukilī*, makes it clear that the *caraka sautrāmaṇī* is the simple and therefore in all probablities the primary form of the rite, and the *kaukilī sautrāmaṇī* more elaborate form of the same. It is noticed that certain rites are added in the ritual of the *kaukilī*. The main additions are those of the rice-pap to Aditi, both at the beginning and at the end of the sacrifice, an animal to Indra at the beginning of the sacrifice and an animal to Indra Vayodhas at the end of it, the offerings of the three cups of milk to the deities, the *abhiṣeka* of the sacrificer and the singing of the *sāman*, and also in the procedure of preparing *surā*.

If we assume that the description of the *kaukilī sautrāmaṇī* occurring in the *ŚatBrā* is the oldest one and the ritual found in the *Śrauta Sūtra*s is based on it, it is observed that the ritual procedure found in the *ŚatBrā* is not followed by all the *sūtra*s. Conspicuously different is the procedure found in the *MānŚS*. According to it, the rice-pap to Aditi is not offered, either at the beginning of the sacrifice or at the end of it. The addition of the milk-cups is also not a feature special to the *kaukilī sautrāmaṇī* according to this *sūtra*, since, in the ritual of the *caraka* also this *sūtra* prescribes the offerings of the three milk-cups together with the *surā*-cups to the three deities. Thus, according to the *MānŚS* an animal to Indra at the beginning of the sacrifice, an animal to Indra Vayodhas at the end of it and the *abhiṣeka* of the sacrificer are the only additional elements in the ritual of the *kaukilī sautrāmaṇī*.

In connection with the *abhiṣeka* also, the procedure found in the *MānŚS* is different. In all the other texts, except the *MānŚS*, the *abhiṣeka* is performed with the fat which is remaining after the offerings are made with the help of the hoofs of the animals; whereas in the *MānŚS* the *abhiṣeka* is performed with the milk remaining after the *vājaprasavya* offerings. Similarly, it is only according to the *MānŚS* that the *vājaprasavya* offerings are found offered in connection with the *sautrāmaṇī*. The ritual sequence of the *abhiṣeka* and the rites which are performed before and after it is also, as is noted in the chapter *abhiṣeka*, different from that, in the other texts. It is stated before, that the singing of the *sāman*, in connection with the *abhiṣeka* of the sacrificer is prescribed only in the *Śukla YV* tradition. No other Vedic text has prescribed it.

Some variations are found in the ritual of the *kaukilī*, about the procedure of the preparation of *surā*. While preparing *surā* in connection with the *caraka* milk is not added to it, whereas in the *kaukilī*, milk is poured in it for three days. Further, in the *ĀpaŚS* and in the *HirŚS* the use of curds or buttermilk and the use of the remnants of the *agnihotra*-offerings are also additionally prescribed in the procedure of preparing *surā*. In this matter also, the *MānŚS* has proved its speciality. It has prescribed (and also the *VārāŚS* together with it) that the milk is to be poured in *surā* only for two days and not for three days like the other texts.

Generally it is found that the *Brāhmaṇa* texts always offer an explanation of or a justification for each and every act or offering. It is true in respect of the ritual of the *caraka* also. Regarding the ritual of the *kaukilī*, however, it is surprising, that the *ŚatBrā* which elaborately discusses the ritual is silent and does not offer any explanation of the additional offerings, viz. the rice-pap to Aditi and the offerings of the animals to Indra and Indra Vayodhas at the beginning and at the end of the sacrifice. Explanations however are given of the various acts in the *abhiṣeka* and of the additions in the ritual procedure of preparing *surā*, while lauding the ritual of the *abhiṣeka*, it is mainly considered as a rite of reestablishing the strength and vigour of the sacrificer, whereas while glorifying the ritual acts in the preparation of *surā*, the main purpose is to establish similarity of *surā* with the *soma*-juice and also that of the *surā*-ritual with the *soma*-ritual

Conclusion

THE study about the origin of the *sautrāmaṇī* makes it evident that the chapters 33 to 40 of the *AitBrā* are very important. The discussions and descriptions occurring in this final part of the *Brāhmaṇa* bring into sharp focus the relations between the kṣatriya and the brāhmaṇa caste, the importance of the priestly class, the position and the growing importance of the kṣatriya in Vedic sacrificial institution.

It is after reading the description of the *rājasūya* ritual in this *Brāhmaṇa*, that one comes to know, that at first, the kṣatriya, be he a king, had no right to perform a sacrifice. Later, when he was granted this right he had to perform certain preparatory rites and to become a brāhmaṇa to be able to perform a sacrifice.

However, even though, the kṣatriya was entitled to perform a sacrifice, some reservations were made by the priests in order to maintain their own power and supremacy over the kṣatriya caste. And, as a result of this, the kṣatriya sacrificer was denied a share in the sacrificial *soma*-drink. He was given the juice of certain fruits and roots instead. Also, at the end of the sacrifice, he was given the *surā*-drink and it was considered to be the *soma*-drink of the kṣatriya sacrificer.

After the performance of the sacrifice was over, the kṣatriya sacrificer had to be a kṣatriya again and for that purpose he had to perform certain redressing rites. The *punarabhiṣeka* was one such redressing rite and included the *surā*-ritual in it. After a careful study of this rite and its comparison with the *sautrāmaṇī* ritual, one can safely arrive at the conclusion that the *punarabhiṣeka* is the precursor (or, a rudimentary form) of the *sautrāmaṇī*.

Thus it is, that the *surā*, which is severely condemned in the Vedic texts, was introduced in the Vedic hieratic religion, when the kṣatriya sacrificer was allowed to perform a sacrifice and further, the rites of the kṣatriyas were admitted in Vedic *śrauta* ritual. *Surā* then was glorified mainly in connection with the kṣatriya, and to elevate it, further it was compared with *soma*. Therefore it is, that in the *punarabhiṣeka* and in the *sautrāmaṇī*, the *mantra*s used for *surā* are those which are addressed to *soma*.

Once *surā* was introduced in Vedic *śrauta* ritual, its other magico-medicinal qualities were also taken into consideration and it was prescribed for one, who had vomited *soma* or was purged by *soma*. The rite was prescribed to be performed after the *agnicayana* also. It was so done, perhaps in order to increase the importance of the rite and to elevate its place in Vedic ritual.

Later, however, it is found that the rule that the kṣatriyas are not entitled to the right of drinking the sacrificial *soma* is not observed very strictly. Even in the period of the *Śrauta Sūtra*s it is seen that the *KātyŚS* and the *LāṭyāŚS* waive this condition and allow the sacrificer to have the share of the sacrificial *soma*. Thus *LāṭyāŚS*, IX.2.4 prescribes, *evam itareṣām ekaikaṁ yāvatā daśa pūryeran yajamānacamasād anyān*, "Thus, besides the goblet for the sacrificer, ten cups should be filled for others, one for each." The commentary on this *sūtra* is still more specific. It reads, *yajamānacamasaṁ tu yajamāna eva bhakṣayet nānyaḥ* "The goblet taken for the sacrificer should be drunk only by himself and not by anybody else" (see also *KātyŚS*, XV.8.19-21). And this causes the relevant changes in the sacrificial ritual. As a result of it, the redressing rites like the *sautrāmaṇī* have lost their original importance, as is seen even in the Saṁhitā and *Brāhmaṇa* texts. Due to the social and ritual changes the need of such rites is further diminished. The real significance of the rites has disappeared and it is observed that even in the *sūtra*-period, the characteristic feature of the *sautrāmaṇī*, viz. the use of *surā* is vanishing. This might perhaps be the reason why milk is introduced in the ritual of the *caraka sautrāmaṇī*, sometimes together with *surā* and sometimes as its substitute.

It might perhaps be on account of this that, in the discussion of the *kaukilī sautrāmaṇī*, we notice deliberate attempts of the author of the *ŚatBrā* to establish the importance of the rite. He has, for that purpose, repeatedly stressed the point that the *sautrāmaṇī* is both an *iṣṭi* and an animal-sacrifice. His attempts to elevate *surā* to the dignity of the *soma*-drink are also seen clearly in the comparison of the procedure of the preparation of *surā* to that of *soma*.

Later, it is seen in the *prayoga*s that the real significance of the rite has totally disappeared. There are neither animal-offerings, nor are *surā*-offerings.[1] The reason given for it is that, since the use of *surā* is prohibited in *kali yuga*, it is used neither in the *vājapeya* nor in the *sautrāmaṇī*. There are prescribed the milk-offerings instead of *surā*. As a justification of it, they have quoted the authority of *ĀpaŚS*, XIX.2.13 in their support.

No explanation can be sought, however, as to why it is said in *MāṭhVr*, II(7.23) *sautrāmaṇyāṁ surāpānaṁ raṇḍayā saha svecchālāpaś ca* "The priests indulge in drinking *surā* and chatter with prostitutes in the *sautrāmaṇī*." The Vedic texts do not contain any such description.

While examining the exact relationship between the *agnicayana* and the *sautrāmaṇī*, it is noted that the *Pūrva-Mīmāṁsā* school plays a significant role in the development of some of the *śrauta* rites. The Vedic texts prescribe that the *sautrāmaṇī* should be performed after the *agnicayana*. However, there is a difference of opinion in the Vedic texts. The *Taittirīya* tradition prescribes the *caraka sautrāmaṇī* after the *agnicayana*; whereas the *KātyŚS* of the white *YV* connects the *kaukilī sautrāmaṇī* with the same. It seems that the influence of the *Pūrva-Mīmāṁsā-Sūtra*s on the author of this *Śrauta Sūtra* has caused this variance. It is a need,

1. Falk has rightly remarked in this connection that even though the offerings of a particular rite change, the name remains the same. 'Ein Opfer mag Verändert werden, aber sein Nāme bleibt dabei erhalten', *ZDMG*, Band 134, Heft 1, 1984, p. 116.

therefore, that the *Pūrva Mīmāṁsā* texts should be studied carefully and the aphorisms stated in them should be compared with the *Śrauta Sūtra*s. A comparative study of these two branches will probably shed some light on the causes of the changes and the development of the *śrauta* ritual

Similarly, while studying the primeval myths regarding the *sautrāmaṇī*, it is observed that the scholars have given importance only to some particular myths, viz. those of Indra and Namuci, which occur in the *ŚatBrā*, XII.7.1.1-14 and XII.7.2.1-4. But they are later myths and therefore, the undue importance, which is attached to them has caused the interpretation of the myths and also of the ritual to be lop-sided. It was only after taking into consideration all the myths regarding Indra and Viśvarūpa — occurring not only in connection with the *sautrāmaṇī* but also with some other rites — that a possible explanation regarding the origin and the exact nature of the *sautrāmaṇī* could be sought. It was after the holistic study of all these myths that the picture of the relation between the brāhmaṇa and the kṣatriya caste became vivid.

I feel it necessary, therefore, that a particular rite should be studied together with all the myths, which have occurred in connection with some other rite or rites. It is possible then, as has been pointed out by Leeming,[2] that the myths then will lead to discoveries in other fields — in history, in anthropology and also in archaeology.

---

2. David Leeming, *Mythology*, *Newsweek Book*s, New York, 2nd printing, 1979, p. 35.

Bibliography

Sanskrit Texts

Aitareya-Brāhmaṇa, with the comm. of Sāyaṇa, Ānandāśrama Sanskrit Series, Poona, Vol. 32, 33; 1896, 1931.

Āpastamba-Śrauta-Sūtra ed. by R.,Garbe, Bibliotheca Indica, Calcutta, work 92, 1882-1902.

Aṣṭāṅga-Hṛdaya, ed. by Aṇṇa Moresvara Kuṇṭe, Nirṇaya Sāgara Press, Bombay, 1891.

Aṣṭāṅga-Saṁhitā ed. by G.S. Tarte, Ganpat Krisṇaji Mudraṇālaya, Bombay, 1888.

Āśvalāyana-Gṛhya-Sūtra, Bibliotheca Indica, 1869.

Āśvalāyana-Śrauta-Sūtra, with the comm. of Gārgya Nārāyaṇa, Rāmnārāyaṇa Vidyāratna, Bibiliotheca Indica, Calcutta, 1874.

Atharvaveda-Saṁhitā (*Śaunaka*), ed. by R. Roth and W.D. Whitney, Berlin, 1924.

Baudhāyana-Śrauta-Sūtra, ed. by W. Caland, Calcutta, 1904-13.

Bhāradvāja-Śrauta-Sūtra, ed. by.C.G. Kashikar, Vaidika Saṁśodhana Manḍaḷa, Poona, 1964.

Bhela-Saṁhitā, Journal of the Department of Letters, University of Calcutta, Vol. IV, 1920-1.

Caraka-Saṁhitā, ed. by V.K. Datar, Nirṇaya Sagara Press, Bombay, 1922 and 1941.

Drāhyāyaṇa-Śrauta-Sūtra, ed. by J.N. Reuter, London, 1904.

Gautama-Dharma-Sūtra, ed. by Ganesh Shastri Gokhale, Anandasrama Sanskrit Series, Poona, 1910.

Gopatha-Brāhmaṇa, ed. by Bieuke Gaastra, Leiden, 1919.

Hiraṇyakeśī-Śrauta-Sūtra, ed. by Kashinath Shastri Agashe,

Anandāśrama Sanskrit Series, Poona, No. 58, 1907-32.

Kāṭhaka-Saṁhitā, ed. by L. Von Schroeder, Leipzig, 1900.

Kātyāyana-Śrauta-Sūtra, with the comm. of Vidyadhara, Acyutagranthamāla Karyalaya, Varanasi, Saṁvat 1987. (For references to *KātyŚS* this edition is used).

——— with the comm. of Karkācārya, ed. by V.P. Madanmohan Pathak, Varanasi, 1903-8.

——— with Devayājñika Paddhati, ed. by Pt. Vidyādhara Śarma, Chowkhamba Sanskrit Series Banares no. 415, 1933.

Kauśikapaddhati, ed. by V.P. Limaye and others, Tilak Maharashtra Vidyapeeth, Poona, 1982.

Lāṭyāyana-Śrauta-Sūtra, ed. by Ānandacandra Vedāntavāgīśa, Bibliotheca Indica, Calcutta, 1870-2.

Mādhava-Nidāna, with the comm. Madhukośa, Nirṇaya Sagara Press, Bombay, 1955.

Mahābhārata, critical edition, ed. by V.S. Sukhathankar, and others, Bhandarkar Oriental Research Institute, Poona, 1927-61.

Maitrāyaṇī-Saṁhitā, ed. by L. von Schoeder, Leipzig. 1881-6.

Mānava-Śrauta-Sūtra, ed. by Jeannette M. van Gelder , Śatapitaka Series, No.17, International Academy of Indian Culture, New Delhi, 1961.

Māṭhara-Vṛtti, ed. by P. Viṣṇu Prasad Sarma, Chowkhamba Sanskrit Series, Banares, No. 296, 1922.

Mīmāṁsā-Sūtras, in six vols., Anandashrama Sanskrit Series, 97, 1929-34.

Pañcaviṁśa-Brāhmaṇa, ed. by Anandacandra *Vedāntavāgiśa*, Bibliotheca Indica, 1870.

Ṛgveda-Saṁhitā, with the comm. of Sāyaṇa, ed. by Max Müller, London, 1849-74.

Śābara-Bhāṣya ed. by T. Subbaśastri, Anandaśrama Sanskrit Series, 97, 1929-34.

Śāṅkhāyana-Brāhmaṇa, ed. by B. Linder, Jena.

Śāṅkhāyana-Gṛhya-Sūtra, ed. by S.R. Seghal, New Delhi, 1960.

Śāṅkhāyana-Śrauta-Sūtra, ed. by A. Hillebrandt, Bibliotheca India, Calcutta, 1889-91, 1897.

Śatapatha-Brāhmaṇa, ed. by A. Weber, Chowkhamba Sanskrit Series, no. 96, 1964.

Suśruta-Saṁhita, ed. by Jādavi Trikamji Acarya, and Nārāyaṇa Rām Acārya, Nirṇaya Sāgar Press, Bombay, 1883.

Taittirīya-Brāhmaṇa, with the comm. of Sāyaṇa, Anandashrama Sanskrit Series, 37, 1898. With the comm. of Bhaṭṭa Bhāskara, ed. by A. Mahadevashastri, Bibliotheca Sanskrita No. 36, Mysore 1908.

Taittirīya Saṁhitā, with the comm. of Sāyaṇa, ed. by E. Roer and E.B Cowell, Bibliotheca Indica, 1860-99.

Vaikhānasa-Gṛhya-Sūtra, ed. by W.Caland, Bibliotheca Indica, 242, 1927.

Vaikhānasa-Śrauta-Sūtra, ed. by W. Caland, Bibliotheca Indica, 265, 1941.

Vaitāna Sūtra with the comm. of Ākṣepānvidhi of Somaditya, ed. by Viśveśvarānanda Viśvabandhu, Indological Institute, Hoshiarpur.

Vājasaneyi-Saṁhitā, with the comm. of Uvaṭa and Mahīdhara, ed. by Jagdisha Shastri, Delhi, 1971.

Vārāha-Śrauta-Sūtra, ed. by C.G. Kashikar in *JBBRAS*. (N.S.) 1, pp. 10ff.

Modern Texts

Aalto, Pentti, "Madyam Apeyam", *Commeoration Volume in Honour of Johannes Nobel,* ed. by Claus Vogel, Delhi, 1959, pp. 17-37.

Aiyangar, Narayan, *Essays on Indo Aryan Mythology*, Parts I and II, Madras, 1901.

Allchin, F.R., "India, the Ancient Home of Distillation?", in *Man —The Journal of the Royal Anthropological Institute*, New Series, Vol. 14, 1979, pp. 55-63.

Bagchi, P.C., "Some Linguistic Notes", in *Indian Historical Quarterly*, Calcutta, Vol. 9, 1933, pp. 253-65.

Von Bartholomae Christian, *Altiranisches Wörterbuch*, Berlin, 1961.

Basham, A.L., *Aspects of Ancient Indian Culture*, Bombay, etc., 1966.

Bergaigne, A., *La Religion Védique après des Hymnes du Ṛgveda*, parts I-V Paris, 1878, 1881, 1883, 1897, Engl. Tr. by V.G. Paranjape,

Parts I and II, Poona, 1969, 1971.

Bhargava, P.L., *India in the Vedic Age*, Aminabad, 1971.

Bhattacharya, N.N., *Ancient Indian Rituals and Their Social Contents*, Delhi, 1975.

Black, William George, *Folk-Medicine*, London, 1963.

Bloomfield, M., "Contributions to the Interpretation of the Veda", *JAOS*, Vol. 15, 1893, pp. 143-63.

Bodewitz, F.W., *The Daily Evening and Morning Offering (Agnihotra) According to the Brāhmaṇas*, Leiden, 1976.

Böhtlingk, Otto and Roth, R., *Sanskrit-Wörterbuch*, Vol. I-VII, St. Petersburg, 1855-75.

Briggs, D.E., *Barley*, London, 1978.

Buddha Prakash, *Indus Valley Civilization*, Hoshiarpur, 1966.

Van Buitenen, J.A.B., *The Pravargya*, Poona, 1968.

Caland, W., *Das Vaitāna Sūtra des Atharvaveda*, Amsterdam, 1910.

———, *Das Śrauta Sūtra des Āpastamba*, Bände I-III, Göttingen, 1921, Amsterdam, 1924, Amsterdam, 1928.

Chinnasvami Shastri Pt., *Yajñatattvaprakāśa*, Calcutta, 1953.

Collins, John J., *Primitive Religion*, New Jersey, 1978.

Coomaraswamy, A.K., "Angel and Titan — An Essay on Vedic Ontology", in *JAOS*. Vol. 55, 1935, pp. 373ff.

Crawley, A.E., "Drinks and Drinking", in *Encyclopaedia of Religion and Ethics*, Vol. 5, 1912, pp. 72ff.

Darby, William J., *et al.* (ed.), *Food, the Gift of Orisis*, Vol. 2, London, 1977.

Dumezil, G., *Tarpeia*, 1947.

Eggeling, J., *Śatapatha Brāhmaṇa*, tr. Vol. 1-5, SBE Series, ed. Max Müller, (reprinted) Delhi, 1963.

Eliade, Mircea, *Myths, and Reality*, London, 1964.

———, *Myths, Rites and Symbols*, a Mircea Eliade Reader, Vol. 1, ed. by Wendell C. Beane and William G. Doty, New York.

Falk, Harry, "Die Legende von Śunaḥśepa vor ihrem rituellen Hintergrund," *ZDMG*, Band 134 — Heft 1, 1984, pp. 115-35.

Forni, Getano, "The Origin of Grape-wine: A Problem of Historical-Ecological Anthropology", in *Gastronomy*, *the Anthropology of*

Food and Food Habits, Margaret L. Arnott (ed.) The Hague, Paris, 1975, pp. 69ff.

Frazer, G.J., *Golden Bough*, (abridged), London, 1963 (Reprint).

Garge, D.V., *Citations in the Śābara Bhāṣya*, Poona, 1952.

Garvin, J.L. (ed.), *Encyclopeadia Britannica*, 14th edition, 1929, Vol. 3.

Geldner, K.F., *Ṛgveda Übersetzt*, III, Cambridge (Mass), 1957.

Ghosal, U.N., "The Vaitānasūtra" (Eng. tr. with Notes), *IHQ*, Vol. 5, 34,6.

———, "The Besprinkling Ceremony of the Rājasūya", *IHQ*, 19(4), 1943.

Ghurye, G.S., *Vedic India*, Bombay, 1979.

Gogoi, P. and S. Boissya, "A Method of Preparation of Beer from Rice . . .", *Anthropos*, 1979-84, 1-3. pp. 248-50.

Gonda, J., *Four Studies in the Language of the Veda*, S-Gravenhage, 1959.

———, *Die Religionen Indiens*, I, Stuttgart, 1960.

———, *Savayajñas*, Amsterdam, 1965.

———, *The Ancient Indian Kingship from the Religious Point of View*, Leiden, 1966.

———, *History of Indian Literature*, Vol. 1, Fasc. 2, Vedic Literature, Wiesbaden, 1975.

———, *The Ritual Sūtras*, Wiesbaden, 1977.

———, *The Mantras of the Agnyupasthāna and the Sautrāmaṇī*, Amsterdam etc., 1980.

———, *Vedic Ritual -- The Non-Solemn Rites*, Leiden, 1980.

———, "*Vedic* Gods and the Sacrifice", N*umen*, Vol, Fasc.1, July 1983, pp. 1 to??

Griffith, J., *Śukla Yajurveda* (tr.), Delhi, (1899, 1916).

Hastings, J., (ed.), *Encyclopadia of Religion and Ethics* (*ERE*), New York, 1912.

Haug, M., *Aitareya-Brāhmaṇa of the Rigveda*, Allahabad, 1922.

Heesterman, J.C., *The Ancient Indian Royal Consecration*, (Thesis, Utrecht, 1957) 'S-Gravenhage, 1957).

Hillebrandt, A., *Das Altindische Neu-und Vollmondsopfer*, Jena, 1879.

———, *Ritualliteratur, Vedische Opfer anu Zauber*, Strassburg, 1897.

———, *Vedische Mythology*, Breslau, 1927.

Hoens, D.J., *Śānti — A Contribution to Ancient Indian Religious Terminology*, 'S-Gravenhage, 1957.

James, E.O., *Comparative Religion*, London, 1961.

Jayaswal, K.P., *Hindu Polity*, Calcutta, 1924.

Jayne, *Healing Gods of Ancient Civilization*, New York, 1962 (reprint).

Jha, Ganganath, *Śābara-Bhāṣya*, Translated into English, Vol. I-III, Baroda, 1933.

Joshi, Lakṣmanashastri, *Vaidik Saṁskṛtīcā Vikāsa*, Wai, 1972.

———, (ed.), *Mīmāṁsākośa*, Vol. 1-7, Wai, 1952-66.

Kane, P.V., *History of Dharmashastra*, Poona, 1941.

Kashikar, C.G. (ed.), "Vārāha Śrauta Sūtra (revised Sautrāmaṇī text)", in *JBBRAS*. (N.S.) 1, pp. 10ff.

———, "A Survey of the Śrauta-Sūtras", in *Journal of the University of Bombay*, Vol. XXXV. (N.S.) 1968.

———, *Vaidik Saṁskṛtīce Pailū*, Poona, 1972.

———, *Śrautadharmācī Svarūpacikitsā*, Poona, 1977.

———, *et al.* (ed.), *Śrautakośa*, Part I and II (Sanskrit and English Section), Pune, 1958, 1962, 1970.

Kassirer, Ernst, *An Essay on Man*, New Haven, 1951.

Keith, A.B., *The Veda of the Black Yajus School*, Cambridge (Mass.) 1914.

———, *Ṛgveda Brāhmaṇas Translated* (*HOS*, Vol. 21) (reprinted) Delhi, 1971.

———, *The Religion and Philosophy of the Veda and the Upaniṣads*, *HOS*, Vol. 32.

Kirk, G.S., *Myth — Its Meaning and Functions in Ancient and Other Cultures*, Cambridge, 1970.

Kluckhohn, Clyde, "Myths and Rituals: A General Theory", *The Bobbs-Merril Reprint Series in the Social Sciences*, S, 1146, Pam. 156.

Leeming, David, *Mythology*, New York, 1979, 2nd Printing.

Lévi Strauss, Claude, *Myth and Meaning*, London and Henley, 1978.

Macdonell, A.A., *Vedic Mythology*, Delhi, 1963, Reprint.

Manning, *Ancient and Medieval India*, Vol. 1, London, 1869.

Mitra, Rajendralal, "Spirituous Drinks in Ancient India", *Journal of the Bengal Asiatic Society*, Vol. 42, Part, I, 1873, pp. 1-23.

———, *Indo-Aryans*, Vol. 1, Calcutta, 1881.

Monier-Williams, *A Sanskrit-English Dictionary*, New Edition, Delhi, 1970.

Muir J., *Original Sanskrit Texts*, Trübner & Co. 1868.

Oldenberg, H., *Ancient India, Its Language and Religions*, Calcutta, 1962, translated from German by A.H. Gunlogsen and Otto Weyer.

Oldenberg, H., "Indra und Namuci", in *Kleine Schriften*, Teil I, Wiesbaden, 1967, pp. 635-42.

Om Prakash, *Food and Drinks in Ancient India*, Delhi, 1961.

Ostergaard, K., "Three-headed God", *Kuml*, 1954, pp. 55-77.

Potdar, K.R., *Sacrifice in the R̥gveda*, Bombay, 1953.

Raghavan, V., *Festivals, Sports and Pastimes of India,* Ahemedabad, 1979.

Ram Gopal, *India of the Vedic Kalpa Sūtras*, Delhi, 1959.

Regmi, Delli Roman, "The Control of Liquor in Ancient India", *New Review*, Calcutta, Vol. 12, Nov. 1940, pp. 381-91.

Renou, L., *Les Ecoles Védiques et la Formation du Veda*, Paris, 1947.

———, *Vocabulaire de Rituel Vedique*, Paris, 1954.

———, *Vedic India,* translated from the French by Philip Spratt, Delhi, 1971.

Roth, R., "Die sage Von Śunaḥśepa", (Zweiter Artikel), *Indische Studien*, Vol. 2, pp. 112-23.

Sharma, R.N., *Brahmins through the Ages*, Delhi, 1977.

Siegerist, *History of Medicine*, Vol. 1, New York, 1957.

Thite, G.U., "Significance of Dikṣā", *ABORI*, Vol. LI, Poona 1971, pp. 163-73.

———, "Antipathy to the Rājasūya", *Sambodhi*, Vol. 1, Oct. 1972, No. 3, pp. 43-58.

———, "Vapāmārjana in the Śrauta-Sūtra", *Archiv Orientalny*, Vol. 46, pp. 338-40.

———, "Non-attractive dakṣiṇās in Śrauta Rituals", *Viśveśvarānanda*

Indological Journal, Hoshiarpur, Vol. 7, 1969, pp. 36-44.

———, *Sacrifice in the Brāhmaṇa Texts*, Poona, 1975.

———, *Medicine, Its Magico-Religions Aspects*, Pune, 1982.

Thomas, F.W., "Abhiṣeka", in Hastings' *ERE*, Vol. 1, pp. 20-4.

Viśvanātha Shastri, (ed)., *Śrautapadārtha-Nirvacana*, Varanasi, 1919.

De Vries, Jan, *Perspectives in the History of Religions*, tr. by Bolle Kees W., Berkeley, 1977.

Waren, C.A., and H. Lloyd, Hind, "Beer", in *Encyclopaedia Britannica*, Vol. 3, pp. 313-15.

Weber, A., *History of Indian Literature*, tr. into English by John Mann and Theodor Zachariae, 2nd edn., London, 1882.

———, *Über die Königsweihe den Rājasūya*, Berlin, 1893.

———, "Collectanea über die kasten-verhältnisse in den Brāhmaṇa und Sūtra", *Indische Studien*, Vol. 10, 1868, pp. 1-160.

———, "Zur Kenntniss des Vedischen Opfer-rituals", *Indische Studien*, Vol. 10, 1868, pp. 321-96.

———, "Einiges Über das Kāṭhakam", *Indische Studien* Vol. 3, 1855, pp. 451-79.

Glossary

Ahutāda: Those who are not entitled to partake of the remnants of the sacrificial offerings, i.e., the kṣatriyas, the vaiśyas and the śūdras.

Ajītapunarvaṇya: Name of offerings. The thing lost is called *ajīta* and the means for getting it back is called *ajītapunarvaṇya*.

Avabhṛtha: Concluding bath after the completion of the sacrifice.

Cappa: A kind of vessel.

Caraka: Name of a form of *sautrāmaṇī* sacrifice, which is prescribed to be performed after the *rājasūya*.

Caru: Cooked rice.

Cātvāla: In an animal sacrifice or *soma*-sacrifice some earth is dug out from the northern part of the sacrificial place to prepare the northern altar. The pit formed is called *cātvāla*.

Cayana: Piling of the fire-altar in various shapes with bricks of various shapes.

Hautra: The duties of the Hotṛ in connection with a sacrifice.

Havis-sacrifice: A Śrauta sacrifice in which oblations are given of milk, curds, ghee, clarified butter or of grains such as paddy, barley, etc.

Hutāda: Those who are entitled to partake of the remnants of the oblation-material after the offerings, i.e., the brāhmaṇas.

Iṇḍva: A supporting ring on which pots, jars, etc., are placed.

Iṣṭāpūrtasyāparijyāni: Name of offerings. Lit. the absence of the destruction of (the fruit acquired by) the *iṣṭa*, i.e., the duties performed by the sacrificer and the *pūrta*, i.e., the benevolent deeds performed by him.

Kārotara: According to *BaudhŚS* it is a lid to be put on a pitcher. It is made either of wood or bamboo or clay. It is covered with hide on all sides. According to *ĀpaŚS* and *HirŚS*, *kārotara* is a bamboo vessel. The jar of mixture of *surā*, ready for fermentation is put first in the *kārotara* and then in a pit or in a *kārotara* instead of a pit. Then the *kārotara* is covered with hide. A spout is attached to it. According to *KātyŚS*, *kārotara* is a sieve, through which *surā* is strained.

Kaṭhina (or *pājaka*): A kind of bamboo vessel or a perforated pot in which the rice cooked for preparing the *surā* is poured and which afterwards is hung to collect the scum of that rice.

Kaukilī: A form of *sautrāmaṇī* sacrifice. It is obligatory, optional and also incidental. According to Weber, this might have been named after a prince 'Kokila Rājaputra', who might have introduced it first, in Vedic sacrificial ritual.

Kuval: A kind of berries.

Lājā: Parched rice-grains.

Māsara: The mixture of the ingredients of *surā* which is ready for fermentation. Sometimes the dregs of *surā* are also called *māsara*.

Nagnahu: According to *BaudhŚS* the flour of pulses is called *nagnahu*. According to Karkācārya, the commentator on *KātyŚS*, it is a kind of root used as a catalytic agent in the preparation of *surā*, which accelerates the process of fermentation. According to *ĀpaŚS*, the coarse barley is mixed with the remnants of the *agnihotra* offering; this mixture is called *nagnahu*. According to Mahīdhara, the commentator on *VājaS*, *nagnahu* is some medicinal herbs.

Nidhana: The words to be added at the end of a *sāman*.

Pājaka (or *Kaṭhina*): A kind of bamboo vessel or a perforated pot in which the rice cooked for preparing the *surā* is poured and which afterwards, is hung to collect the scum of that rice.

Parisrut: The mixture of the ingredients of *surā* kept for fermentation is called *parisrut*. Sometimes, *surā* itself which is ready for performance and which is being strained through the sieve is also called *parisrut*.

Payasyā: Some sour thing like lemon-juice or curds is poured in the boiling milk and it is separated. The solid portion is called *payasyā* and the liquid is called *āmikṣā* or *vājina*.

Praiṣa: The suggestion given by the sacrificer or the priest.

Pratigara: When a *śastra* is being sung, either the Adhvaryu or the Pratiprasthātr̥ stand and stand bending before the singer and utter certain words, viz., *oṁ*, *othamodaiva*, etc. These are called *pratigara*.

Prayoga: A manual which describes procedure of a particular rite in minute details.

Pr̥ṣadājya: An oblation material. The mixture of curds and ghee.

Punarabhiṣeka: Name of a rite in which the sacrificer is anointed again after the anointment in the *rājasūya*.

Puronik: Lit shining before or 'fore-shining'. Designation of the formulas preceding the *upayāmagr̥hīto'si*...' you are taken with a support . . . etc.

Puronuvākyā: Invitatory verses. The verses recited by the Hotr̥ or the Maitrāvaruṇa to invoke the gods at the time of the principal offerings.

Saṁhiti: Wholeness.

Samr̥ddhi: Perfection and appropriateness in a sacrifice.

Samśāna Sāman: Name of a *sāman* which is sung in the *kaukilī sautrāmaṇī*.

Saṁsrāva: The remnants of the oblation-material of the *agnihotra* offering.

Śaṣpa: Sprouted barley

Sata: Name of a pot. *Surā*, when ready for offering is poured into it.

Śatātr̥ṇṇā: A vessel with hundred holes.

Sautrāmaṇī: A *havis*-sacrifice in which *surā*, a kind of beer is offered into a *Śrauta* sacrificial fire. It is the only sacrifice in which *surā* is consumed by the sacrificer and also sometimes by the priests.

Somavāmin: One, who has vomitted *soma*.

Somātipūta: One, who is excessively purged by Soma.

Sphya: A wooden sword.

Stambayajus: In an *iṣṭi* while preparing the altar, the earth dug is carried and is thrown on the *utkara*, 'the rubbish heap'. That earth together with some *darbha* blades is called *stamba-yajus*.

Śuṇḍā: Spout.

Surā: A kind of beer, prepared by the fermentation of grains, especially sprouted paddy, barely, parched rice, etc

Surāsoma: Ingredients of *surā*.

Sutāsutī: According to *BaudhŚS* the *kārotara* is called *sutāsutī* also for, the beer which flows out, conduces to the attainment of heaven, while that which does not flow out indeed causes one to remain on earth.

Sutrāman: An epithet of Indra. Lit. one, having fine protection (to offer to others). In this context, however, it means — one who has good protection from others; who is well-protected.

Śyāmāka: Millet.

Tarī: The rice grains which do not burst open even after being parched.

Tokma: Sprouted paddy or sprouted barley.

Udavasānīyā iṣṭi: The concluding *iṣṭi*.

Upavāka: Indra grains.

Vālapavitra: A strainer or a sieve prepared from the hair of a goat or a ram, or from the hair of an ox or a horse.

Varuṇapraghāsaparvan: Name of a rite in *cāturmāsya* sacrifice.

Veda: A broom prepared of *darbha* blades used for cleaning in a sacrifice.

Viloma: Not in proper order.

Vyr̥ddha: Imperfect.

Yājyā: The offering or oblatory verses, to be recited by the Hotr̥ at the time of the principal offerings.

Yūpa: A quadrangular or octagonal sacrificial wooden post, to which the animal to be offered is tied.

Sanskrit Index

General Index